How the Streets Were Made

How the Streets Were Made

*Housing Segregation and
Black Life in America*

Yelena Bailey

The University of North Carolina Press CHAPEL HILL

© 2020 The University of North Carolina Press
All rights reserved
Set in Merope Basic by Westchester Publishing Services
Manufactured in the United States of America

The University of North Carolina Press has been a member of the Green Press Initiative since 2003.

Library of Congress Cataloging-in-Publication Data
Names: Bailey, Yelena, author.
Title: How the streets were made : housing segregation and black life in America / Yelena Bailey.
Description: Chapel Hill : University of North Carolina Press, 2020. | Includes bibliographical references and index.
Identifiers: LCCN 2020018379 | ISBN 9781469660585 (cloth : alk. paper) | ISBN 9781469660592 (paperback : alk. paper) | ISBN 9781469660608 (ebook)
Subjects: LCSH: African Americans—Segregation. | Segregation—United States—History. | African Americans—Social life and customs. | African Americans—Social conditions—1975- | African Americans—Economic conditions—History—20th century.
Classification: LCC E185.615 .B266 2020 | DDC 305.896/07301732—dc23
LC record available at https://lccn.loc.gov/2020018379

Cover illustration: Manhattan Bridge Tower in Brooklyn (photo by Danny Lyon, 1974). Documerica, Record Group 412: Records of the Environmental Protection Agency (1944–2006), National Archives, College Park, Maryland.

Excerpts from Ann Petry's *The Street: A Novel* are copyright © 1946, renewed 1974 by Ann Petry. Reprinted by permission of Houghton Mifflin Harcourt Publishing Company. All rights reserved.

Excerpts from Ta-Nehisi Coates's *Between the World and Me* are copyright © 2015 by Ta-Nehisi Coates. Used by permission of Spiegel & Grau, an imprint of Random House, a division of Penguin Random House LLC. All rights reserved.

For my mother

Contents

Acknowledgments xi

Introduction 1

CHAPTER ONE
How the Streets Were Made 15

CHAPTER TWO
The Secret of Selling the Negro 44
The Creation of Black Urban Consumerism

CHAPTER THREE
From *The Street* to the Streets 76
Black Literary Production and Urban Space

CHAPTER FOUR
Music Born of the Streets 99
Hip-Hop's Articulations of Urban Life and Identity

CHAPTER FIVE
A Hood Genre 124
Visualizing the Streets in TV and Film

Conclusion 156

Notes 171
Bibliography 187
Index 201

Figures

1. "The Man Who Owns His Home" poster 47
2. "How Glad I Am" poster 49
3. Advertisement for Bassett furniture 64
4. Advertisement for Ultra Wave hair straightener 70
5. Advertisement for Artra skin tone cream 74
6. Cover image for "Fu-Gee-La" single 109

Acknowledgments

Friends and colleagues at Seattle Pacific University (SPU) and the University of Washington helped foster this project through their time, conversation, and support. My colleagues in the Department of English and Cultural Studies, my department chair, Mark Walhout, and my Dean, Debra Sequeira, went above and beyond to support me while I finished this project. My friends and colleagues Eunsong Kim, Shannon Smythe, Chris Chaney, Becky Hughes, Zhiguo Ye, Traynor Hansen, Linh Thủy Nguyễn, Kim Seagall, Kate Ness, and Will Hartmann helped sustain me in this work through their kindness and conversation. I want to especially thank Eunsong for taking me to see Kendrick Lamar perform and helping me work through the material in chapter 4. Likewise, I need to thank Olushade Unger, Jade Parker, Nicole Cotton, and Janelle Bobbitt for supporting me as a fellow Black woman by fostering community. I also want to thank Dennis Childs, my former adviser at the University of California, San Diego, whose example and support helped me see that I could do this kind of work as a young Black scholar. All of these people have been an invaluable source of support.

My students in the social justice and cultural studies major at SPU played an important role as I completed this project. While I was initially content to identify and analyze the problem of how the streets came to be, these students urged me to provide concrete avenues of redress. Their generation holds mine accountable in many ways.

This project has also greatly benefited from the guidance of the University of North Carolina Press. My peer reviewers provided incredibly helpful feedback and pushed me to make this the best work possible. I would like to especially thank my editor, Lucas Church, whose advice, patience, and guidance ushered this project to full fruition.

Finally, this project would not have been possible without the support of my family. Naomi Windham, who has become my adopted sister, encouraged me along the way through many late-night video calls. I also need to thank my mother, Shelly Lucore, and my stepfather, Michael Lucore, and my father, Jote Betel. In addition to giving me the experiences that inspired this project, my mother continues to be my greatest source of encouragement. She and my stepfather have read every draft of every piece of writing I have produced. My family's love and support continue to ground me and remind me why I do this work.

How the Streets Were Made

Introduction

Soon after musician Nipsey Hussle (Ermias Joseph Asghedom) was murdered on March 31, 2019, social media was flooded with the reactions of Black artists, authors, and activists mourning his death. Originally from Crenshaw, Los Angeles, Nipsey Hussle made a name for himself through the release of several mixtapes. It was his community activism, however, that drew wider attention. The rapper invested in companies and real estate in Crenshaw with the goal of helping Black youth find a path to success and economic self-determination. He was also working to address policing and gun violence in his community. In fact, he managed to set up a meeting to discuss these issues with Jay-Z's entertainment agency, Roc Nation, and the Los Angeles Police Department. He never lived to see the meeting, however, because he was murdered the day before it was scheduled to take place.

In the wake of this loss, writer and creative strategist Duanecia Evans tweeted, "The hood is a construct. The deepest underbelly of survival and poverty. The science project of classism and elitism. If you get out you have survivors [sic] guilt forever, if you stay in . . . man. Ain't no middle. Rest easy, @NipseyHussle."[1] Evans's description of the hood, or the streets, as something more than physical geography is at the heart of this project. Whereas Evans describes the hood as a construct that can't be escaped or reformed by people like Nipsey Hussle, *How the Streets Were Made* examines the streets as a sociocultural construct stemming from U.S. geographic segregation that continues to define the contours of Blackness and belonging in the United States today.

The notion of the streets as a sociocultural construct resonates with me personally and professionally. On a personal level, although I did not grow up in the streets, I was raised by a mother whose parenting was in no small way shaped by her determination to keep me from them. My mother spent most of her childhood in the projects of North Minneapolis. She is intimately familiar with the streets and the threats they pose to Black life. She is equally familiar with the way such spaces foster community and belonging. Despite this, her parenting was shadowed by the threat of the streets. Her story is an exception to the norm. Her mother, like many other African Americans, did all she could to move out of public housing projects. Eventually, this meant marrying a Black veteran in the 1970s who managed to secure a home in a first-ring suburb of Minneapolis.

Although my mother made it out of the hood, throughout my childhood she was painfully aware of just how little separated us from that life. This awareness created a ferocious determination in her. Although we did not have much money, she was resolved to keep me from the fate of other poor Black folks. This often meant moving us from place to place, actively fighting against the social, economic, and cultural forces that attempted to corral us back into poor urban neighborhoods. Even when we lived in the projects, my mother moved us across town just so we could get into one of the few available suburban public housing projects. We may have been poor, but she would be damned if I didn't get a middle-class education.

When those housing and school opportunities ran out, my mother was willing to relocate to another suburb or another area of the city. I say this not to exalt her as an example of exceptional perseverance or determination to raise oneself up but rather to highlight the way the streets, even in their strict absence, radically shaped my childhood. My mother accepted a life of transience just so her daughter could have a shot at a decent education and a childhood free from the violence of the streets. Reflecting on my own experience has helped me to recognize the streets as much more than a physical space associated with urban Blackness.

On a professional level, I am continually interested in the way this understanding of the streets appears in cultural production, ranging from literature and film to advertisements. Author Ta-Nehisi Coates does this particularly well. When I first read Coates's book *Between the World and Me*, I was captivated by his articulation of the streets—not only as a place but also as a construct with its own set of cultural ideologies, social practices, opportunities, and limitations. Coates revisits this concept in a more recent book, *We Were Eight Years in Power*. Discussing his reluctance to embrace a liberal vision of linear racial progress during the Obama administration, Coates specifically cites his experience growing up in West Baltimore as evidence to the contrary. Initially, Coates accepts the explanation that urban poverty and crime are the "unfortunate consequence" of deindustrialization. It is not that Coates fails to understand the role of White supremacy, but rather that "white supremacy was not in direct evidence because there were no white people around."[2]

For Coates, the streets merit a more complex explanation than White supremacy alone. As he explains: "When I recalled the Baltimore of my youth, it did not seem to suffer from anything so quaint and simple as 'segregation' or 'white supremacy,' terms that conjured COLORED ONLY signs, night rides, and thuggish sheriffs with ominous nicknames. Instead, the pox represented itself in an abundance of men hanging out on corners, single mothers working night shifts, teen parents in all my high school classes, and kids with ready and easy access to guns."[3] In this passage, Coates dispels the myth that geographic segregation was merely about determining who could exist where and was thus resolved with antisegregation policies. Beyond physical separation, geographic segregation determined *how* people were made to exist in certain spaces, creating a set of beliefs and practices that came to define Blackness in twentieth and twenty-first-century America.

The beliefs and practices associated with the streets are what Coates alludes to when he claims that "the streets [are] a country and like all others, the streets [have] anthems, culture, and law."[4] At times, this culture is known only to those intimately familiar with the streets. A prime example of this is Coates's statement that the realities of the streets are "observable . . . on any Martin Luther."[5] What Martin Luther King Jr. Boulevard, Street, or Avenue signifies for Black people in nearly every city across America is almost universally understood. As someone who has moved across the country several times, I can distinctly remember my mother telling me to "go drive by Martin Luther at night to get a feel for the city" before each move. Understanding what urban Blackness looked like in a new city gave me a basis for understanding how I would be perceived and treated in any space. In *The Beautiful Struggle*, Coates differentiates between those who are *of* the streets and those who are *from* the streets.[6] I would add to this those who, like myself, are shaped by the streets despite residing outside of them. These distinctions are important to avoid an oversimplification of the heterogeneous ways Blackness exists in America. What started as a project to confine Blackness to specific geographic spaces eventually created a set of beliefs about how all Black people exist in all spaces.

In an effort to analyze this phenomenon, *How the Streets Were Made* examines the creation of the streets not just as a physical, racialized geographic space produced by segregationist policies but also as a sociocultural entity that has influenced our understanding of Blackness in America for decades. Drawing from fields such as media studies, literary studies, history, sociology, film studies, and music studies, this book engages in an interdisciplinary analysis of the how the streets have shaped contemporary perceptions of Black identity, community, violence, spending habits, and belonging. I argue that because the physical, social, and cultural creation of the streets is rooted in White supremacy and anti-Blackness, it produced myths of urban Black pathology, financial irresponsibility, and inherent violence that have fueled the economic and social divestment of Black communities, as well as a broader divestment from Blackness as a part of U.S. identity. Nevertheless, Black Americans have contested these myths through literature, film, and music, through both overt political messages and personalized narratives that assert the fundamental humanity of Black people. What all of this illustrates is that creation of the streets is significant when discussing not only geographic segregation and the racial wealth gap but also the contested racial imaginary of American life.

More Than a Rap Lyric: Understanding the Racialized Geographies of the Streets

Whether one refers to "the streets," or instead uses terms like "the ghetto" or "the hood," the geographic space of reference is the same. As a concept, however, the streets occupy a liminal space. Sociologists Douglas Massey and Nancy Denton address this point when they write: "The term 'ghetto' means different things to different people. To some observers it simply means a Black residential area; to others it connotes an area that is not only Black but very poor and plagued by a host of social and economic problems."[7] Thus, while nearly everyone understands the space we are referring to when we discuss the streets, the cultural, racial, political, and economic significance of the streets varies greatly depending on the persons using and/or hearing the term.

Scholars have wrestled with this broader significance for decades. In 1944, Gunnar Myrdal argued that geographic segregation in America operates on a social level as well as a physical one. In his words, it creates "an artificial city" where schools, hospitals, social circles, and institutions are racially segregated.[8] Thus, the result of geographic segregation is the proliferation of prejudice. Twenty years later, Kenneth B. Clark, who was Myrdal's student, defined the United States' segregated spaces as "dark ghettos." By using "dark" as a qualifier, Clark took the already racialized Italian term for marginalized Jewish space and added another layer of exclusion by applying it to the context of U.S. White supremacy and anti-Blackness. Furthermore, Clark argued that there was something unique about U.S. ghettos, making them more than segregated spaces. Rather, he posited that these "dark ghettos" were "social, political, educational, and—above all—economic colonies. Their inhabitants are subject peoples, victims of the greed, cruelty, insensitivity, guilt, and fear of their masters."[9] Both Myrdal and Clark articulate how the racially segregated spaces in America called ghettos are much more than sites of physical separation. They are complex structures of socioeconomic relations. Moreover, both scholars highlight the way such spaces have been historically tied to Blackness.

More recent studies of urban segregation have described Black space in similar ways. In *Code of the Street*, sociologist Elijah Anderson describes the streets as a "social context of persistent poverty and deprivation, [and] alienation from broader society's institutions."[10] Much like Myrdal and Clark, Anderson suggests that the streets are made up of complex social relations and practices that dictate the terms of Black life in very particular ways. In their study of urban segregation, Massey and Denton describe the ghetto as "a set of neighborhoods that are exclusively inhabited by members of one group, within which virtually all members of that group live. By this definition, no ethnic or racial group in the history of the United States, except one [urban Blacks], has ever experienced ghettoization."[11]

Anderson, Massey, and Denton capture the nature of the streets as both a physical space created through government policy and a social space of isolation. These scholars also recognize that while poverty and geographic segregation affect a number of communities within the United States, the specific way these factors have converged through government engineering had a unique impact on Black Americans. A number of sociologists, historians, and other scholars have executed thorough studies of how geographic segregation impacts Black Americans socially and economically.[12] However, much of this scholarship fails to fully address the cultural and ideological meanings of the streets.

George Lipsitz's discussion of racialized space and the spatial imaginary is a useful framework for addressing this issue. In *How Racism Takes Place*, Lipsitz uses the theoretical framework of cultural geography to link government housing policies to the creation of White and Black space as something more than physical geography. He argues that these spaces are not merely the product of racist government policies, but that "it takes places for racism to take place."[13] The significance of this reality is not only the creation of a new understanding of Black urban space but also the recognition that "American whiteness [is] one of the most systematically subsidized identities in the world."[14]

Lipsitz's argument illustrates the connections between geographic segregation and our national understandings of Whiteness and Blackness. From the Homestead Act of 1862 to the Federal Housing Act of 1934, Whiteness and American belonging have been intimately connected to the ownership of land and homes. Unsurprisingly, both of these polices, which radically subsidized ownership for White Americans, were rarely, if ever, applied in the service of Black Americans. Today, the wealth accumulated over generations thanks to these policies has resulted in a nearly insurmountable racialized wealth gap. Black Americans possess approximately 5 percent of the wealth of White Americans.[15] Arguably, the systematic imposition of geographic segregation through these policies has impacted Black Americans in a way that is second only to slavery and mass incarceration.

What Lipsitz's work helps us understand, however, is that these policies have done more than create vastly different economic realities for White and Black Americans. Along with the physical, social, and economic segregation generated by these government policies, divergent perceptions of Black and White space were created. As Lipsitz explains: "The white spatial imaginary portrays the properly gendered prosperous suburban home as the privileged moral geography of the nation. Widespread, costly, and often counterproductive practices of surveillance, regulation, and incarceration become justified as forms of frontier defense against demonized people of color. Works of popular film and fiction often revolve around phobic representations of Black people unfit for freedom. These cultural commitments have political consequences."[16] The delineation of Black and White space has entrenched itself in the American imaginary. The way White space and Black space are imagined in literature, music, and across television and movie screens is evidence of a larger cultural and ideological battle for power and belonging.

The negative racialization of Black space discussed by Lipsitz is far from new. Black geographies have long been framed in such a way as to justify the horrors of slavery and colonization. One of the farthest-reaching philosophical examples of this is Hegel's claim that Africa "is no historical part of the world."[17] In fact, for Hegel, Africa's nature as the "land of childhood . . . originates, not merely in its tropical nature, but essentially in its geographic conditions."[18] Thus, it is the geography of Africa itself that is responsible for the fact that "the Negro . . . exhibits the natural man in his completely wild and untamed state."[19] Despite attempts by intellectuals such as Léopold Senghor to refute these notions, Hegel's claim that Africa is an uncivilized space continues to be heard in public discourses on the continent today.[20]

Hegel's lectures on Africa were first published in 1837, a little less than a hundred years before the federal government instituted nationwide redlining practices through the Home Owners' Loan Corporation (HOLC) and the Federal Housing Association (FHA). Despite this century-long gap, the origins of segregation and the racialization of American urban space are not far removed from the logic of White supremacy that fueled slavery and colonization. The legacy of these ideologies is an important part of understanding how and why the discourse surrounding cities after the Great Migration not only took on a decidedly anti-Black tone but also began another century-long process of inscribing derogatory meaning onto Blackness.

While on the one hand the history of anti-Blackness in the West is closely tied to geographic belonging, on the other hand antiracist resistance has utilized geographic space in similar ways. Scholars such as Kathleen Kirby, Ruth Wilson Gilmore, and Katherine McKittrick have long argued for the need to examine the intersections between cultural meaning, dominance, resistance, and geography.[21] As McKittrick explains, "The relationship between black populations and geography—and here I am referring to geography as space, place, and location in their physical materiality and imaginative configurations—allows us to engage with a narrative that locates and draws on black histories and black subjects in order to make visible social lives which are often displaced, rendered ungeographic."[22] McKittrick's understanding of Black geographies is an important counter to the idea that geographic space is somehow neutral, or merely the physical location where social and economic relations take place.

Drawing on her work, as well as that of George Lipsitz, *How the Streets Were Made* examines the way Black artists and intellectuals use their work to both carve out discursive space and create new imaginative geographic meanings for the streets. Only one who is intimately familiar with the streets can define them as something more than a space of unbelonging. This is because such an individual is aware not only of how the streets are perceived externally but also of what the streets are like experientially. They bear witness to dominant ideologies and external processes of socialization, as well as the ways in which these ideologies and processes are internalized and lived out. This is one of the reasons Ta-Nehisi Coates's description of the streets resonates so strongly with me.

Coates's description is not unique, but rather represents a conspicuous concept throughout Black American literature, film, and music. However, a unique facet of Coates's work is the explicit, albeit cursory, connection between government housing policies and the creation of the streets as a physical, cultural, and ideological entity. Toward the end of *Between the World and Me*, the narrator tells his son, "'Black-on-black crime' is jargon, violence to language, which vanishes the men who engineered the covenants, who fixed the loans, who planned the projects, who built the streets and sold red ink by the barrel."[23] What Coates articulates so well is that the streets are not just a pejorative term for Black space. Rather, they are an engineered product of American policy.

From a Culture of Poverty to Superpredators and Welfare Queens: The Public Discourse on the Streets

In the wake of increased Black urbanization and racialized inequalities, several theories emerged to explain the vast social and economic disparities between Black and Brown urban inhabitants and their White American counterparts. Perhaps the most infamous explanation of urban poverty is Daniel Patrick Moynihan's report *The Negro Family* (1965). Basing much of his research on sociologist E. Franklin Frazier's work, Moynihan attempted to explain the widening educational and economic disparities between White and Black Americans.[24] He argued that "at the heart of the deterioration of the fabric of Negro society is the deterioration of the Negro family."[25] To support this claim, Moynihan devoted a large part of his report to detailing Black divorce rates, births outside of marriage, and single-mother households. All of this, he argued, was caused by a poor family structure. Relying heavily on psychoanalytic and heteronormative understandings, Moynihan argued that the process of natal alienation irrevocably shaped Black familial structures.[26]

On the one hand, Moynihan attempted to recognize the lasting impact of slavery on Black life, as well as the more recent history of Jim Crow segregation. Yet, in doing so, he simultaneously relegated Black women to the periphery and blamed them for urban social ills. For instance, when discussing how segregation stripped Black Americans of their personhood, Moynihan states: "Keeping the Negro 'in his place' can be translated as keeping the Negro male in his place: the female was not a threat to anyone."[27] Yet, while Black women were apparently not the target of Jim Crow racism, they were to blame for young men never learning to take up their so-called proper role as the head of the family. This issue, he argued, was particularly linked to Black life in the city.[28] For Moynihan, "In every index of family pathology . . . the contrast between the urban and rural environment for Negro families [was] unmistakable."[29]

Criticisms of the Moynihan Report are plentiful.[30] To be fair, Moynihan recommended policies that would have aided urban Black inhabitants, including a minimum income and job programs, but these policies were not included in the final report.[31] However one might interpret Moynihan's intentions or political leanings, arguably his greatest contribution to American politics was the bipartisan narrative of Black pathology. In many ways, his words are reminiscent of Thomas Jefferson's claim that "blacks, whether originally a distinct race, or made distinct by time and circumstances, are inferior to the whites in the endowments both of body and mind."[32] Whether he explained it as existential or circumstantial, by arguing that inequality is a result of Black pathology, Moynihan provided fuel for the argument that inferior conditions are merely the product of being from an inferior race.

Moynihan was not the only one who attempted to shape the national discourse on race and poverty. In 1966, anthropologist Oscar Lewis published his "culture of poverty" thesis.[33] Lewis argued that, rather than the result of individual character flaws, the reality of racial and economic disparities in America was that they were the product of a way of life developed over many generations. Focusing mostly on urban Puerto Ricans, Lewis suggested that the conditions of generational urban poverty result in a distinct subculture. Although, according to Lewis, his intention was to depart from the dominant narratives that blamed individuals for their lot in life, his culture of poverty thesis ultimately reinforced the emerging stereotypes of urban people of color. His observations of the "culture of poverty" posited that communities of color had developed poor impulse control and a disproportionate focus on instant gratification as a way to cope with the hopelessness of their surroundings.

Lewis also argued that sexual promiscuity and families with single mothers were an inherit part of this "culture of poverty." To be fair, Lewis was attempting to move away from the assumption that such family structures were particular to Black Americans due to their history of slavery. In lieu of this, he suggested the real issue was the nature of class-based identities within the West. However well-intentioned, Lewis's thesis did far more to reinforce the idea that the words "poor," "urban," and "nonwhite" are synonyms than it did to challenge racist assumptions about people of color. Furthermore, while Lewis attempted to frame his "culture of poverty" thesis as evidence against the belief that members of urban communities of color were living disordered, chaotic lives, he ultimately defined these communities by "the inexorable repetitiousness and the iron entrenchment of their lifeways."[34]

Lewis's and Moynihan's theses on race and urban poverty are significant not only for the narratives they tell of the streets but also for their direct impact on U.S. policy. At the time, President Lyndon B. Johnson was engaged in his War on Poverty and seeking research to explain the nature of racialized poverty in America. After serving as the assistant secretary of labor for Johnson, Moynihan went on to advise President Nixon, and his work provided fuel for conservative politicians who wanted to explain away racial disparities as a matter of cultural difference. If Black culture made urban inhabitants promiscuous and prone to focus on the present rather than the future, then both the government and White Americans were off the hook for their problems.

Another common explanation for the disparities that affect urban communities of color, and one that continues to be used today, is that Black urban inhabitants are trapped in a cycle of poverty because the welfare state does not force them to become socially mobile. This explanation first emerged in the 1970s when conservative theorists and politicians such as Charles Murray and Lawrence Mead argued that liberal social programs encouraged unemployment. They argued that the liberal welfare state existed in such a way that Black urban inhabitants either did not have to work hard or did not want to work hard for fear of losing their benefits.[35] This theory was also used to explain the growth of Black single-parent households and unemployment.

Throughout the 1980s and 1990s, the narrative of Black pathology continued to fuel the racialization of the streets, particularly when deployed by conservative politicians. The culture of poverty thesis, for example, continues to be an integral part of social conservative thought and a key explanation for the so-called failures of the welfare state and the dangers of big government. This rhetoric has appeared in everything from advertisements to speeches and posters as part of what media studies scholar S. Craig Watkins calls "the symbolic organization of social conservatism."[36] This symbolic organization, he argues, was quite intentional. During the latter part of the twentieth century, "social conservatives [deployed] their rhetorical devices, vast resources, and political imagination to create sharp and decisive symbolic boundaries that [constructed] an image of society under siege from a number of subversive forces—feminists, gays and lesbians, liberals, racial 'minorities,' and labor unions."[37] As Watkins also points out, the increasing reach of social conservatism in the latter part of the twentieth century was not merely economic or political; it was cultural and ideological. This often played out through the imagining of Blackness and urban life across television and movie screens. I address the result of such cultural labor in chapter 5 of this book.

While social conservativism positioned itself as a protective force against a number of social threats, urban Black Americans were often the most prominent among these in the 1980s and 1990s. This is perhaps best exemplified through Reaganism. Rather than a movement built up by Ronald Reagan alone, Reaganism can be defined as an ideological "return to old-fashioned

Republicanism — large tax cuts for the rich, less government help for the poor, weaker enforcement of civil rights, fewer controls on industry, less protection for the environment, and emotional rhetoric on the virtues of hard work, family, religion, individualism, and patriotism."[38] This return to "old-fashioned Republicanism" also meant a return to anti-Blackness, albeit in less overt terms.

The us-versus-them rhetoric of social conservatism often manifested itself in public discourses on the perceived social and economic threat of urban crime and poverty. This resulted in a frequent call for law and order by Reagan, directed almost exclusively toward communities of color.[39] The most infamous product of this thinking was the War on Drugs, but a series of so-called tough love laws also proliferated in the 1980s and 1990s.[40] The positioning of urban Black space as a site in need of discipline went far beyond the sphere of policy. The "just say no" campaign, for example, turned the War on Drugs into a moral conflict with White middle-class America on one side and urban Black America on the other.

While the criminalization of urban Blackness was focused largely on Black men, Black women also faced a gendered facet of this discourse. The stereotype of the welfare queen, for instance, emerged as an example of the failure of liberal policies. In many ways, the welfare queen is the linchpin of conservative representations of the culture of poverty. As Patricia Hill Collins explains, "In contrast to the welfare mother . . . the welfare queen constitutes a highly materialistic, domineering, and manless working-class Black woman. Relying on the public dole, Black welfare queens are content to take the hard-earned money of tax-paying Americans and remain married to the state."[41] Not only this, but the welfare queen is often portrayed as being guilty of fraud. She does not just benefit from the state but actively attempts to cheat it. Much like the War on Drugs, the discourse on the welfare queen extends beyond the economic and political sphere and into a moral one. It is not just that Black women are dependent on the state, but that they remain so due to poor moral fiber. This depiction of Black women runs counter to the dominant ideologies of meritocracy and the Protestant work ethic. As such, it places urban Black women firmly outside the boundaries of normative American identity and belonging.

In addition to seeing the emergence of the welfare queen stereotype, this era also marks the moment John J. Dilulio Jr.'s superpredator thesis became a key way of describing Black urban youth as a violent threat.[42] All of these new terms and images worked together to define Black urban space in new, very specific ways through the lens of racial and moral deficiency. As Watkins

Introduction 11

explains, "This law-and-order spectacle emphasized images of inner-city villainy—gang violence, crack cocaine, delinquency, and moral degeneracy—as a major urban pathology."[43] This "inner-city villainy" was almost always embodied by Black and Brown people.

As a result of the rise of social conservatism and its emphasis on policing the inner city, urban Blackness was increasingly demonized and framed as the antithesis of mainstream American life. In 1990, a survey conducted by Tom Smith for the University of Chicago's National Opinion Research Center found that 62 percent of non-Black Americans believed Black people were lazier than others, more than half felt they were more violent and less intelligent, and almost 80 percent thought they were prone to live off welfare rather than work to support themselves.[44] These findings are just one example of how the narratives of Black pathology, moral deficiency, and criminality became hegemonic ideologies. Furthermore, the rhetoric of social conservatism during this era resulted not only in the increased incarceration of Black Americans but also in the widespread criminalization of urban Blackness itself. The poison fruit of this era is still evident today, both in the overwhelming number of Black Americans who are incarcerated and those who have been unjustly assaulted or killed at the hands of police.

Conservatives were not the only ones theorizing the root cause of racialized urban poverty. Many liberal theorists and politicians correctly identified the systemic issues that produced urban poverty, such as deindustrialization.[45] Still, even these theories failed to locate geographic segregation as the genesis of these broader systemic issues. Douglas Massey and Nancy Denton diverge from other scholars by specifically aiming their work at redirecting conversations about racialized social and economic disparities back to the topic of geographic segregation. In addition to making this important intervention, Massey and Denton also contest the culture of poverty with their own "culture of segregation" theory. They posit that "segregation created the structural conditions for the emergence of an oppositional culture that devalues work, schooling, and marriage and that stresses attitudes and behaviors that are antithetical and often hostile to success in the larger economy."[46]

Massey and Denton go on to explain that their theory is not representative of all urban inhabitants and, in fact, many diverge from these patterns and behaviors. Rather than provide a totalizing narrative of urban Blackness, Massey and Denton attempt to explain the broader limitations imposed on Black urban inhabitants. However, while their theory offers a refreshing departure from narratives of Black pathology, it also reinforces a binary understanding of urban Blackness. Either one succumbs to the "culture of segregation," or one is an exception. The reality of urban Blackness, as articulated by those intimately familiar with it, is far more complex. Aspects of urban Black identity may seem oppositional to White middle-class norms, but this is not the sum of urban Blackness. Recognizing this fact is an essential part of acknowledging the humanity of Black people and further challenging narratives of Black pathology.

Still, what Massey and Denton provide that most scholars do not is a clear understanding of how Black geographic segregation exists unlike anything else seen in the United States. As they put it: "Black segregation is not comparable to the limited and transient segregation experienced by other racial and ethnic groups, now or in the past. No group in the history of the United States has ever experienced the sustained high level of residential segregation that has been imposed on blacks in large American cities for the past 50 years. This extreme racial isolation did not just happen; it was manufactured by whites through a series of self-conscious actions and purposeful institutional arrangements that continue today."[47] Massey and Denton wrote these words twenty-five years ago. Yet, despite the fact that their book maps out these historical and sociological realities, little has changed in the way of our understanding of how the streets were created and, more important, how they continue to impact and shape Black life today.

How the Streets Were Made attempts to explain why racialized spaces like the streets exist, why it is that "urban and ghetto" most often signify Black, and, most important, how we might approach the topic of redress in a more robust and practical way. As a cultural studies scholar, I abide by the claims of Raymond Williams and Stuart Hall that institutional, political, and cultural practices are inextricably linked to economic ones and therefore must be studied together.[48] As such, my methodology for examining how the streets were made is highly interdisciplinary. I draw from sociology, history, media studies, music studies, literary studies, and American studies, among other disciplines. The purpose of this approach is to create a picture of the streets that accounts for their multifaceted nature.

How the Streets Were Made has three main objectives. First, I want to establish that the streets—as they are described by Coates, appear in the media, and exist geographically—are the direct result of government policies that responded to increased Black urbanization after emancipation, specifically the housing policies that began under President Franklin D. Roosevelt and lasted until President Johnson signed the Fair Housing Act of 1968. To that end, chapter 1 details the government policies and practices responsible for creating segregated Black urban spaces, as well as the long-lasting social and economic impact of geographic segregation.

The second objective of *How the Streets Were Made* is to disentangle the meaning of the streets by examining their use in various cultural media throughout the twentieth century. I am particularly interested in how Black writers and artists have used their work to theorize the streets' existence and their impact on Black life. In chapters 3, 4, and 5, I examine the way the streets are depicted in literature, hip-hop, and television and film, respectively. These chapters focus on the creation of specific sociocultural meanings associated with Black urban space.

The final objective of this project, and perhaps the most important, is to investigate the cultural, social, and ideological implications of the creation of the streets for Black American life. While this last objective is addressed throughout the book, chapter 2 provides a concrete example of how the creation of the streets shaped perceptions of Black consumerism and economic practices. While the post–World War II housing boom forged the cultural connections between White middle-class consumerism and homeownership, Black consumerism was cultivated in such a way as to create an image of urban Blackness as flashy, brand conscious, and overly concerned with physical appearance. This racialization of urban consumerism continues to permeate public discourses on Black life and work ethic today.

While much of *How the Streets Were Made* is about examining the broader social, cultural, and economic impact of geographic segregation on Black Americans, I am also interested in how this understanding of the streets lends itself to conversations about redress. In "The Case for Reparations," Ta-Nehisi Coates argues that reparations are more than economic redress. Rather, he calls for "an airing of family secrets, a settling with old ghosts."[49] In the conclusion, I consider arguments about reparations for housing and geographic segregation. Drawing from Coates, Kimberlé Crenshaw, and others, I attempt to map out what this process might look like.

CHAPTER ONE

How the Streets Were Made

When I think about the way public housing policy and geographic segregation led to the creation of the streets as a sociocultural construct, I think about the experiences of my mother and stepfather, both of whom grew up in housing projects in Minnesota. My stepfather, a White American, grew up in a housing project in Duluth in the 1950s. His family moved into the housing after World War II. For them, public housing was transitional, and they eventually were able to purchase a home and settle into middle-class American life. In contrast, my Black American mother grew up in the housing projects of North Minneapolis. Her mother, a young single parent, moved into this housing in the 1960s. My mother jokingly recalls that the only time the police dared to come into the area was when they were rounding someone up.

My parents' divergent experiences are significant because they speak to the radically different ways subsidized housing operated for Black and White Americans. Experiences like my stepfather's are often used to explain away the specific anti-Blackness of U.S. housing policy. If White people lived in the projects too and managed to become socially mobile, then there was no excuse for Black people. These types of broad generalizations represent both a misunderstanding of history and a misunderstanding of how race and space function in America. Ta-Nehisi Coates addresses this misconception in "The Case for Reparations" when he claims that "an unsegregated America might see poverty, and all its effects, spread across the country with no particular bias toward skin color. Instead, the concentration of poverty has been paired with a concentration of melanin. The resulting conflagration has been devastating."[1] Coates points to the fact that in contemporary America, race and poverty are largely intertwined thanks to segregationist housing policies.[2] Understanding how the physical spaces of the streets came to be, as well as how they were linked to certain racialized behaviors and social patterns, helps us confront the untruth of questions such as, if White Americans were able to transition out of public housing and into their own homes, why didn't Black people? If, instead, we know that the housing projects designed for Black Americans were a subpar counterpart to the New Deal economic support being extended to White Americans, we can begin to truly understand the roots of current racialized geographic space and economic disparities.

While the rest of *How the Streets Were Made* focuses on the ways the streets operate socially and culturally in marketing, literature, music, film, and television, this chapter recounts the history of geographic segregation and the policies that created the streets. This history has been well explored by scholars, but I intentionally begin this project with its retelling for several reasons.[3] First, the fact that geographic segregation has only grown since the mid-twentieth century (as has the racial wealth gap largely created by the policies that kept Black Americans from owning high-value homes, if they owned homes at all) illustrates that the significance of this history has yet to be fully realized by many. Second, I argue that this history is about more than just federal policy, or even the contrasting creation of Black urban and White suburban identities in mid-twentieth-century America. I argue that this history demonstrates a complex joint effort between federal, state, local, and private powers to create physical, social, and cultural confines for Blackness. Finally, as I explained in the introduction, the creation of Black urban spaces through segregationist policies led to a proliferation of anti-Black ideologies and sentiments. By 1990, 62 percent of non-Black Americans believed Black people were lazier than others, more than half felt they were more violent and less intelligent, and almost 80 percent thought they were prone to live off welfare.[4] I argue that the way Black space was designed lent itself to the creation of narratives of Black pathology, moral deficiency, and criminality that are present in U.S. society today.

Mapping America in Black and White

The history of urban geographic segregation in the United States begins not with government housing policy but with the migration of Black Americans following the Emancipation Proclamation. In the century after plantation slavery was officially abolished, Black Americans went from living predominantly in the rural South to living predominantly in urban areas throughout the country.[5] Before 1900, Black Americans in the North were largely integrated into neighborhoods based on their socioeconomic status, although Black Americans were undoubtedly overrepresented among the poor and working class. This integration was due in part to the fact that Black people rarely made up more than 30 percent of northern neighborhoods.[6] Whatever the rationale, Black Americans living in the North before the twentieth century were in constant contact with White Americans and were afforded certain opportunities Black southerners were not. These circumstances gave rise to Black middle-class leaders such as W. E. B. DuBois and Charles Chesnutt. As one might imagine, circumstances in the South were much different. The majority of Black Americans in the South were enslaved, and to thwart escapes and separate families, southern Black people were spread across White inhabited spaces. Overall, even with the existence of slavery, pre-twentieth-century America was not characterized by geographic segregation.[7]

It would be naive to assume that the geographic integration that existed before the Great Migration signified sociocultural integration. As many Black authors and scholars have established, the supposed dichotomy of North and South, where the North was a haven of integration and racial harmony and the South alone was the hotbed of White supremacy, is a false one.[8] Still, there were some differences in White and Black interactions in each area. In southern cities, the regular contact between Black and White Americans was largely based on a master-slave or master-servant relationship. Even among free Black Americans and nonslaveholding White Americans, the cultural practices that eventually became Jim Crow laws established a strict binary of White superiority and Black inferiority. These cultural and ideological practices were not limited by the Mason-Dixon Line, however. On the contrary, although Black Americans who migrated north were no longer disproportionately working as sharecroppers, or de facto slaves, their conditions did not drastically improve with migration. On the one hand, migration gave rise to greater autonomy, as illustrated through cultural and social movements such as the Harlem Renaissance, the civil rights movement, Black Nationalism, and the Black Arts Movement. On the other hand, many of these artistic and political movements were the direct product of or response to U.S. racism and the continued fight for equal rights.

Some scholars argue that anti-Blackness did not become a major problem in the North until White Americans felt threatened by the mass migration of the early 1900s, particularly in terms of employment competition.[9] In *Black Metropolis*, St. Clair Drake and Horace R. Cayton note that before 1910, Black Americans were tolerated in cities such as Chicago when they "filtered into" White neighborhoods. Still, Black Americans were made to compete with newly arrived southern and Eastern European immigrants for social mobility and integration. Unsurprisingly, the hegemonic nature of anti-Blackness meant that while European ethnic groups found economic opportunity and social mobility in the city, Black Americans did not. The perceived economic threat of Blackness gave way to race riots and northern segregation. Among these racial tensions, housing became a key issue, as White Americans no longer wanted to inhabit the same space as Black Americans. Sociologists Douglas Massey and Nancy Denton argue that this history laid the foundation for the urban ghetto long before postwar discriminatory housing policies. By 1930, for instance, Black people in Chicago lived in neighborhoods that were more than two-thirds Black, while Black people in cities such as New York, Cleveland, and Chicago were living in neighborhoods that were at least half Black.[10]

While other ethnic groups were similarly living in ethnic-dominant neighborhoods, their circumstances were significantly different from those of Black Americans. For one, immigrant enclaves, such as those inhabited by Jewish or Polish communities, were rarely truly homogeneous; they were often perceived and named as such, but were in fact quite heterogeneous. Second, most ethnic enclaves did not host the majority of their respective populations. In Chicago in 1933, for instance, only 3 percent of the Irish population lived in the designated Irish neighborhood. Even among southern and Eastern Europeans, only 50 percent of Italians lived in Little Italy, and 61 percent of Poles lived in the Polish neighborhood. In contrast, 93 percent of Black Americans lived in designated Black areas. The final difference between segregated Black spaces and other ethnic enclaves is that urban Black space has become a permanent feature of American geography, whereas most other ethnic neighborhoods were transient.[11] I argue that the high concentration of Black Americans in geographically segregated areas, along with the permanence of these spaces, is due to the unique social and cultural perceptions of Blackness in contrast to other racial and ethnic groups. Rather than a group transitioning into the melting pot of White American identity, Black urban inhabitants are perceived as an incompatible threat to this identity.

In addition to this early spatial-cultural separation of Blackness from American identity, geographic segregation also had dire physical consequences for Black Americans, who were regularly subjected to violence throughout the twentieth century. After the housing shortages during World War I, Black people in Chicago were corralled into the city's Black Belt, as Drake and Cayton call it, on the South Side. When I say corralled, the allusion to how one would treat an animal is intentional. Black Chicagoans faced terrorism by White neighborhood associations trying to force them into segregated spaces. Between July 1917 and March 1921, for example, fifty-eight Black homes were bombed. That translates to a bombing nearly every three weeks.[12] By the mid-1920s, direct violence had been largely replaced by intricate systems of restrictive covenants and real estate association guidelines that ensured Black exclusion from White neighborhoods.

Even after such physical violence had died down, those few upper-middle-class Black families who managed to overcome the obstacles to securing a mortgage and getting a realtor to sell them a home in a White neighborhood found that their battle had only just begun. Many were harassed, not just by Ku Klux Klan members who burned crosses in their yards, but also by neighborhood residents who formed mobs outside their homes. Local police often did little to stem the violence. In fact, some joined in with the anti-Black protesters. In one particular case that Richard Rothstein documents, White neighbors rented a house next door to a Black family and turned it into a White supremacist clubhouse. They raised a Confederate flag, blasted music from the house at all hours, and threw rocks and yelled racist slurs at the family on a regular basis. Unfortunately, this experience is not exceptional. Rather, Black families who dared to traverse the boundaries separating White and Black space were frequently the victims of physical violence, ranging from thrown rocks and beatings to firebombings well into the late 1980s.[13] The history of this violence is an important reminder that geographic segregation was not some loosely enforced concept by government officials but rather a tangible reality that shaped Black life in dangerous ways. Moreover, the convergence of local policy and neighborhood violence demonstrates the various scales on which anti-Blackness operated at this time.

While geographic segregation can be explained by increasing anti-Blackness after the Great Migration, its institutionalization and sustainment were a direct result of federal, state, and local policy. Rothstein examines this in *The Color of Law*, where he challenges the public belief that Black urban space is the result of de facto segregation—the socially and culturally embedded practices that exclude African Americans from specific spaces, activities, and rights. Instead, he argues that Black urban space is the product of the unconstitutional practice of de jure segregation—the legally embedded exclusion of African Americans from specific spaces, activities, and rights.[14] Rothstein's argument is not new, but his emphasis on the unconstitutionality of these practices is uniquely compelling. Housing segregation policies dictated where African Americans and other people of color were allowed to live until at least 1968, when President Lyndon B. Johnson signed the Fair Housing Act. Thus, for much of the twentieth century, Black Americans were systematically denied their constitutional rights through these practices. The issue of constitutionality raised by Rothstein has clear legal significance. However, I argue that it is also one of the strongest examples of the social and cultural consequences of geographic segregation. Constitutional rights are the foundation of American exceptionalism. By disenfranchising Black Americans from these rights, federal, state, and local policies solidified the separation of Blackness from mainstream U.S. spatial, political, and cultural belonging, evidencing the inherent contradictions of American exceptionalism itself.

The Origin of Public Housing: When the Projects Were for the White Middle Class

If you were to survey people today about what comes to mind when they hear "the projects," you are likely to get responses such as poor, urban, Black, or ghetto. Despite their contemporary connotations, public housing projects emerged during World War I as a means of offering residences to White defense workers living near military bases and munitions plants. In fact, Black people were banned from using public housing, even if they worked in the same factories as White beneficiaries. During World War I, there were more than eighty public housing projects in twenty-six states, housing around 170,000 White workers.[15] While this vast network of government-funded housing was linked to patriotism and productivity during World War I, in the forty years that followed it became the emblematic representation of Black urban poverty.

Contrary to the imagery public housing projects might conjure in contemporary minds, the homes built to stem the early twentieth-century housing shortage were not dense, high-rise apartments. Rather, most of these early projects were low-rise, single-family homes. The design of public housing projects, serving their original purpose as temporary shelter for working- and middle-class White Americans, is significant. Public housing for White Americans blended in with private housing, signaling normalcy. However, when public housing was finally opened up to Black Americans, not only did its racialization shift, but so did its very design and infrastructure. As the projects became increasingly associated with Blackness, they became decreasingly associated with family life. Rather than sheltering families in transition, the projects became a means of warehousing urban Black Americans. Still, despite the ubiquitous association of poor urban Blackness and public housing projects today, the process of creating this cultural meaning was not a smooth one.

Initially, Black Americans had to fight for access to public housing. When World War I ended, an influx of veterans returned to the United States without adequate housing. In addition to the return of veterans to urban spaces, recent Black migrants were looking for housing in various city centers. The result was a gross shortage of housing, one that the federal government sought to resolve through President Franklin D. Roosevelt's New Deal economic development policies. The primary goal of this policy change was not only to meet growing housing demand but also to stimulate the economy through construction jobs. These efforts were led in large part by the Public Works Administration (PWA), which expanded the use of public housing, making it available to civilians who were not working in the defense industry. Housing projects were also made accessible to Black Americans, although these new housing projects were segregated by race based on the rationale that Black people preferred to be among themselves.[16]

Despite this segregation, access to public housing was a victory of sorts because it meant receiving a share of national public provisions. The effort to open public housing to Black Americans was driven by the secretary of the interior, Harold Ickes. A former president of the Chicago chapter of the National Association for the Advancement of Colored People (NAACP), Ickes is often described as a liberal champion of African American rights. While this may be true to an extent, Ickes was still a product of his historical context and held a somewhat ambivalent position on the widespread implementation of antisegregation policies. For instance, although he desegregated many of the spaces under his direct control, such as public parks and office restrooms, he did not believe that states should be forced to desegregate until African Americans "improved themselves." He explained himself by saying, "I have always been interested in seeing that the Negro has a square deal, I have never dissipated my strength against the particular stone wall of segregation. I believe that wall will crumble when the Negro has brought himself to a high educational and economic status."[17]

Ickes's belief that racism would ultimately be eliminated by Black self-improvement, rather than systemic change, framed his work with the PWA. Richard Rothstein credits Ickes for the fact that eventually one-third of all U.S. public housing projects were occupied by African Americans by the mid-twentieth century.[18] Of course, these were segregated projects. In advocating for Black occupation of public housing, Ickes argued that housing projects should reflect the racial composition of the area. In other words, projects in White cities would be restricted to White Americans, while those in racially mixed or Black neighborhoods would house mixed or Black populations, respectively.[19] When one considers Ickes's perception of Black Americans as a group of people in need of improvement, the cultural and ideological significance of this segregationist policy becomes clearer. Black and White Americans were separated not due to neighborhood composition but due to a perceived difference in their social and moral composition.

Still, one might argue that Ickes's focus on matching an area's racial composition was merely a rhetorical strategy meant to help Black Americans gain access to public housing. Because public housing was still seen as primarily a service for White Americans, a number of methods were used to discourage or disqualify Black applicants. For instance, in cities such as New York and Boston, public housing applicants could be disqualified by a number of unsurprising factors, including having a criminal record, a narcotic addiction, or mental illness. However, other factors were even more subjective and open to being deployed as a means of racial discrimination, such as being a single-parent family or having an inconsistent employment record, poorly behaved children, poor housekeeping habits, or insufficient furniture.[20] Within this context, Ickes's strategy may seem like a reasonable compromise that provided greater access to public services.

However, when one considers the broader, systemic context of city building in the mid-twentieth century, Ickes's policy becomes more clearly detrimental. Ickes's racial composition rule was often applied in conjunction with the work of city planners who either at that time or previously had designated certain geographic areas as Black. In areas that were racially integrated, the PWA's policies meant that only segregated, Black public housing was made available. In cities such as Oakland, Atlanta, and New York, for instance, White and Black workers lived in the same areas due to the necessity of being near to factory jobs. However, the work of city planners and the PWA separated these communities. As such, their policies not only further isolated and marginalized Black Americans but also displaced other, non-Black low-income families.[21] Since many of these White Americans were of southern and Eastern European heritage, they were still in the process of being integrated into mainstream White America. The PWA's policies helped facilitate their entrance into Whiteness while simultaneously distancing urban Blackness from the rest of mainstream America.

The fact that integrated urban spaces existed before the PWA's policies is just one example of how federal policy played a direct role in creating America's racialized geography. We will never know how these cities may have grown and thrived as racially heterogeneous spaces. Moreover, when integrated neighborhoods in cities such as Atlanta, New York, or Oakland were designated Black or White and cleared for public housing use, the result was not only the racialization of city space but also the fixed association of class, race, and space. While people of various economic classes inhabited White and Black space, respectively, it was the city that became synonymous with poverty. Thus, the PWA's policies ensured that interracial class solidarity was disrupted and that poverty itself was racialized as Black and confined to the city.

Despite all that it accomplished in terms of created segregated urban space, the PWA only oversaw public housing for four years. After it built twenty-six new projects, the responsibility for public housing shifted from the PWA to the newly established U.S. Housing Authority (USHA) in 1937. Much like the PWA, the USHA maintained the policy that public housing should reflect neighborhood composition.[22] Initially, the USHA created only a limited number of new housing projects due to the focus on supporting the military during World War II. Even in 1940, when Congress passed the Lanham Act that financed the construction of housing projects specifically for defense workers, this new housing was designed to be demolished or sold off to private companies after the war.

After World War II, however, the large number of returning veterans and the birth of baby boomers created an increased demand for housing. This time, however, President Truman faced opposition from Republicans, who preferred that the new housing market be private. To thwart Truman's Housing Act of 1949, Republicans included an amendment that specified segregation would no longer be allowed in public housing. Rather than representing racial progress, however, this amendment was a strategic way to sink the bill. Republicans of the time knew that southern Democrats would not pass a bill that forced integration in public housing.[23] Despite these attempts to halt Truman's bill, it was eventually passed without any stipulations about integration. The bill not only supported the federal subsidization of mortgage programs but also funded urban renewal programs and the construction of more than 800,000 public housing units. It was touted by Truman as a means of "building decent homes in wholesome surroundings for low-income families now living in the squalor of the slums."[24] The racially coded language of "wholesome surroundings" for "families," which were decidedly perceived as two-parent, heterosexual households, is abundantly clear when one considers the practice of segregation that was integral to the construction and allocation of public housing at the time. Now that Black Americans had access to public housing, it became necessary to delineate between different types and uses of the projects. This is one example of how specific narratives around Black public housing inhabitants as pathological or morally deficient first emerged.

Another way Black space was coded in policy was through referrals to "slums" and slum clearance. As much as the 1949 Housing Act was discussed as a means to provide housing to American families, it was equally designed for slum clearance. In fact, Truman established the federal Division of Slum Clearance, which essentially operated by clearing out Black neighborhoods to make room for new public housing projects.[25] Unsurprisingly, this coincided with the period when public housing became more exclusively used by Black Americans. In the years that followed World War II, the reality of Truman's promise was the movement of "wholesome" White families to the suburbs through subsidized mortgage programs. The result was that those who remained dependent on public housing in the city were predominantly Black. This was also due to Truman's "racial equity formula," which proposed an increase in Black-only public housing.[26] The same segregation occurred on state and local levels. In states where city officials wanted to build integrated housing projects, such as my home state of Minnesota, most state constitutions prevented this with amendments requiring local referenda for low-income family housing. While on the surface these referendums appeared to promote democratic involvement, in practice they allowed White neighbors to vote to maintain their racial exclusivity. The blatantly racist nature of these amendments becomes even clearer when one realizes such referendums were not required for low-income senior housing but only housing that might serve the Black population.[27] Overall, the result of these federal, state, and local policies meant that while the White middle class was being ushered into a period of homeownership and prosperity, Black Americans were systematically relegated to the domain of public housing and/or lower-value homes due to their confinement to racialized urban neighborhoods. Ironically, this divestment from Black ownership felt like progress due to the historical exclusion of Black Americans from public housing.

The little progress that was made by opening public housing to Black Americans was undercut when Dwight Eisenhower became president in 1953. At the time, the United States was undergoing a dramatic political shift. With Republicans now more socially conservative than Democrats, Eisenhower's win meant a reversal of the minimal efforts that had been made toward equitable housing. For instance, although rarely enforced, federal policies did exist to ensure that Black Americans received housing of the same quality as White housing, and others required the provision of public housing to those most in need, regardless of race. These policies were abolished under Eisenhower.[28]

At the same time that these modest protections for Black Americans were being eliminated, the federal government was subsidizing White middle-class American homeownership, exacerbating the racial and economic divide between urban and suburban geographies. Additionally, throughout the 1950s and 1960s, public housing income caps were created and enforced in such a way as to push out remaining White families, as well as middle-class Black families.[29] As a result of these income caps, public housing projects earned less income to support their maintenance. Moreover, the cultural identity of public housing became even more decidedly poor and Black. By the end of the 1960s, shifts in public housing policy had a stark impact on America's geographic imaginary. Blackness and poverty defined urban spatial belonging, whereas Whiteness and social mobility defined the suburbs.

Local Housing Segregation

While federal and state policy played a key role in the way U.S. geography was historically segregated and racialized, the same cultural and ideological powers operated on a local level. Long before the PWA made geographic segregation a federal practice, America's racialized geography was enforced by local governments and neighborhood covenants. Throughout the 1910s, as Black urbanization increased, cities across the country began adopting zoning laws that separated White and Black urban populations. For example, Baltimore established an ordinance banning African Americans from purchasing homes in White neighborhoods in 1910.[30] It was one of the first cities to do so and set a precedent that many others followed. Similarly, cities such as Indianapolis passed ordinances requiring the written consent of White residents before African Americans could move into their neighborhoods. Although the NAACP filed a lawsuit against these cities and the Supreme Court ruled such ordinances unconstitutional in 1916, urban segregation continued to proliferate during the early twentieth century.[31]

Once overt racial segregation through zoning laws was outlawed, many communities relied on neighborhood covenants to maintain their racial composition. Most of these covenants did not exist before 1900, but they were frequently used in the early twentieth century to enforce racial segregation. Because these covenants were based on the choice of private owners and residents, they were legal and did not require government approval. However, government offices, from the federal all the way down to the local level, enforced these covenants through evictions, committee organizations, credit ratings, and Supreme Court decisions that upheld their legality.[32] What is particularly significant about the way local powers enforced geographic segregation is that they did so under the guise of democratic choice. Local communities argued for their right to collectively determine who belonged in their neighborhoods. Unsurprisingly, Black voices were left out of these conversations.

The assertion of local control did not go uncontested. Several of these segregationist ordinances were declared illegal by the Supreme Court in 1948. Nevertheless, cities continued geographic segregation through city planning policy.[33] In Austin and Atlanta, for example, city planning documents designated Black and White spaces. Atlanta city planner Robert Whitten maintained that racial zoning was "essential in the interest of the public peace, order and security" and demonstrated as much in his 1922 city zoning plan.[34] Despite the fact that this plan was deemed unconstitutional by the Atlanta Supreme Court in 1924, it continued to guide city planning for the next few decades.[35] Lest one think this was only a southern problem, in the 1920s then secretary of commerce Herbert Hoover organized the production of a manual on house zoning as well as an Advisory Committee on Zoning, both of which strongly supported racial zoning.[36] In fact, the committee included city planners such as Frederick Law Olmsted Jr. and Alfred Bettman, both of whom were outspoken segregationists who argued that racial zoning was necessary for economic and national well-being.[37] Much like the narrative of local control, "national well-being" was another way of tying geographic segregation to American identity. The preservation of separate White and Black spaces signaled the protection of an American way of life.

Overtly racist policies were not the only way of enforcing geographic segregation. Economic zoning was another method of segregation that worked by limiting homeownership to those who could afford single-family homes, typically White middle-class families. These policies used the language of class to continue racial segregation.[38] Often, highways and industrial zones were constructed as a buffer between Black and White neighborhoods, based on the rationale that this would preserve home values in White neighborhoods. More often than not, the design of these buffer zones devalued Black neighborhoods. Beyond physical separation, economic zoning also permitted different businesses to build in White and Black neighborhoods. The result was a disparate characterization of Black and White space. For instance, bars, nightclubs, and brothels were permitted to be built in Black neighborhoods.[39] Rather than contribute to these neighborhoods' economic value, these policies were meant to simultaneously protect White space from such vices and codify Black space as synonymous with socially unacceptable behavior such as drinking, prostitution, and crime. Over time, Black space became increasingly associated with pathological behavior. A prime example of this is a 1941 campaign to raise funds to treat syphilis in the Black community of Chicago. Mainstream local newspapers promoted the campaign by calling Chicago's South Side a "cesspool of disease."[40] This seemingly innocuous activity, a public health campaign, took on a decidedly negative, racialized tone when connected to urban Black space. This is one example of how quickly public policy produced racialized meanings associated with U.S. geography.

This negative characterization of Black space extends beyond the geographic boundaries of the city. As I mentioned in the introduction, the meanings ascribed to the streets through public policy impact perceptions of Blackness and belonging across spatial boundaries. Cultural geographer Carolyn Finney's work *Black Faces, White Spaces* provides a prime example of this. Finney discusses how the proliferation of sundown towns, where the threat of physical violence or death after dark was almost guaranteed for Black people, served to limit Black movement in the country and further restrict Black behavior.[41] In one instance, as Finney recounts, a middle-class Black family reported to the *New York Times* that their fear of sundown towns directly impacted their plans to vacation in Montana.[42] Finney's work highlights the fact that the policies and practices that created the streets and ascribed derogatory meanings to Blackness attempted to confine Blackness to urban spaces both literally, through violence, and ideologically, through fear.

Another way Black space was defined in very specific ways was through industrial zones that often adjoined or overlapped with Black-designated neighborhoods. The construction of new factories and plants not only posed a serious health hazard to residents but also characterized Black urban space as a site for production rather than community. There continues to be a debate about whether or not this industrial zoning is the result of explicit racism or merely the discriminatory impact of unrelated policies.[43] Given the larger history of anti-Black zoning and housing laws, the former seems more probable. Arguably, the desire to call this the result of discriminatory impact, rather than the product of systemic racism, seeks to avoid any sense of legal, social, or cultural responsibility for redress. Regardless of what one calls them, these policies turned predominantly Black areas into the so-called slums that would later give rise to urban renewal projects.

The urban renewal projects that were implemented throughout the early to mid-twentieth century displaced the low-income Black urbanites formerly forced to live in industrial zones. This so-called slum clearance made way for new highways, hospitals, universities, and offices. Unsurprisingly, these new public services were not meant for Black use. Rather, efforts at urban renewal primarily served the purpose of making the commute between downtown business and shopping centers and White suburbs easier. Such was the case, for example, with the Cross Bronx Expressway, which displaced poor communities of color, so that suburban travelers would never have to be reminded of the cost of their own easy lives. Former vice president Henry Wallace made as much clear when he proposed that urban renewal could bring about "the elimination of unsightly and unsanitary districts."[44] Rather than integrating displaced Black communities into higher-income areas, these policies further concentrated urban poverty, thus reinforcing Black spatial segregation.[45] Instead of solving issues of urban crime and poverty, these programs simply moved them farther away from White America.[46] Historian Arnold Hirsch calls this the creation of a "second ghetto," where patterns of geographic segregation were further solidified through government policy.[47]

The impact of government policies that sequentially created Black spaces through zoning and then reinforced their separation through urban renewal programs cannot be overestimated. Massey and Denton point out that this represented a "new segregation of Blacks—in economic as well as social terms—[that] was the direct result of an unprecedented collaboration between local and national government. This unholy marriage came about when private actions to maintain the color line were overwhelmed by the massive population shifts of the 1950s and 1960s."[48] Where federal policy provided large-scale economic and social spatial separation along racial lines, local government reinforced this segregation under the guise of community control. Public housing policy, racial and economic zoning, neighborhood covenants, and slum clearance worked together to define increasingly Black urban spaces as synonymous with poverty, immorality, and underdevelopment.

Creating White Suburbia: The Federal Subsidization of Homeownership

While geographic segregation was produced by a combination of racist federal, state, and local policies, federal housing policy played a particularly significant role in racializing the suburbs as the antithesis of the streets. Just as urban areas were becoming increasingly Black, New Deal federal housing policies were ushering city-dwelling White Americans into the suburbs and subsidizing homeownership for them. Analyzing the creation of White suburbia contextualizes the streets as a place of exclusion by identifying exactly what Black urbanites were excluded from: homeownership, wealth accumulation, and national belonging.

Although the scale of White suburbanization under the federal housing policies of the mid-twentieth century was unprecedented, the push for White homeownership has much deeper historical roots. In the 1920s, for instance, then secretary of commerce Herbert Hoover led the Better Homes in America (BHA) movement. The Advisory Council of Better Homes in America included leaders such as Vice President Calvin Coolidge and Franklin D. Roosevelt, who at the time was the president of the American Construction Council. The political trajectory of those involved reflects the political nature of homeownership and its perceived relationship to American identity.

The BHA movement launched itself into the public eye in 1922. One of its key methods was campaigning through pamphlets and magazine ads. For example, ads were often placed in the *Delineator*, a magazine produced by the Butterick Publishing Company that targeted female consumers. These ads appealed to "the intuition of woman" whose "first thought is always of the home."[49] The movement did more than just sell the idea of homeownership to White Americans though; pamphlets titled *How to Own Your Home* also provided the cultural capital necessary to pursue homeownership.[50] Despite the widespread campaigning, the BHA movement could not overcome the financial barriers most Americans faced when trying to buy a home. Until the early twentieth century, home mortgages often required a down payment equal to 50 percent of the home value and provided only a five- to seven-year repayment period.[51] The financial difficulty of homeownership was only made worse by the Great Depression, during which many of the families who had managed to purchase homes under these terms ended up in foreclosure.

Regardless of these failures, the BHA movement laid the cultural and ideological foundations for White homeownership, as is evident in the way Hoover resurrected the movement's discourse during the 1930s. In his 1931 address to the White House Conference on Home Building and Home Ownership, for example, Hoover argued that the desire for homeownership is distinctly American: "I am confident that the sentiment for homeownership is so embedded in the American heart that millions of people who dwell in tenements, apartments, and rented rows of solid brick have the aspiration for wider opportunity in ownership of their own homes. To possess one's own home is the hope and ambition of almost every individual in our country, whether he lives in hotel, apartment, or tenement."[52] The seeming universality of the dream of homeownership becomes much more specific as

Hoover continues to describe what homeownership signifies culturally, claiming, "This aspiration penetrates the heart of our national well-being. It makes for happier married life, it makes for better children, it makes for confidence and security, it makes for courage to meet the battle of life, it makes for better citizenship. There can be no fear for a democracy or self-government or for liberty or freedom from homeowners no matter how humble they may be."[53] Twentieth-century homeownership is tied not only to the heterosexual nuclear family but also to American belonging.

The connection between homeownership and patriotism is not altogether surprising. However, a closer analysis also reveals the ways in which this patriotic desire is racialized. Hoover attempts to capitalize on early American nostalgia as he describes the need for homeownership:

> Those immortal ballads, Home, Sweet Home; My Old Kentucky Home; and the Little Gray Home in the West, were not written about tenements or apartments. They are the expressions of racial longing which find outlet in the living poetry and songs of our people. They were written about an individual abode, alive with the tender associations of childhood, the family life at the fireside, the free out of doors, the independence, the security, and the pride in possession of the family's own home—the very seat of its being. That our people should live in their own homes is a sentiment deep in the heart of our race and of American life.[54]

One might argue that Hoover is referencing the human race here, but any reasonable analysis of the cultural and historical context of his comments reveals otherwise. For one, Hoover refers to songs that emerged distinctly out of the White, Anglo-Saxon American tradition. The power to create these songs and sentimentalize westward expansion was in the hands of White men. Who else could sing in such a way about freedom, independence, and security in the nineteenth century? Moreover, these songs are reflective of ideologies such as Manifest Destiny. This is significant because it signals a specific racial hierarchy and ties the notion of Manifest Destiny to the twentieth-century pursuit of the American Dream.

Hoover's vision for American homeownership was made a reality by President Roosevelt. Only two years after Hoover presented his address on homeownership, Roosevelt created the Home Owners' Loan Corporation (HOLC), which took over mortgages that were close to default and refinanced them under longer terms (typically fifteen to twenty-five years). In addition to changing mortgage terms, HOLC loans allowed purchasers to build equity by applying their payments to both the principal balance and the loan interest. By amortizing loans in this way, HOLC turned homeownership into a means of building wealth.[55]

While HOLC can be credited with transforming home mortgages in a way that greatly benefited existing homeowners, it must also be credited with initiating the government use of redlining. The nature of HOLC mortgages meant there was a greater need to ensure homeowners could make payments. To assess default risk, HOLC contracted with local realtors to conduct home appraisals. These evaluations, however, were often based on neighborhood racial composition. Organizations such as the Association of Real Estate Boards, for instance, operated under a code of ethics that stated realtors "should never be instrumental in introducing into a neighborhood . . . members of any race or nationality . . . whose presence will clearly be detrimental to property values in that neighborhood."[56] The association between neighborhood racial composition and home values manifested itself in the way realtors mapped metropolitan neighborhoods. Areas that were low risk, meaning all White, were colored green. In contrast, the riskiest neighborhoods, meaning all Black, were colored red. Regardless of class or income levels, all African American neighborhoods were redlined.[57] Because HOLC produced maps for every major metropolitan area in the United States, it systematically instituted the practice of redlining across the country.[58] Furthermore, because private lenders often modeled their practices after HOLC policies, including using HOLC city maps for credit decisions, this government-created system of redlining permeated both the private and the public sector.[59]

The Home Owners' Loan Corporation was not the only federal organization created under the New Deal to serve homeowners. In fact, the Federal Housing Administration (FHA), created by the National Housing Act of 1934, and the Veterans Administration (VA) had a much larger impact on Americans due to their focus on first-time home buyers. Much like HOLC, the FHA changed the mortgage industry by providing insurance for mortgages with longer terms, typically twenty years, and smaller down payments of around 15 to 20 percent. Authorized by the Servicemen's Readjustment Act of 1944 (G.I. Bill), the VA provided many veterans with low-interest home loans requiring zero down payment.[60] These new mortgages were also amortized, meaning new home buyers could immediately begin to build equity in their homes.[61]

Unlike HOLC, the FHA conducted its own home appraisals, although these were sometimes contracted out to local real estate agencies. Nonetheless, one would have hoped that without the explicitly racist practices of realtors getting in the way, people of color would have had greater access to these new loans. Unsurprisingly, this was not the case. Instead, the FHA made neighborhood racial composition a fundamental part of its appraisal process as outlined in its *Underwriting Manual*, which was first published in 1934, with yearly editions to follow. According to the manual, "If a neighborhood is to retain stability, it is necessary that properties shall continue to be occupied by the same social and racial classes."[62]

Black and racially integrated neighborhoods were marked as financially risky, as were White neighborhoods that were in close proximity to Black neighborhoods.[63] As Ta-Nehisi Coates puts it, "Black people were viewed as a contagion."[64] This policy is what led to the now infamous case of White residents building the Detroit Eight Mile Wall in 1941 to further separate their neighborhood from a Black one.

Another means of redlining was offering better credit ratings to new construction. While this practice may appear logical and innocuous on the surface, new suburban housing was zoned in such a way as to be available almost exclusively to White Americans. Likewise, the FHA's prioritization of single-family homes over multifamily units and its rules about lot size, setbacks, and separation from existing structures essentially built in a systemic preference for White suburban homeowners.[65] In the late 1940s, the explicitly racist language was removed from the FHA's *Underwriting Manual*, although the practice of geographic segregation was still encouraged under the guideline of evaluating "compatibility among neighborhood occupants" as a criterion for appraisal.[66] During its tenure, the FHA evaluated 239 cities across the United States, redlining districts that were predominantly of color. This large-scale evaluation took the process of creating racialized geographic spaces to a national level. Moreover, much like HOLC, the FHA's policies impacted the private sector. Without FHA backing, private banks were often unwilling or unable to issue loans to Black Americans, even those who had the financial means for homeownership.

Between HOLC, the FHA, and the VA, not to mention the private lenders that followed their lead, homeownership was placed systematically and disproportionally in White hands. Moreover, the way neighborhoods were evaluated, along with new construction and zoning policies, meant that White homeowners were spatially segregating themselves from Black urbanites. Whereas during the early twentieth century White city dwellers attempted to maintain segregation through local policies, violence, and intimidation, now they were simply leaving the city altogether. As Massey and Denton poignantly observe, "Although whites were still highly resistant to racial integration in housing, withdrawal to the suburbs provided a more attractive alternative to the defense of threatened neighborhoods."[67]

As White flight became the norm, the suburbs emerged as a more concrete cultural space. White suburbia involved more than housing. White suburban space meant federally funded highways, public transport, communications infrastructure, schools, and a host of other public goods.[68] There was an inpouring of government funds to make these spaces livable. One of the best-known examples of White suburbia in the twentieth century is Levittown, Long Island. Developed by William Levitt after World War II, Levittown consisted of 17,000 new single-family homes, built exclusively for White Americans. Each home was equipped with the latest home appliances. In essence, Levittown homes were the starter pack for young, White American dreamers.[69]

In addition to embodying the dream of midcentury American suburbia, Levittown also represents the way in which entire suburban communities were constructed on the basis of racial exclusion, expediting the racialization of American suburbia. It also represents the codependent nature of private business interests and government policy. The Levittown developments relied on the FHA's new mortgages to supply residents. William Levitt testified to this before Congress in 1957, declaring, "We are 100 percent dependent upon the Government."[70] Not long after this, a New Jersey court decided in 1960 that Levittown was essentially public housing due to the FHA's role in its construction, financing, and selling. As such it was deemed illegal to exclude African Americans.[71]

Despite the fluctuating legality of housing segregation, the lived reality for most Black Americans was that they were not allowed to move into White suburban spaces. Robert Mereday, a middle-class African American veteran who owned a small trucking business, is a primary example of this. As a small-business owner and veteran, Mereday had the financial means to secure a loan. However, he was also highly aware of the FHA's racial requirements and thus did not even bother to apply for a loan. He states, "It was generally known that Black people couldn't buy into the development. When you grow up and live in a place, you know what the rules are."[72] What Mereday speaks to is the way structural inequality—in this case, denied access to federally backed loans—gets inscribed into the public understanding. In this way, housing segregation and the denial of homeownership to Black Americans become hegemonic, or cultural common sense. One might argue that had Mereday applied, he may have been able to achieve his dream of purchasing a Levittown home. Perhaps this really was a matter of individual character and persistence. This myth, however, is quickly disproved by the experience of his son's girlfriend's family. This family, which was also Black and middle-class, attempted to purchase a home in another Levitt development after *Shelley v. Kraemer* outlawed restrictive covenants. The family was, unsurprisingly, denied the home.[73]

Mereday's story is not unique. While zoning policies and urbanization weeded out many Black Americans, there were still plenty of middle-class Black families who sought homeownership in the suburbs. Their stories are a prime example of how the sociocultural construct of the streets as a space of poverty and unbelonging shaped the experiences of Black people who had the financial means to move outside of urban geographies. Despite their economic standing and desire for social mobility, Black middle-class families could rarely secure fair home loans, let alone get a realtor to sell to them in a White neighborhood. When they did manage to find someone, they were often swindled by realtors who would act as bankers too, charging much higher interest and requiring a bigger down payment. If these families were late or missed a monthly payment, the realtors would then evict them and resell the house under similar terms. Across the country in cities such as Chicago, Baltimore, Detroit, and Washington, D.C., Black Americans were being preyed upon. In Chicago, 85 percent of Black home buyers were sold contracts of this type.[74] This predatory lending was the beginning of a trend that capitalized on the Black middle class's desire to escape the streets.[75]

When they were not engaged in predatory lending, realtors would purchase homes through blockbusting and then divide them into small, cramped apartment units.[76] They then rented these apartments at exorbitant rates to Black Americans, especially recent arrivals to the city from the rural South.[77] Besides these predatory habits, many real estate agents refused to sell houses in White neighborhoods to Black people altogether. Over 80 percent of real estate agents surveyed by sociologist Rose Helper in Chicago, for example, said that they would not engage in sales that promoted integration. Massey and Denton's research demonstrates that this was not unique to Chicago, but rather a national pattern.[78] This illustrates how these were not just neighborhood or government policies but ingrained social practices fueled by anti-Black ideologies. The result was that the Black middle class was stuck in a catch-22. As they sought to escape the confines of urban segregation, they actually brought it with them. Any property they purchased signified its expansion, rather than their escape.

By the late twentieth century, government housing policies and the creation of White suburbia had solidified patterns of spatial, economic, cultural, and social segregation. In 1940, when these policies were in their early stages, only one in three metropolitan residents lived in the suburbs. By 1970, the majority of metropolitan dwellers lived in suburbia. In contrast, the percentage of Black Americans living in urban centers more than doubled in the 1950s and 1960s.[79] This segregation resulted not only in the racialization of certain spaces but also certain lifestyles and practices. Black Americans were deliberately and systematically pushed into geographic spaces that were coded, or racialized, as poor, Black, and urban. Meanwhile, White Americans were systematically ushered into middle-class suburban spaces that were coded as American, patriotic, and family oriented. This delineation of White and Black spaces reinforced the streets as more than geography. As the experiences of middle-class Black Americans demonstrate, the streets became an inescapable part of Black identity.

Geographic Segregation from the Post–Civil Rights Movement to Today

Despite the fact that many of the policies responsible for creating the streets were outlawed in the late twentieth century, the physical, social, and cultural confines of the streets were sustained by the ideologies and practices that fueled these policies in the first place. By the middle to late twentieth century, the civil rights movement had begun to produce some change regarding housing segregation. In the 1948 case *Shelley v. Kraemer*, the Supreme Court ruled that it was unconstitutional for state authorities to enforce segregation, even if it was privately agreed upon. Still, the federal government, primarily led by FHA commissioner Franklin Richards, refused to change its practice.[80] When the FHA did comply with this ruling, it was by insuring housing that required community approval. Thus, when the FHA could no longer rely on a legal means to enforce racial segregation, it could still rely on cultural and ideological means. Overwhelmingly, White Americans continued to articulate their desire to maintain spatial segregation. In 1942, 84 percent of White Americans answered "yes" when asked if there should be separate towns for Black and White people.[81] Nearly twenty years later, 61 percent of White Americans said it was their right to keep Black people out of their neighborhoods.[82]

In 1968, President Lyndon B. Johnson signed the Fair Housing Act, which was more explicit in making racial discrimination illegal in the housing sector. Despite this, as one might imagine, geographic segregation did not disappear. Forty-seven percent of White Americans continued to argue that it was their right to keep Black people out of White neighborhoods.[83] A key element that allowed housing segregation to continue long after it was outlawed was the association of Blackness with economic risk. In 1961, the chairman of the Federal Deposit Insurance Corporation (FDIC), Erle Cocke, claimed that the FDIC's only responsibility regarding race and home loans was to prohibit the approval of unsound loans, not to force the approval of sound loans to Black Americans.[84] Ironically, Cocke uses the language of nondiscrimination to perpetuate anti-Black policies. His statement reflects the general way economic language was used as code for racial segregation. While there are corresponding material realities to the claims that Black neighborhoods are higher financial risks, these realities are the engineered products of decades of segregationist policies. Because the notion of financial risk is deeply rooted in the racialization of space, it is nearly impossible to disentangle the two.

In the aftermath of the postwar housing boom and subsequent fossilization of segregated metropolitan space, President Johnson appointed the U.S. National Advisory Commission on Civil Disorders to better understand the root causes of the race riots taking place in various U.S. cities. The committee chair, Illinois governor Otto Kerner, concluded in 1968 that the root cause was racial inequality produced by geographic segregation. He went even further by declaring that "white society is deeply implicated in the ghetto. White institutions create it, white institutions maintain it, and white society condones it."[85]

Kerner's statement reflects that, whether fully acknowledged or not, the origin and totalizing impact of racialized geographic segregation have been known for at least fifty years. In contrast to earlier claims and recommendations by the likes of Daniel P. Moynihan, Kerner and his fellow committee members argued in no uncertain terms that the only way to solve the issue of geographic segregation was to pour social and economic resources into U.S. cities, to redress gaps in social services, and to systematically integrate suburban spaces.[86] Despite their recommendations, when President Johnson signed the Fair Housing Act in 1968, the issue of housing segregation was treated as resolved. Yet, because the Fair Housing Act failed to, as the Kerner Commission suggested, address the streets as more than a geographic space tied to policy, it had little effect on the disparities of White and Black space. Unsurprisingly, rather than improve, the social, cultural, and economic disparities between urban Black Americans and White suburban Americans continued to grow exponentially.

In the decades that followed the civil rights movement and the Fair Housing Act, small changes in geographic segregation occurred. During the 1970s, Black migration to northern cities slowed down significantly, and the South actually saw an increase in Black migration. The result was that urban White northerners felt slightly less threatened by the influx of Black Americans. Black people were even beginning to integrate into the suburbs. Scholars such as Massey and Denton argue that up until the recession of 1973, the economic status of Black people was improving, and anti-Black discrimination was decreasing. The proof of this is that Black poverty reached a historic low in 1973.[87] Despite this initial trend, by the end of the 1970s, geographic segregation and racialized economic disparities were at an all-time high.[88]

While small instances of integration gave a false sense of racial progress, most U.S. cities observed only a minor decline in racial geographic segregation, and places such as New York and Newark even saw an increase. The trend in metropolitan areas across the United States was to have a Black urban core surrounded by a White suburban ring. The main exception to this pattern was in southern cities where Black people were geographically integrated but forced to live in subpar housing.[89] By the end of the 1970s, more than 70 percent of White Americans in the North lived in suburbs, whereas only 23 percent of Black Americans lived there. The situation was only slightly better in the South, where 65 percent of White Americans and 34 percent of Black Americans lived in the suburbs.[90] Given the fact that the population of White Americans was much higher, these percentages translate into even more disparate numbers when counting the people who occupy these spaces. Moreover, some of the Black suburbs were still highly segregated spaces. They may have existed outside of the city, but many still suffered from the same socioeconomic marginalization.[91]

Today, more than fifty years after the Fair Housing Act was signed, over a third of Black Americans experience what Massey and Denton call hypersegregation, the confluence of strategies that layer the effects of segregation through population distribution.[92] This is not to say that the remaining two-thirds of Black Americans do not live in racially segregated spaces, or do not suffer from the socioeconomic and cultural implications of geographic segregations, but that over a third of Black Americans live in the most extreme version of urban segregation ever seen in America. This group is unlikely to come into contact with someone who is White in their own neighborhood, or even in any of the nearby neighborhoods. This is the case for Black urbanites living in six of the country's ten largest metro areas.[93]

On the one hand, the continuation of racial geographic segregation long after the legal victories of the civil rights movement might be explained by the remaining realities that race was still closely tied to property value. It could be argued that post-1968 spatial segregation was an economic decision on the part of White Americans, not a racial one. This argument can be quickly dismissed when one considers the persistent cultural and ideological attitudes about Black spatial belonging. For example, in 1985, the Michigan state Democratic Party surveyed White working-class Americans regarding their perceptions of Black people. The interviews revealed that these working-class White Americans "express a profound distaste for blacks, a sentiment that pervades almost everything they think about government and politics. . . . Blacks constitute the explanation for their vulnerability and for almost everything that has gone wrong in their lives; not being black is what constitutes being middle class; not living with blacks is what makes a neighborhood a decent place to live."[94] In a study conducted in 2001, Douglas Massey found that White Americans still viewed racial composition as more significant than property values, schools, crime rates, or class composition when deciding where to purchase a home. The threshold of Black acceptability in a neighborhood was just 15 percent for those surveyed. Interestingly, what has changed is that many of these White Americans found it acceptable to live among other non-White groups but continued to express a distinct anti-Black preference in their home-buying habits.[95] The reality of the streets as a construct that defines and restricts Black life socially, culturally, and economically is stronger than ever despite changes in civil rights law. This is due to the fact that the streets are more than a geographic location; they are a set of interrelated beliefs and practices about Blackness and spatial belonging that have become a solidified part of U.S. society.

The perceptions of Blackness tied to the streets continue to produce economic and social disparities today. The U.S. Department of Housing and Urban Development (HUD) has conducted several studies on housing discrimination over the past few decades, and each study reveals that, despite existing laws, Black Americans are still discriminated against. This discrimination is more covert than it was fifty years ago. Rather than being explicitly told they cannot live in certain neighborhoods, Black buyers in the 1970s, 1980s, and 1990s were often steered toward lower-valued property or away from White neighborhoods, denied financial assistance and fair loan rates, or denied housing altogether.[96]

Even more recently, in 2012, HUD found that Black home buyers are shown fewer homes and continue to face greater scrutiny of their financial ability to purchase a home. Thus, while realtors may have been socialized to show Black Americans homes, they continue to operate under the ideology that Black Americans cannot afford the same homes as White Americans. In contrast, the same realtors often go above and beyond to help White purchasers secure financing. Overall, the 2012 HUD study found that since 1977, Black Americans have faced less discrimination as renters and are far less likely to be denied access to homes for sale, although it concluded: "Discrimination with the number of homes shown, however, does not appear to have changed much over time."[97] I would argue that this fits within a broader cultural pattern. As Blackness has become more synonymous with rentership rather than ownership, discrimination against Black renters has lessened. Of course this is also due to a broader acceptance of Black middle-class and upper-middle-class Americans. Despite these shifts, however, the ideological limitations of our racial progress are demonstrated by the fact that Black Americans still struggle to be perceived as qualified home buyers. As the HUD study concludes, "Taken together, these findings suggest that the most blatant forms of 'door slamming' discrimination observed in the earliest paired-testing study are much less frequent today, but that other, less easily detectable forms of discrimination persist, limiting the information and options offered to minority homeseekers."[98]

Even among Black homeowners today, just over 40 percent of Black Americans, their homes are often worth less than those of their White counterparts by virtue of being in Black neighborhoods.[99] Another way Black American home buyers are targeted and discriminated against is through what Rothstein calls "reverse redlining." In essence, Black Americans are targeted by banks and marketing campaigns as customers for subprime loans. Infamously termed "ghetto loans" by Wells Fargo employees, these mortgages were granted to underqualified buyers with the bank's full knowledge that they were unaffordable.[100] In fact, the bank penalized buyers for being underqualified by charging them higher interest rates. The loans also often had payments that were too low to cover the interest, so Black buyers accumulated no home equity. The exploitative nature of these loans meant foreclosure was almost a certainty.

The widespread nature of this practice in the early 2000s was a key contributor to the 2008 recession, and lest one think this was a matter of class more than race, low-income Black Americans were twice as likely to receive these loans as low-income White Americans. The ratio is even worse for higher-income Black Americans, who were three times as likely to receive such loans as their White counterparts.[101] The grave impact of these recent practices was articulated by HUD secretary Shaun Donovan as he addressed the Countrywide Mortgage Company settlement hearing: "From Jamaica, Queens, New York, to Oakland, California, strong, middle-class African American neighborhoods saw nearly two decades of gains reversed in a matter of not years—but months. Any way you look at it, that's an absolute tragedy."[102]

While Black Americans were still resisting their relegation to the streets and attempting to buy their way into middle-class American belonging, White Americans were amassing wealth from their subsidized homeownership. From the inception of the FHA mortgage program until 1962, the federal government underwrote $120 billion in new housing. However, less than 2 percent of that amount went to people of color. This staggering statistic only begins to reveal the larger implications of government housing policy for the racial wealth gap.[103] The homes that Black Americans were prohibited from buying became essential sources of equity and wealth building for White Americans. In fact, housing equity constitutes approximately two-thirds of all wealth for the median household.[104] The wealth subsidized by federal mortgage programs and other government protections of White-owned space grew exponentially after the Fair Housing Act was signed. According to economic scholars, about 50 to 80 percent of Americans' lifetime wealth accumulation today is directly attributed to past generations.[105] This often takes the form of financing children's education (through a higher tax base as well as paying for higher education), cosigning loans, and providing a cost-free space for children to live while they pursue higher education and/or a career. Government-subsidized homeownership also provided the base wealth for White Americans' retirement, small businesses, investments, and inheritances.

Over the past few generations, these housing policies, and the social practices they generated, have resulted in the exponential growth of racialized wealth disparities in America. In fact, scholars have found that the racialized wealth gap quadrupled in size between 1984 and 2007.[106] Between 1990 and 2030, the baby boomer generation will inherit $9 trillion, mostly from wealth created by subsidized homeownership before 1968.[107] Lipsitz points out that, rather than stave its growth, post–civil rights policies have actually aided in increasing this gap. For instance, laws that reduce taxes on inheritances and capital gains have served to compound White wealth.

Likewise, larger deductions for property taxes disproportionately benefit White Americans.[108]

This history is important because it directs us to the issue of America's racial wealth gap, one that is much more drastic than our racial wage gap. While Black Americans earn roughly 57 percent of what White Americans do, the wealth disparity is far worse. Today, for every hundred dollars White American families have in wealth, Black families have just over five dollars.[109] Moreover, one in four Black people have zero or negative wealth. In contrast, this is true of only one in ten White people.[110] Without this safety net, Black families suffer a great deal more during times of economic crisis. It is also increasingly difficult for Black families in particular to finance higher education for their children.

Even when Black professionals attempt to overcome these disparities by pursuing higher-paying professional careers, studies show that the racialized wealth gap results in these young Black professionals holding disproportionately more debt than their White counterparts. In essence, even among Black professionals who manage to close the wage gap, the racialized wealth gap still impacts them in grave ways.[111] This reality resonates with me personally. My mother was able to move out of the projects, finish high school, and eventually earn a bachelor's degree. Yet, despite her achievement, she still earned a lower income and, like her, I spent the first part of my childhood living in government-subsidized housing. Even today, after having managed to earn a doctorate and secure a tenure-track job at a university, I have no net wealth. Like many young Black professionals, the disproportionate amount of debt it took for me to move into the middle class professionally means that I have yet to do so economically.

Despite how gross this economic disparity is, and how much it continues to shape Black life, a recent study conducted at Yale University found that most Americans continue to underestimate the racial wealth gap and that there is "a systematic tendency to perceive greater progress toward racial economic equality than has actually been achieved, largely driven by overestimates of current levels of equality."[112] Acknowledging the vastness of America's racialized wealth gap, and its clear roots in government housing discrimination, is a fundamental step in deconstructing the myths of meritocracy that suggest that White middle-class American families have somehow pulled themselves up by their bootstraps while Black families have not. Instead, it reveals that White social mobility and the creation of the White middle-class were in fact direct products of government assistance. As legal scholar John A. Powell puts it, this history reveals how "whites moving to the suburbs were being subsidized in the accumulation of wealth, while Blacks were being divested."[113] While not as explicitly violent, government housing segregation policies emerged out of the same ideological roots as White supremacist lynching, subpar education, social segregation, and civil disenfranchisement, yet the effects of these policies have yet to be fully understood, let alone addressed.

In addition to direct economic disparities, geographic segregation also created generations of social and educational disparities. Black areas where home values were rated lower, and renters often outnumbered homeowners, had a much lower tax base than their White counterparts. A lower tax base translates into less funding for public schools and social services. Thus, racialized neighborhoods had an immediate impact not only on economic accumulation but also on access to education and opportunities for social mobility.[114] As scholars such as Douglas S. Massey, Camille Z. Charles, Garvey Lundy, and Mary J. Fischer have argued, there is a strong correlation between different types of capital disparities.[115] Without sufficient wealth, it is difficult to pursue social mobility through education, entrepreneurship, and so forth. However, these racialized spaces also limited cultural capital (knowledge of the norms and mannerisms necessary for social mobility) and social capital (networks and connections to successful, often middle- or upper-class, individuals) by physically and socially confining Black Americans to certain spaces. This is just one of the ways in which these policies worked to solidify a particular social meaning attached to the streets. By restricting their economic, social, and cultural capital, these policies contributed to the racial formation of urban Blackness as lazy, uneducated, and unenterprising.

The racialization of the streets continues to harm urban Black inhabitants today by reinforcing Black spatial isolation. This formation limits employment opportunity (who wants to start a business in the ghetto?) and even determines the food available to Black urbanites (save for gentrification, there are no Whole Foods stores in the hood). These perceptions have tangible effects on Black economic potential and health.[116] Unsurprisingly, these perceptions are largely responsible for heavier policing in Black neighborhoods. In addition to the physical threat Black urban inhabitants face, the presence of such policing has also proved to have detrimental effects on Black mental health and life expectancy.[117]

In these ways, the creation of the streets through segregationist government housing policies continues to have a drastic impact on Black life today.

The streets now exist as a self-sustaining entity that continues to produce greater socioeconomic inequality and reinforces negative perceptions of urban Blackness that serve to justify that inequality. It is also self-perpetuating, because its spatial isolation makes it difficult for Black Americans to physically escape poverty. Studies have shown that young Black Americans (aged thirteen to twenty-eight) are ten times more likely to live in poor neighborhoods due to generational disinheritance than are poor, young White Americans.[118] The way that poverty compounds over generations for Black Americans is contradictory to U.S. ideologies of social mobility and challenges the idea that White and Black poverty are the same. Black poverty is localized and culturally reinforced in ways that White poverty never is. The history of housing segregation and the creation of America's racialized wealth gap is one we must confront if we ever hope to build a just and equitable society.

CHAPTER TWO

The Secret of Selling the Negro
The Creation of Black Urban Consumerism

In 1945, a young John Johnson founded what would become the flagship Black magazine of the twentieth century, *Ebony*. During the first few years of *Ebony*'s run, Johnson had to keep the magazine afloat through loans and advertisements for his own mail-order products. "I sold vitamins, wigs, dresses, and hair-care products," he recounts. "I sold anything that I could sell in order to get enough capital to keep *Ebony* going."[1] After being rejected repeatedly by advertising agencies, Johnson took it upon himself to contact White business executives directly. It took persistent phone calls and a grassroots campaign of readers telling companies they would boycott if the companies did not advertise in *Ebony* to gain the kind of marketing attention Johnson desired.[2]

Johnson spent much of the 1940s and 1950s building on these campaigns to get *Ebony* to the height of its marketing success. The fruit of this labor was great economic gain for Johnson Publishing, as well as the solidification of *Ebony*'s place as the leading medium for reaching Black consumers. On average, *Ebony*'s monthly issues during the 1950s and 1960s were about 185 pages in length, with about 75 percent of those pages filled with advertisements. Between 1962 and 1969, the magazine's advertising revenue increased from $3.6 million to nearly $10 million.[3] Through *Ebony*, Johnson created one of the first means of mass Black-targeted marketing of its kind. While this meant that Black consumers received unprecedented economic attention, the attention was segregated from the rest of the national market. After Johnson coined the term the "new Negro market" in a 1954 film coproduced with the Department of Commerce, Black consumers were inundated with ads from White business owners. However, whereas their White counterparts were marketed home goods and luxury products, Black consumers were largely marketed food, clothing, cosmetics, and means of entertainment. I argue that this was due to the way Blackness was tied to urban space and nonownership through the public policies discussed in chapter 1.

The racialized divergence in post–World War II marketing practices facilitated a lasting perception of Black Americans, particularly those who live in urban spaces, as economically illiterate. Many of us are familiar with the stereotypes. Black urbanites are perceived as flashy, caring only about the possession of goods such as clothes, cars, and jewelry. Black consumerism today is understood as materialistic, but without the financial savvy that promotes wealth accumulation and social mobility. These assumptions that Black Americans spend their money on ephemeral things serve as justification for the harsh reality of racialized economic disparities in America. After all, if Black Americans choose to be unwise with their money, whose fault is it that they have not moved up the socioeconomic ladder?

While scholars such as Denver D'Rozario and Jerome D. Williams have analyzed "retail redlining," or the failure to market or provide certain goods in Black urban spaces, I am more interested in the history of how the marketing of particular goods associated with Black space created a specific racialization of consumerism itself.[4] In other words, how did the creation of the streets through geographic segregation shape perceptions of Black consumerism? Based on an analysis of American consumerism during the post–World War II boom, narratives around the so-called new Negro market, and archival research from *Ebony* magazine, I argue that Black consumerism was cultivated in such a way as to solidify an image of urban Blackness as flashy, brand conscious, and overly concerned with physical appearance. Furthermore, I argue that the distinct way in which Black marketing tactics were deployed functioned to further demarcate Blackness as something that exists outside of normative American consumer culture.

The New American Dream of Homeownership

As I discussed in chapter 1, homeownership has long been tied to national identity. Decades before FHA and HOLC policies made the housing boom possible, the government was urging Americans to buy more homes. This push for greater homeownership was motived in large part by a desire to prevent the spread of communism. The Bolshevik Revolution of 1917 sparked fear in U.S. leaders. In response, the Espionage Act (1917), the Immigration Act of 1918, and the Sedition Act (1919) were passed to thwart the spread of communism by deporting "immigrant threats" and incarcerating many leftists. These legal means of preventing the spread of communism were not the government's only strategy, however. Homeownership played an equally vital role in American anticommunism.

Homeownership represented a greater investment in U.S. capitalism, as well as another reason to believe in the veracity of the American Dream. These ideological underpinnings of government housing policy become even more evident when one considers the propaganda that accompanied them. For instance, the U.S. Department of Labor took over an Own Your Own Home campaign started by the National Association of Real Estate Boards (NAREB) in 1917. The campaign was initially a cooperative effort in which the NAREB worked alongside mortgage lenders and construction companies to promote the purchase of homes. In 1919, the Department of Labor instituted an Own Your Own Home Section under the Division of Public Works and Construction Development, as well as the Information and Education Division. This move is significant because it illustrates the historically intimate connection between private business in the United States and public policy. This fluidity between private and public spheres played a key role as homeownership became an increasingly significant part of American identity.

The Own Your Own Home campaign consisted of millions of posters, which were placed in newspapers, factories, and other business, as well as pamphlets that explained how homeownership was a patriotic duty. Additionally, promotional buttons that read "We Own Our Own Home" were used to target schoolchildren. The nature of this campaign is revealing. For one, it targeted White Americans across different class categories by promoting homeownership in factories, a traditionally working-class environment, as well as in middle-class media such as professional businesses and newspapers.[5] This was a clear attempt to combat class solidarity. Furthermore, as is clear from the poster depicted in figure 1, homeownership is tied directly to patriotism. The "realness" of the man's American identity is linked to his possession of a house.

The campaign also relied heavily on the dominant ideologies surrounding nuclear families, heterosexuality, and gender roles. This is illustrated in the poster through the emphasis on the man's ability to provide for his family with text that reads as follows:

> It should be a matter of personal pride with you to own your own home. Pride—in your proved ability to give your family a home of their own. Pride—in the ownership of real property, an ownership that places you among the bigger men of your community.
>
> A home-owner is a marked man—marked in the letters that can't be missed—"Success."
>
> Your family looks to you to give them a home of their own. They know that there is more happiness and comfort in a home of one's own. Let your children grow up in a real "home" atmosphere. Give

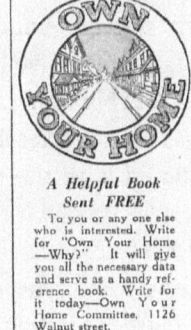

FIGURE 1 "The Man Who Owns His Home" poster. From the General Records of the Own Your Own Home Campaign, U.S. Housing Corporation, 1917–1952, Record Group 3, box 5, U.S. National Archives and Records Administration, College Park, Maryland.

your wife an opportunity to show you that she can be a business woman and a loving wife and mother at the same time.

Own your Home![6]

The repetition of words such as "pride," as well as the language of success, suggests that homeownership is tied to a specific form of masculinity, which is defined by the ability to provide economically. More specifically, the man's economic duty is to furnish the physical space, "a real home," necessary for American domestic life.

In a similar fashion, the mention of the man's wife implicates her in this constructed image of American homeownership. In their article, ". . . Be a Genuine Homemaker *in Your Own Home*," Paul C. Luken and Suzanne Vaughan discuss the specific ways in which women were targeted by the Own Your Own Home campaign. Whereas homeownership was linked to masculine provision for men, for women it was tied to feminine domestic duty.[7] The campaign circulated ads that suggested homeownership was about children's well-being. For instance, the U.S. Department of Labor printed a poster that simply read in large letters: "Own a Home for your Children's Sake." In figure 2, White American women are entreated to seek homeownership through the language of domestic pride. According to the poster, owning your own house allows for a home that "is always in order and much pleasanter and more livable than any rented house," along with a well-kept lawn and garden, "a real home atmosphere."[8]

It is worth noting that almost all of the posters and promotional materials from the Own Your Own Home campaign focus on nuclear families. As Luken and Vaughan conclude based on their archival research, "None of the illustrations depicts unattached people dreaming or thinking of buying a home nor alternative housing structures such as multi-household cooperatives."[9] Arguably, this early government push for White, heterosexual, middle-class homeownership is what led to the American Dream being directly equated with the proverbial house, white picket fence, and 2.5 kids.

The association of American identity and belonging with homeownership only grew as the twentieth century progressed. More so than any government campaign, the degree to which American identity and consumerism were tied to homeownership in the post–World War II period is exemplified by a 1959 exchange between then vice president Richard Nixon and Soviet premier Nikita Khrushchev. As part of a program of cultural exchange, each leader hosted the other in their respective home countries, where the visi-

"How glad I am that I agreed with John when he proposed that we 'Own' our Home!"

"I CAN look back and laugh now at the worries and discomforts that were always with us when we rented our house. With troublesome rent payments, the constant need for repairs that our landlord seldom made, the uncertainty of living in some one else's house, moving from place to place—I sometimes wonder how we stood it as long as we did.

"We wouldn't have remained renters for a minute if we had known then how easy it is to own a home. For four years we paid rent—a total loss.

"One day, this was eleven years ago—John said, 'No more renting for us—We'll own our home!'

"We found that we needed but four hundred dollars in cash to take immediate possession of the very house that we had always wanted. We also found that we could very easily borrow the rest of the money and pay it back in monthly installments.

"Eleven years later we're still here. Eleven happy years, too. It was just as easy as paying rent to pay off our loans—easier, in fact, because every time we paid rent, we realized that our money would never come back to us. Paying for our home, on the other hand, was merely taking money out of one pocket and putting it in the other.

"When repairing or decorating is needed, we have it done. Our home is always in order and much pleasanter and more livable than any rented house could be. Our lawn is well kept, our garden is blooming—in short, we live in a real home atmosphere."

A case of this sort is a common occurrence nowadays. City residents, particularly Philadelphians, are coming to realize that it is just as easy and much more advantageous to own than to rent.

You, yourself—if you can afford to rent—you can afford to own. And it is inevitable that soon you, too, will tire of rent troubles and rent wastefulness and the uncertainty of living in some one's else house. You will decide to own your home.

Attend the "Own Your Home" Exposition, First Regiment Armory, Broad and Callowhill Streets, April 21 to 26, and get a free chance on the bungalow to be given away. Exposition open from noon until 11 P. M. daily. Admission free, no tickets required.

A Helpful Book SENT FREE

To you or any one else who is interested. Write for "Own Your Home —Why?" It will give you all the necessary data and serve as a handy reference book. Write for it today—Own Your Home Committee, 1126 Walnut street.

We have no list of properties for sale. This campaign is purely educational—to teach the advantages of home ownership.

Own Your Home Committee
1126 Walnut Street

FIGURE 2 "How Glad I Am" poster. From the General Records of the Own Your Own Home Campaign, U.S. Housing Corporation, 1917–1952, Record Group 3, box 5, U.S. National Archives and Records Administration, College Park, Maryland.

tor would walk members of the press and government through a display representative of their nation. The Soviet exhibit opened in June 1959 in New York City, while the U.S. exhibit opened in July in Moscow. While the encounter epitomizes the many ideological and economic tensions that existed between the two world powers, it also points to the significant role U.S. homeownership played in America's narrative of prosperity and exceptionalism.

The U.S. exhibit included a display of several technological advances. Its most prominent feature, though, was a full-scale model of a $14,000 home. As Nixon walked Khrushchev through the display, the leaders engaged in a verbal sparring match, aptly dubbed the Kitchen Debate. Nixon argued that homes like the one on display were easily affordable and accessible by most workers and veterans due to recent changes in mortgage terms and government policies.[10] He added that these affordable homes came with all the latest appliances. Pointing to a dishwasher, Nixon claimed that this new model was typical of American homes and produced in mass. "In America, we like to make life easier for women," Nixon explained.[11] Unwilling to accept Nixon's proclamations about the ease of homeownership and modern convenience in the United States, Khrushchev retorted that Nixon's comment represented the sexism inherent in capitalism. Rather than deny his comment was sexist, Nixon countered that "this attitude towards women is universal. What we want to do, is make life more easy for housewives."[12]

Nixon's narrative of America being a place where life is easier for women, housewives in particular, is revealing in terms of who these ideal American women were. While he spoke of appliances and technologies that make life easier, he failed to mention the domestic labor force of Black women who were arguably more responsible for making life easier for White, middle-class women. Overall, Nixon's comments during the Kitchen Debate reveal the dominant image America was constructing of itself as a land of middle-class prosperity and access to the American Dream. His comments equally reveal those who were systematically excluded from this dream.

The Emergence of the Negro Market

While I have established the early twentieth-century connections between American identity, Whiteness, and homeownership, these dynamics took on a new form in the wake of the post–World War II housing boom. While Black Americans were being confined to urban space, White Americans were being ushered into the suburbs through government-subsidized loans, creating the base of a new consumer market. In her comprehensive study of

American advertising, *Soap, Sex, and Cigarettes*, Juliann Sivulka suggests that the postwar boom provided new markets for automobile, furniture, and appliance manufacturers. "Americans bought refrigerators, freezers, washing machines, clothes dryers," and other appliances in "unprecedented numbers."[13] In fact, it was this new housing-oriented market that led to the development of current household staples such as Tide heavy-duty detergent and Cascade dishwasher detergent.

In contrast to the ways in which White consumerism was being linked to homeownership, Black consumers were either ignored or targeted as buyers of superficial goods. The divergent development of White and Black consumerism and its relationship to the post–World War II housing boom become even clearer when one considers the history of Black commerce and consumerism on its own. When W. E. B. DuBois published *The Philadelphia Negro* in 1899, he noted the growth and potential of Black business in the city's Seventh Ward. Still, DuBois was quick to point out how the potential growth of Black commerce was stifled by discriminatory attitudes, disparities in capital, and the exclusion of Black businesses from the mainstream market.[14] Forty years later, M. S. Stuart, the vice president and director of government relations for Universal Life Insurance and a historian for the National Negro Insurance Association, argued that the exclusion of Black business owners from mainstream markets and their confinement to the so-called Negro market represent an "economic detour which no other racial group in this country is require to travel."[15] Both DuBois's and Stuart's works help explain the historical aversion to Black commerce and consumerism.

In their study of Black consumerism in Chicago, St. Clair Drake and Horace R. Cayton found that these negative views of Black business were held not only by White Americans but also by Black consumers. In fact, during interviews of local Chicago residents in the 1940s, Drake and Cayton found a distinct preference for White businesses among Black buyers. Many residents explained that they preferred White businesses because they sold higher-quality goods at more reasonable prices.[16]

While Black consumers preferred White businesses, their attention was often unrequited. As Roland Marchand observes in *Advertising the American Dream*, advertising agencies did not specifically target African American consumers in the first half of the twentieth century because their idealized consumer was White and middle class.[17] On the contrary, Black consumers were subjected to degrading advertisements based on racist stereotypes. Images of Black mammies and Sambos saturated product advertisements. Likewise, derogatory language was equally employed.[18]

As Black urbanites slowly came to be viewed as a new economic market following mass urbanization, some product advertising was directed at them. These ads, however, were mostly for beauty products and music, both of which were driven by racist perceptions. The beauty products were often skin-whitening creams and hair straighteners, which reinforced the superiority of White beauty standards. Likewise, ads for musical instruments affirmed the stereotypical belief that Black people were biologically more inclined to make music and entertain.

The postwar housing boom did little to change marketing efforts directed toward African Americans, at least initially. At the same time that advertising and manufacturing companies were catering to the new housing boom, few of these efforts were aimed at African Americans. In the twelve leading magazines that existed between 1946 and 1965, less than 1 percent of the ads placed featured African Americans.[19] At a time when segregation was a determining factor for housing, schools, and jobs, advertising was no different. The lack of Black representation was a clear signal that the goods being marketed were not meant for Black Americans.

Despite this lack of representation, American advertisers were slowly beginning to recognize the potential of the Black American market. The changes that took place were driven in part by a capitalistic desire to pursue new means of economic gain, but they were also, if not equally, driven by the efforts of Black leaders. Black marketing expert David Sullivan, for instance, published a number of articles on how to best approach the so-called Negro market. One of his articles, titled "Don't Do This—If You Want to Sell Your Products to Negros!," includes a list of stereotypical caricatures and language to avoid.[20] Likewise, newspaper publishers such as Claude Barnett attempted to reshape public perceptions of Black consumerism. As a result of efforts such as Sullivan's and Barnett's, Black-directed marketing changed its derogatory language and imagery.

Although these overtly racist images were disappearing, Black-directed marketing still operated on the basis of assumed racial characteristics. For instance, in 1946 Interstate United Newspapers contracted with the Research Company of America (RCA) to conduct a national survey of African American consumer habits. The survey was given to 5,000 families in twenty-seven cities, including Atlanta, Chicago, Detroit, Los Angeles, and New York. Although the survey was prompted by a coalition of Black newspapers, the data collected turned into a highly racialized narrative about Black consumerism. The survey results listed top brands among African American consumers, as well as a breakdown of how Black Americans were spending their collective

$7 billion in disposable income. According to the survey, $2.5 billion was spent on food, $2 billion on clothing, $750 million on housing, $500 million on beverages, $400 million on medicine, $350 million on home furnishings, $350 million on toiletries and cosmetics, $200 million on tobacco, and roughly $150 to $200 million on automobiles.[21]

The results of the RCA survey raise a number of questions. For example, what constitutes disposable income? Why are products such as food and housing on the list? These may seem like trivial questions, but they reveal the cultural and ideological assumptions that contextualize these data. To include items such as food and housing under "disposable income" raises questions about how the public understands what counts as a right or necessity for Black life and what counts as a privilege or a luxury. The narrative that emerged from studies such as this, and one that continues to shape Black marketing campaigns today, is made abundantly clear by the title of a review in *Advertising Age*, "Food, Clothing Get Most of Negroes' $10 Billion."[22] In essence, the title suggests that Black Americans spend their money on food and appearance (like many Americans), but that for Black Americans this is somehow frivolous.

An interesting explanation for the logic behind this claim appears in an article published by *Sponsor*, the primary trade journal for broadcasting at the time. In a piece titled "Does the Negro Have a Standard of Living (and a Product Consumption) that Compares with the Standard of Living of U.S. Whites?," the author argues that Black consumers have a comparable amount of money to spend on food, clothes, and other goods due to their prohibition from spending money in other arenas. He states: "Negroes are denied many recreations in many parts of the country that whites take for granted. I mean access to theaters, restaurants, night-clubs, beaches, vacation resorts, travel facilities and the like. . . . The Negro therefore will spend much more money on food, clothing, appliances, automobiles, and other items. . . . Negro standards of living, in many categories of goods, are a match for white standards."[23] While on the one hand the author acknowledges the discriminatory exclusion of Black Americans from certain domains of public consumerism, on the other hand he seems to suggest that the happy result of this racism is a level playing ground for businesses wishing to market certain goods.

Despite the eventual embrace of the so-called Negro market, its history reveals that it has always been perceived as distinct and separate from its White counterpart. Thus, as the natural response to growing White middle-class homeownership was the creation of more goods and marketing campaigns related to suburban home life, there was an equally "natural" response to Black segregation and urbanization. Segregation fueled a desire to compete through buying power, something publishing magnate John Johnson used to his advantage when he established *Ebony* as *the* Black middle-class magazine. Similarly, the exclusion of Black Americans from fair home values, or from homeownership altogether, meant that advertisers focused on selling goods that fit into the narrative of Black revelry and conspicuous consumerism. These divergent marketing methods turned into equally divergent notions of Black and White consumerism, notions that continue to inform the public perception of Black urban life today.

The Secret of Selling the Negro Market

The so-called Negro market was defined and promoted in large part by John Johnson. In addition to his work in publishing, in 1954 Johnson coproduced the film *The Secret of Selling the Negro* with the U.S. Department of Commerce and SARRA Production, a company known for producing several National Safety Council films. In the wake of northern migration and Black urbanization, *The Secret of Selling the Negro* tries to entice White business owners by extolling the untapped market of Black consumers. The promotion of *Ebony* magazine, another one of Johnson's holdings, as the ideal site for marketing to Black buyers was just an added benefit, of course.

Undoubtedly, *The Secret of Selling the Negro* signals a historical shift in American media and popular culture as they pertain to the topic of Black consumerism. Black buyers were finally worth White attention. The film attempts to leverage this buying power to promote a sort of economic equality (i.e., Black money spends the same as White money). However, when one situates this film within the context of the discriminatory housing policies that created the streets, it can also be seen as a cultural counterpart to the structural confinement of Black life to segregated spaces. In other words, the film functions as a cultural representation of the confines of Black consumerism within the wider landscape of American capitalism.

The segregated otherness of Black consumerism is prevalent throughout the film. For instance, in the opening scene a telegraph machine rapidly clicks away as it processes an incoming message. After a few seconds of anticipation, the camera shifts and viewers are shown the following message: "Washington—The average Negro wage-earner today gets 4 times more money than a few years ago, the Secretary of Commerce of the United States said today. 'His income has increased more rapidly than the income of all other Americans,' the Commerce Secretary said. We pointed out the family income of the Negro today at a record high."[24] In this scene, the emergency alert about Black consumers frames them as a new discovery, an unexplored territory. The target viewers, White business owners, are given a directive straight from Washington to consider the economic power of Black consumers. While on the one hand this power is framed as an equalizer, on the other hand the constant contrast between the "Negro" and "all other Americans" parallels the segregation produced by public housing policies.

The separation between the consumerism of "all other Americans" and the "Negro market" is highlighted in a particularly ironic way in the film's title. The most obvious source of irony here is the double meaning of "selling the American Negro." Given the history of chattel slavery in the United States, the "who" and "what" of buying and selling would have been interpreted quiet differently less than a hundred years prior to the film's release. Another point of irony is that a Black-owned media company is responsible for publishing a guide on "selling the Negro." Given the heightened awareness of racism in the 1950s, one cannot help but wonder at the title choice.

Even more fascinating than the title itself is the question of what exactly it means to "sell the Negro" in mid-twentieth-century America. This question is one that is answered throughout the remainder of the film. Shortly after the opening scene and credits, the main presenter, Robert Trout, addresses the viewer directly and proclaims the good news of the "Negro market." With $15 billion of spending power, these new consumers represent an enormous potential for economic gain. Before ever naming who the consumers are, Trout uses phrases such as "fresh" and "still full of opportunities" to prime the viewer. Lest someone watching the film questions why they have not heard of such a lucrative opportunity before, Trout explains this market is a secret because it "grew up so fast" and "got so big in a hurry that few of us realized its scope."[25] The last description is interesting as it divorces the emergence of a Black consumer market from historical factors such as slavery, emancipation, and northern migration.

After throwing in a few more convincing comments about how much money there is to be made and how no reasonable person would miss an opportunity to do so, Trout finally identifies this new market as the "Negro market." In many ways, it seems as though the film's producers and presenter are "selling the Negro" to White business owners in this scene. Trout continues to tell the "story of the Negro market" while images of Anglo-Saxon last names posted next to house numbers flash across the screen. As the narrator introduces "the New Negro family," he assures viewers that they go by names such as "Wells," "Wilson," or "Brown." The rhetoric of a "new Negro" is a clear appropriation of Harlem Renaissance language. However, whereas early twentieth-century Black American writers such as Alain Locke used this term as a means of self-fashioning against dominant stereotypes, it is used here as a way of proclaiming Black Americans to be somehow changed by recent historical events and therefore ready to be considered worthy consumers.

Black consumers' worthiness is represented in the film by the appearance of smiling, middle-class Black families. In one scene, a Black woman wearing pearls emerges from a pristine house and collects her mail, all while directing her gaze at the camera. As she returns inside, the viewer is shown her modernly furnished home and her husband and two children. These images situate Black consumers within a reality that is familiar to the viewer, that of middle-class suburbia. However, this reality was largely inaccessible to most Black Americans at the time. These images represent the film's two-pronged approach to promoting Black consumers. The first element of this approach is to establish the legitimacy of Black consumers through the frame of respectability. The second is to use this respectability as a guide for new marketing strategies.

The narrative of respectability can be seen in the way the film's narrator explains the past neglect of the "Negro market" and the rationale for change. He emphasizes that this market has been overlooked due to "mistaken" and "out-of-date" ideas about "how the Negro lives and how he buys."[26] What is interesting here is that these mistaken ideas have nothing to do with how Black people themselves are valued and understood, but rather represent a misevaluation of their buying power and consumeristic tendencies. In fact, the few times that questions of recognition or dignity are addressed are when the film presents strategies for selling to Black customers.

These "out-of-date" ideas are articulated by a shaky, malicious voice that states, "I don't like to do business with Negroes. They're drifters. You can't keep track of them."[27] The film's narrator responds to these comments with statistics about Black American credit ratings and payment records, as well as the statistic that one in three Black Americans who live in cities own their own home. At a time when White Americans were purchasing homes in droves, this figure highlights the disproportionate number of Black Americans who were renting, never mind the systematic devaluation of Black-owned property. This statistic is used to demonstrate that the filmmakers were far less concerned with the reality of Black homeownership than they were with making business owners aware that Black Americans now live in established spaces where they may be targeted for material consumption without fear that they might disappear before paying their bills.

The film goes even further in its promotion of Black consumers by telling the viewer that this market is particularly desirable for those selling high-end items. The narrator rattles off another series of statistics about Black Americans buying more quality items than any other racial group. This is followed by the appearance of former U.S. secretary of commerce Sinclair Weeks, who lists even more figures and statistics as evidence of Black buying power. What is most interesting is that this purchasing power is based on a perceived increase in wages. Predictably, there is no mention of the fact that these wages were mostly nonexistent during slavery ninety years earlier and minimal in the decades that followed. Likewise, as increased enrollment in schools is given as evidence of the "New Negro's improvement," there is no mention that access to such education was previously denied. Rather, the discourse on Black consumerism frames Black money as something that miraculously appeared out of thin air, a fruit that is now ripe for the picking by any White business owner willing to sell to Black people.

On the surface, the film's descriptions of Black consumers as a stable, socially improved group with great spending power seem to challenge the historical disregard for Black buyers. As such, it would be easy to miss what *The Secret of Selling the Negro* has to do with the sociocultural construct of the streets. Admittedly, the film's narrative represents a certain amount of progress. However, I argue that rather than signaling the economic integration of Black consumers, the attempt to shift the perception of Black consumers in the film is primarily about what Black consumers can offer White business owners. Robert Weems Jr. makes this argument in *Desegregating the Dollar* when he claims, "Changes in business practices among white-owned companies resulted from pragmatic white conservatism, rather than from altruistic white liberalism."[28] Despite the public recollection of the 1960s as a time of great liberal progress, Weems argues that advances in Black marketing were driven primarily by economic conservativism and a capitalistic tendency to adapt in the pursuit of greater profit. This does not mean that businesses did not take up the narrative of social responsibility, but rather that this narrative was often disingenuous.

This reality is evident at certain points in the film. For instance, in one scene a salesperson is explaining to the viewer how to do business with Black customers. He instructs the viewer to focus on transactions, treat Black people with respect, and avoid talking about race and politics. While this narration is taking place, a Black store owner and a White salesman stand in front of grocery shelves looking at a product together. In the background the viewer can see several images of Aunt Jemima products. Each of these products features a racist caricature of a mammy. This scene is telling. While the viewer is meant to focus on the exciting potential for economic transactions, the reality of anti-Black racism manifests itself on the very products being discussed.

The underlying impulse for targeting Black consumers was evident even to the Black leaders who championed the cause of Black consumerism. John Johnson reflects on these realties in his autobiography. Recalling his work in corporate America, he states: "I held the unofficial position of special ambassador to American Whites. . . . Enlightened self-interest: that was my theme. I asked corporate leaders to act not for Blacks, not for civil rights, but for their corporations and themselves. . . . What it all boiled down to was that equal opportunity was good business."[29] Johnson's words are refreshingly honest. They not only reveal a deep understanding of American capitalism but also challenge the linear narrative of racial progress. Moreover, they reflect the fact that Black Americans played a role in complying with these practices, even if the ends appeared to justify the means. Regardless of their respective motives, Johnson and the White business owners he worked with fostered the idea of Black consumers as a distinct, separate market poised to produce White economic gain. In many ways, this narrative fits within the broader patterns of Black economic exploitation seen in the banking and leasing policies discussed in chapter 1.

While *The Secret of Selling the Negro* caters mostly to White American business owners, it also constructs a narrative for Black consumers to follow. This narrative is that they should live up to the narrator's defense of them by fulfilling the label of the "New Negro," purchasing expensive goods and keeping up on payments. These expensive goods often revolve around appearance and entertainment. The focus on these types of goods is illustrated in the narrator's praise of the number of Black consumers who purchase record players and television sets. Likewise, he declares that Black Americans buy more toiletries and cosmetics than any other racial group. These statistics represent a proactive framing of Black consumerism around disposable goods and appearance.

In a similar way, brand consciousness for the sake of social status is a common association made with Black consumerism throughout the film. In fact, one of the key strategies listed in the film for selling to Black Americans is providing brand names. The narrator of this section plainly states, "For a long time the Negro has been sold a lot of shoddy, second-class merchandise. So now, he asks for name brands in order to make sure he gets his money's worth. Buy by brand. That's the first important Negro buying habit."[30] These instructions reflect Johnson's own opinion that brand names were an important way for Black consumers to ensure equal access to quality merchandise. However, even this suggests that Black consumerism must be performed in a way that is distinct from White consumerism. To be seen as equal, one must spend more; Black consumers do not have the luxury of frugality.

In addition to this first strategy, the narrator lists the other two key habits as selling "symbols of quality and prestige" and not "switching at point of sale." The former is explained by the narrator as the result of Black Americans' tendency to be heavily influenced by the thoughts and opinions of others. Thus, Black Americans buy brand-name, high-quality items to garner the approval of those around them. Johnson seems to affirm this idea to an extent in an *Ebony* editorial titled "Why Negroes Buy Cadillacs." Johnson argues that Cadillacs are "an instrument of aggression, a solid and substantial symbol for many a Negro that he is as good as any white man. . . . To a Negro indulgence in a luxury is a vindication of his belief in his ability to match the best of white men."[31] As Johnson points out, the drive for approval is not necessarily motivated by a desire for assimilation. Calling the purchase of luxury items "an instrument of aggression" points to its use as a means of registering one's frustration with the laws and practices that limit Black economic and social mobility.

Johnson's views on purchasing luxury items like Cadillacs are not unique. In *The Warmth of Other Suns*, Isabel Wilkerson records the story of a Black physician who desired a Cadillac as a symbol of success. The physician, Robert Joseph Pershing Foster, had recently settled in Los Angeles and opened a new practice. Struggling to live up to his wife's upper-class expectations and deal with discriminatory treatment by White Americans, Foster sought to buy a Cadillac as a way to "make them respect him more." Foster did not necessarily want to prove his worth to those around him; rather, he wanted to "blow 'em outta the water" by subverting their expectations of someone Black.[32]

While Johnson and Foster narrate the complex motivation behind luxury purchases such as Cadillacs at that time, this nuance was lost within the dominant narratives being formed about Black urban consumers. Rather than registering their purchasing habits as a response to inequality, Black Americans were simply seen as more brand conscious and less financially savvy by nature. In fact, marketing leaders, such as H. A. Haring, the editor of

Advertising and Selling, published claims that Black Americans were drawn specifically to brand-name foods, instruments, radios, clothing, and accessories. Much like those made in the film, these claims allude to a unique need Black Americans have for status symbols, despite lacking the financial means to make larger purchases such as home appliances.[33]

Likewise, a 1960 report prepared by Batten, Barton, Durstine & Osborn for the B. F. Goodrich Tire Company argued that Black consumers were drawn to brand names and therefore companies should design specific marketing approaches for them. Discussing the nature of the "Negro market," the authors explain, "Conspicuous consumption is an important factor in the Negro's buying phsychology [sic]."[34] They elaborate further: "Research shows that a majority of Negro consumers prefer to buy national brands (they represent acceptance, equality and assurance of honest value), and that Negroes are inclined to favor those national brands that advertise directly to them."[35]

For Black women, the narrative of brand consciousness takes on a particularly gendered form. A *Sponsor* article written by the director of the Women's Interest Bureau, titled "How to Sell Today's Negro Woman," gives general advice on which language to use when selling cosmetics to Black women. The author, Elsie Archer, tells advertisers that Black women's "needs are different" but does so by saying, "She does not want a blue-eyed suburban housewife telling her to use a particular product when she is faced with urban living."[36] The fact that the contrast between Black and White womanhood revolves around the dichotomy of suburban homeownership and urban dwelling emphasizes just how much racial identity and belonging were, and are, tied to space. Even in mid-twentieth-century advertising, there was an awareness that Whiteness signified suburban ownership, whereas Blackness signified urban rentership. In this particular instance, this separation is also classed and gendered in explicit ways. Suburbia is tied to blue-eyed Whiteness and the domestic labor of being a housewife, a privilege afforded only to middle-class women. In contrast, Blackness is tied to urban space and the suggestion of a working-class identity by default of *not* being a housewife. This is one example of how marketing tactics were already being informed by the dichotomy between the streets and White suburban America.

Films such as *The Secret to Selling the Negro* and marketing guides like *Advertising and Selling* and *Sponsor* reflect the ways Black consumerism was being shaped by new marketing tactics and narratives in the mid-twentieth century. In contrast to the marketing of home and family goods to White suburbanites, Black Americans were urged to prove their worth through spending power. Moreover, White business owners were urged to see Black consumers as a segregated market ripe for economic exploitation. The cultural separation of Black consumers from the rest of the American market is reflective of the geographic confinement of Black Americans to urban space through housing policies. Together, these forces worked to collapse Black consumerism and urban identity in a way that made the streets, and those who live there, synonymous with superficial brand consciousness and financial frivolity.

"The Happier Side of Negro Life": The Case of *Ebony* Magazine

In the 1940s, Johnson Publishing established a series of specialized magazines to target Black consumers. *Negro Digest, Ebony, Jet,* and *Tan* were designed to be the Black equivalent of mainstream staples such as *Reader's Digest* and *Life* magazine. Out of the four new magazines, *Ebony* was Johnson's flagship publication. Founded in 1945 as a general-interest magazine, *Ebony* was one of the primary media through which advertisers reached out to Black consumers. To say that consumerism was at the heart of this magazine is an understatement. Even Langston Hughes, in his guest article in the magazine's twentieth anniversary issue, explains that *Ebony*'s greatest success is its ability to garner "advertisements of high caliber" directed explicitly at the Black public where little attention had been paid previously.[37] It is this emphasis on Black-targeted marketing that makes *Ebony* the best medium for analyzing how, exactly, Black consumerism was cultivated through advertisements. I argue that *Ebony* enacted the tactics promoted in *The Secret of Selling the Negro* throughout the 1950s and 1960s, simultaneously reinforcing the stereotypes of Black consumers and segregating them from the goods reserved for the White suburban market. Ironically, this often took place alongside poignant political essays about anti-Black racism, as well as success stories of Black social mobility.

Although I take a critical view of the type of marketing that appears in *Ebony*, I must also acknowledge that Johnson's ability to garner such a strong advertising presence at a time when Black consumers were largely ignored by White business owners was an accomplishment in and of itself. While other Black publishing magnates, such as Claude Barnett, who ran the Associate Negro Press, were equally interested in increasing marketing campaigns aimed at Black Americans, Johnson managed to accomplish what no one else could. He turned *Ebony* into *the* publication for reaching Black consumers.

One of the ways Johnson accomplished this was by emphasizing the magazine's middle-class readership. In a 1950 article in *Advertising Age*, for example, *Ebony*'s editors boasted that 27 percent of their readers went to college and 36 percent owned homes (compared with 55 percent of all Americans and 34.5 percent of African Americans, according to the 1950 census).[38] In many ways, the targeted marketing in *Ebony* converges with narratives of racial respectability.

When *Ebony* magazine began in 1945, it claimed its purpose was to "mirror the happier side of Negro life—the positive, everyday achievements from Harlem to Hollywood. But when we talk about race as the No. 1 problem of America, we'll talk turkey."[39] In his autobiography, Johnson explains that his goal with *Ebony* was to reach Black veterans during the postwar boom with "more glamour and more pizzazz" than his other magazine in order to provide "relief from the day-to-day combat with racism."[40] In addition, Johnson was motivated by the lack of positive Black images in the media, and he saw *Ebony* as the solution to this problem.[41] This self-definition by the editor frames *Ebony* as a Black magazine that is concerned not only with bringing attention to a unique economic market, but also with using this attention to elevate the status of Black Americans through their power as consumers.

Because *Ebony* collaborated with Google to preserve public access to its archives, starting with its November 1959 issue, I was able to analyze the nature of Black targeted marketing in the magazine. I decided to focus my analysis on advertisements placed during the de jure practice of discriminatory housing policies. As I discussed in chapter 1, these polices continue to be practiced by private lenders today. However, for the purposes of this study, I am interested in the point of origin of contemporary ideologies related to Black consumerism. In order to contrast Black and White targeted marketing, I narrowed my analysis to focus on ads related to home goods, vehicles, and beauty. Throughout the early part of the twentieth century, what little targeted advertising that did exist in Black publications was primarily for over-the-counter medicine, mail-order novelties, and beauty products. This stands in stark contrast to the pervasive advertising of home appliances, cars, food, and other home goods present in mainstream publications.[42] I chose to examine home goods advertisements because they are an obvious point of contrast to the mainstream marketing boom around homeownership and its relationship to the American Dream. I posit that rather than an emphasis on home appliances or other goods associated with ownership, magazines such as *Ebony* include more advertisements for vehicles, products used by renters, and disposable goods such as food and cosmetics. I argue that these advertisements are a means of directing attention away from the limited opportunity of homeownership and the lower value of Black property.

Finally, I also focus on beauty products because historically these have been tied to issues of acceptance, respectability, and assimilation. Additionally, as Susannah Walker discusses in *Style and Status*, the beauty market occupies a unique space within the historical narrative of Black consumerism. On the one hand, the production of Black cosmetics has long been viewed as an exclusive opportunity for Black entrepreneurial success. On the other hand, it has been viewed as a ripe niche market by White cosmetic companies. By the 1930s, a large number of the beauty products advertised in Black magazines were created and funded by White-owned companies. Thus, by the mid-twentieth century the market for Black beauty products came to represent a contested territory tied to a wide range of ideologies from Black Nationalism to racial assimilation. As Walker puts it, Black "beauty culture both demonstrated the possibilities and revealed the limits of black consumer citizenship in the context of segregation, racial discrimination, and economic inequality."[43]

After examining each of the issues available in *Ebony*'s online archive, I found that, in contrast to their White counterparts, Black Americans were disproportionately targeted for the sale of clothes, cosmetics (often ones used to whiten skin and straighten hair), accessories, cars, and musical instruments. Of course, these same goods were sold to White Americans, with the exception of skin-whitening and hair-straightening products, but White-targeted marketing was distinct in a few ways. For one, there was a great variance in branding. Car ads in *Life* magazine (the magazine *Ebony* was modeled after) included luxury brands and imports, whereas *Ebony* did not. A second clear difference was in the amount and type of home goods marketed. On average, there were three times as many ads for home goods in magazines such as *Life*. Moreover, there were ads for windows, flooring, and other products tied to ownership that rarely, if ever, appeared in *Ebony*.

One of the few consistent home ads in *Ebony* comes from Bassett furniture, a Virginia-based company whose ads eventually even used Black models. However, the Bassett advertisement depicted in figure 3 seems self-aware in terms of audience and emerging stereotypes around Blackness.

The advertisement uses the language of luxury to promote the furniture. Technically, furniture sets are considered home goods, but furniture does not necessarily signify ownership. On the contrary, it only gives the appearance of ownership, an investment in one's home environment. However, the window at the top left corner of the ad reveals an elevated city landscape, which suggests that the Black mother and her child are in an apartment. This is an interesting example of one of the ways advertisers in *Ebony* were able

FIGURE 3 Advertisement for Bassett furniture, *Ebony*, May 1965.

to simultaneously cater to Black middle-class readers while maintaining the narrative that Blackness and homeownership were mutually exclusive.

Ebony's Take on the Streets

One of the most interesting and explicit connections between my analysis of *Ebony* and my broader discussion of the creation of the streets is the way in which these spaces and the policies that created them are discussed within the magazine. The November 1959 issue, for example, features a photo-editorial titled "Six Ways to Stop Negro Crime." The article itself resists the notion that crime perpetrated by Black Americans is the result of a pathological predisposition. Instead, the author claims that the increasing rates of Black arrests are due to a combination of racial profiling and structural inequity. "If Negroes are to assume a share of the responsibility for reducing their high rate of crime, they must demand equality of opportunity," he states.[44] Lest equal opportunity be interpreted as an abstract concept, the author plainly lists this as "equal transportation, health and sanitation services, housing, home financing, jobs, schools, teachers and recreational facilities, . . . hospitals opened to all patients and doctors, sufficient traffic signals and street lights installed, rat abatement programs launched to protect their babies."[45] In essence, equality includes all of the social services that are underrepresented in, or absent from, Black urban space.

A few years after the article on "Negro crime" was published, *Ebony* featured an article about James Del Rio, a real estate broker who was working to circumvent discriminatory housing policies. The article is meant to describe how one real estate agent overcame systemic adversity by getting Black families into government-owned homes. According to the article, Del Rio figured out that the Veterans Administration was not publicly listing available homes, so he petitioned it to change this policy. Once it did, he was able to sell homes in predominantly White neighborhoods in Pontiac, Michigan, to Black families. Rather than cause White flight or blockbusting, this resulted in "the picture of racial harmony" where "Negro and white youngsters played harmoniously and obviously unconcerned about differences of race."[46] Del Rio sums up his perspective on how easy this process was by saying Black Americans could buy homes like they did in Pontiac "throughout the country and the whole damn business of segregation would be wiped out overnight," if only they knew they could do so.[47]

On the surface, this article is a kind attempt to disseminate knowledge about government-funded housing. However, both Del Rio and the editors of the magazine assume that this knowledge is somehow enough to solve the problem. Even when the author acknowledges the explicitly discriminatory "code of ethics" held by the National Association of Real Estate Boards at the time, he dismisses these policies as short-lived pending a lawsuit by Del Rio and the Detroit Real Estate Boards. Perhaps this article is emblematic of a moment when middle-class Black Americans thought housing discrimination would be temporary or easily dismantled. Regardless of the rationale, this piece highlights the difficulty of challenging such policies when they are so grossly underestimated.

Just eight months later, *Ebony* published a more sober perspective on government housing policy. In an article titled "I Sold a House to a Negro," a Florida real estate broker named Elizabeth Moore tells of how she lost her license for selling a house to a Black family. Moore was approached by a client who had purchased the new home from a bankrupt builder. The client came to her offering to sell her the home *and* provide a buyer. The catch was the buyer was an African American doctor. The client said he was "too old for such stuff" as having someone "burn a cross in [his] yard."[48] Initially, Moore refused the client's offer. She had no desire to deal with the backlash of selling to a Black person.

Despite her reservations, Moore found herself contemplating the fate of the Black buyer, Dr. John Chenault. Interestingly, it was his existence as a middle-class man in "the Negro ghetto" that troubled her most. She wondered, "Where did a man trained in antiseptic cleanliness live in the Negro ghetto? Where was his house among the old frame shacks with children, chickens and dogs tumbling about the streets deep in dust or mud?"[49] It is not the existence of the streets or the plight suffered by their inhabitants that moves Moore to act. Rather, it is the inconceivable notion that a member of the middle class, Black or otherwise, would have to live in such a space. This becomes even more evident when she questions, "Are Negroes satisfied with their lot? What about the well-educated, cultured ones?"[50] This focus on the Black middle class as a means of instigating social change fits well within *Ebony*'s broader narrative. From its presentation to potential advertisers to the articles that fill the magazine's pages, *Ebony* consistently presents itself as a publication by and for middle-class Black Americans.

Regardless of what prompted her, Moore became adamant about selling the house to Dr. Chenault. She confronted colleagues and spent time working alongside the doctor to carve out a place of belonging in the community. She arranged dinners with future neighbors and met with local religious leaders to ensure that the Chenault family would be welcomed. At first, the article reads like a story about Moore and Chenault overcoming racial barriers. The article lists Chenault's successes: degrees from the University of Minnesota and the University of Chicago, dinner with President Roosevelt, a successful career and membership in a network of Black professionals. Yet just when Moore thought she had achieved her goal, she started receiving backlash for selling the house to a Black family. The same neighbors who had dinner with Dr. Chenault and proclaimed their lack of prejudice were now furious that Moore had actually sold the home to him. She started receiving threatening phone calls and letters.[51]

In an attempt to remove the doctor, Moore's colleagues suggested that she renege on the contract. Local neighbors tried to pool their money in order to buy Dr. Chenault out. They sent letters to other White neighbors with the slogan "You are obligated to do your duty."[52] Eventually, after these attempts failed, Moore was accused of violating Florida real estate guidelines and made to stand before the Board of Realtors' Ethics Committee. Although this charge was dropped, the committee found her guilty of being unethical during a sale that had taken place years earlier due to a clerical error. Moore fought the charges but was not victorious. She was expelled from the Board of Realtors.[53]

What this article shows, especially in contrast to what was published months earlier, is that discriminatory housing policies were becoming stronger and more ingrained in both structural and cultural practice. It also reveals how this reality was obfuscated by narratives that hid the racial motivation behind these practices. Moore's story is a personal reflection on the way geographic segregation had become a fundamental part of American cultural identity and hegemonic understanding. Yet, technically, she did not lose her real estate license for selling a house to a Black man. She was charged with trickery. When members of the Board of Realtors spoke publicly about her expulsion, they stated that it had nothing to do with race or prejudice, but rather the board's commitment to high ethical standards.[54]

In the case of Dr. Chenault, it was not a government policy that threatened him but instead the cultural understanding that he did not belong in middle-class suburbs. Regardless of his economic status, Dr. Chenault's Blackness meant that he was defined by the streets. Interestingly, this was expressed through economic language reminiscent of the policies that sustained redlining in the mid-twentieth century and, arguably, still sustain it today. Moore was told repeatedly, "The presence of any Negro, no matter how distinguished would devaluate their property."[55] This response highlights how the reality of geographic segregation is often suppressed by the discourse of property value and economic logic. However, if this were really the case, the neighbors would not have responded emotionally with "hissed insults" and "anonymous letters."[56] Moreover, the original client who sold the house to Moore would not have specifically mentioned the KKK's potential involvement as a discouraging factor.

As the reality portrayed in "I Sold a House to a Negro" became more conspicuous, *Ebony* began to shift its focus from "the happier side of Negro life" to address these impasses to Black upward mobility. In the years that followed, *Ebony* published, along with its typical celebrations of Black middle-class achievement, numerous articles discussing the adversity faced by Black Americans. Along with the expected topics of voting and anti-Black violence, housing discrimination was often at the center of these articles. For example, the August 1965 issue was dedicated to the topic "The White Problem in America," a subversion of the nomenclature for racial discourse at the time, which often framed it as "the Negro problem." Quite explicitly, one of the magazine's contributing writers states, "There is no Negro problem in America. The problem of race in America . . . is a white problem."[57] Given the idealistic picture of racial harmony presented just months earlier, this statement represents a significant turning point in the way *Ebony* addressed race.

In addition to confronting racism more directly, the special issue includes several articles that address housing discrimination as "one of the most deeply rooted, most doggedly defended forms of racial discrimination."[58] Within these articles, the magazine's contributors define urban space in a way that clearly articulates its man-made origins. Harlem, arguably the most emblematic Black urban space, is described as "a white-made thing."[59] Similarly, Whitney Young, then executive director of the National Urban League, argues that the conditions of Black urban life are part and parcel of racist design. He states: "The white man creates the ghettos and brutalizes and exploits the people who inhabit them—and then he fears them and then he flees from them. He builds Harlem and then he runs from Harlem. He created second-class schools and then he fears for his children. . . . He denies Negroes jobs and then he curses them for robbing his stores. He creates a climate of despair and then acts surprised when the protest marches fill the streets and riots erupt."[60] Beyond his articulation of the way the streets are a direct product of discriminatory design, Young captures the fact that they amount to much more than segregated space. The "ghettos," as he calls them, are the sum of confined space and limited opportunity that gives rise to internalized despair and externalized violence.

Rather than merely identify these origins, writers such as Lerone Bennett Jr. (executive editor at the time) suggest that the public begin asking,

"Why did you create it? And why do you need it?"[61] This last question suggests that Black urban space is not merely a by-product of past discriminatory policies but a sustaining element of Whiteness and racial inequality. By proclaiming that ghettos are "created and sustained by white power," these articles articulate their negative impact on Black life, as well as on public perceptions of Blackness.[62] This latter part is made evident when Bennett states that "the real problem is an irrational and antiscientific idea of race in the minds of white Americans . . . a rationale for giving Negroes poor schools, poor jobs, and poor housing."[63]

In making this last claim, the author gets to the heart of urban Blackness as a socially constructed identity linked to poverty, broken families, and criminality. In this construction, what separates Black poverty, family structure, and criminality from their White counterparts is a belief that "Negroes, by virtue of their birth, have within them a magical substance that gives facts a certain quality."[64] These "facts" about Black urban life are only deemed to exist due to preconceived notions about Blackness and the assumption that Black Americans have some sort of biological predisposition to crime and poverty. In contrast to this "magical substance" that is used to explain the deviant behavior of Black Americans, Bennett argues that "racism in America was made by men, neighborhood by neighborhood, law by law, restrictive covenant by restrictive covenant, deed by deed."[65] Bennett's language suggests that housing discrimination and the emergence of the streets were perceived as central aspects of racism at the time.

Civil Rights Consumerism

Ironically, astute observations about racism and the creation of the streets, like the ones made by the magazine's executive editor, Lerone Bennett Jr., often appeared alongside the very advertisements responsible for furthering racist perceptions of Black consumers. A prime example of this juxtaposition is *Ebony*'s special issue titled "The White Problem in America." Within the issue, which focuses on the state of anti-Black racism in America, an ad for Ultra Wave hair straightener for men shares a page with a critical exploration of White liberalism (figure 4).

On one side, *Ebony*'s readers are urged to think critically about racial progress. On the other, they are offered a way to assimilate to White beauty standards. These starkly contrasting ideologies challenge *Ebony*'s self-construction as a publication geared toward Black progress. More interestingly, they offer insight into how readers could be simultaneously critical of

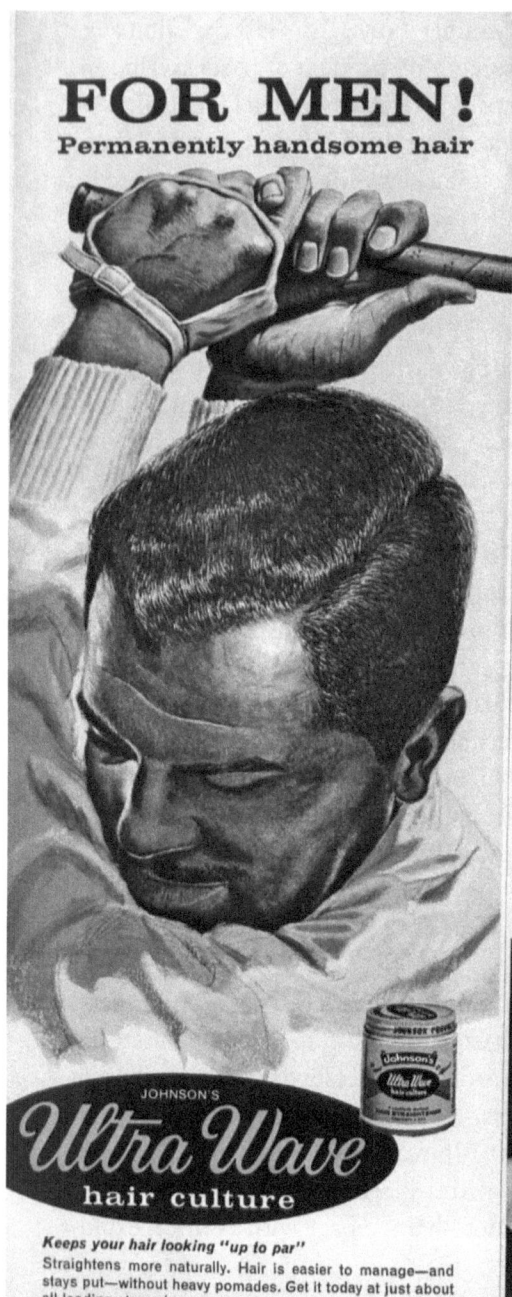

FOR MEN!
Permanently handsome hair

JOHNSON'S Ultra Wave hair culture

Keeps your hair looking "up to par"
Straightens more naturally. Hair is easier to manage—and stays put—without heavy pomades. Get it today at just about all leading stores/JOHNSON PRODUCTS COMPANY, INC.

First civil rights demonstration for which white liberals turned out en masse was the 1963 March On Washington which found whites from all walks of life journeying to the Capital to protest discrimination. Participation was almost spontaneous.

THE WHITE LIBERAL Continued

disfranchised and impoverished blacks would much prefer to see the entire structure come down and make way for a new building. Thus it is that white liberal money and bodies have moved in and taken over every national civil rights organization with the exceptions of ACT, CORE and the Student Non-Violent Coordinating Committee. Let the truth be told: Lyndon Baines Johnson is now the number one "Negro" Leader.

The new power elite has a strong ally in the black bourgeoise. The alliance, I predict, will get stronger once the middle class Negro and the white liberal discover how much they really have in common. Their economic interests and value systems are much the same, and their views of humanity are identical: they are honestly concerned

Martyred Mrs. Viola Gregg Liuzzo was shot from speeding car as she ferried marchers back to Selma in her auto after March on Montgomery. Mrs. Liuzzo was fourth white person murdered in South while aiding Negroes in fight for full civil rights.

FIGURE 4 Advertisement for Ultra Wave hair straightener, *Ebony*, August 1965.

the way the sociocultural construct of the streets was shaping their lives and accepting of its influence.

These kinds of contradictions are present throughout *Ebony*, but they are perhaps most conspicuous in the September 1963 issue, which celebrates the centennial of the Emancipation Proclamation. In contrast to the colorful photos of celebrities that typically appeared on the magazine's cover, this issue features a stark, black-and-white image of Frederick Douglass, which sets the tone for somber reflection rather than the usual celebration of Black upward mobility. Within the issue, John Johnson himself issues a statement from the publisher that notes that this anniversary is not so much a time for celebration as it is a sober recognition of continued struggle. He states, "The freedom proclaimed by Abraham Lincoln is not yet a reality. It is restricted today by state laws in the South, by moribund customs in the North, by the fear, anxieties and rigidities of millions in the South, North, East and West."[66] Johnson's statement is followed by four commentaries on the centennial and the continued fight for racial equality in America by then president John F. Kennedy and former presidents Herbert Hoover, Harry Truman, and Dwight Eisenhower. Truman references his 1948 civil rights message to the Congress of the United States, in which he argued that "all men are entitled to equal opportunities for jobs, for homes, for good health, and for education."[67] Ironically, it was under Truman's "racial equity formula" that public housing projects became increasingly tied to Blackness and poverty.

Herbert Hoover is noted in the magazine as being "too ill to write a personal letter," so the editors included an excerpt from his book *The Challenge to Liberty* instead. This excerpt reads, "American Liberty denies that special privileges come to men by birth."[68] Yet, it was Hoover who, as secretary of commerce, put together the national Advisory Committee on Zoning, made up of outspoken segregationists. Despite these historical contradictions, the inclusion of these statements highlights parallels between the struggle for emancipation and the struggle for civil rights.

Of all the articles in the *Ebony* emancipation issue that address major political events or social issues, I find the statement from Johnson to be of particular significance due to how he defines the magazine's cultural role. Johnson uses his statement to affirm *Ebony*'s identity as a magazine that has always documented the struggle of Black Americans, as well as the ways in which exceptional Black Americans have managed to rise above this struggle. This issue especially is meant to be the epitome of this work. Johnson notes that the issue was the largest one to date, with 236 pages in total, and that all of these were "devoted to the dramatic story of 100 years of hope and struggle."[69] Yet, more than 60 percent of this special issue on Black civil rights consists of advertisements for clothes, food, cosmetics, liquor, television sets, radios, and cars. There is only one advertisement for a major home appliance; in contrast, there are twenty ads for alcohol and eight for cigarettes.

When one considers the almost 200 pages that fill each issue of *Ebony*, one gets the impression that the magazine is equally, if not more, interested in curating Black consumerism as it is with discussing racial struggle and progress. As much as *Ebony* frames itself as a magazine that champions positive Black representation, it is also somewhat self-aware of its unique role in generating attention to the Black American market. The first issue of *Ebony* did not include any advertisements. However, by the time of its fifteenth anniversary issue, *Ebony* was "second only to *Holiday* magazine in total advertising among general interest monthlies."[70] Johnson goes on to state that the magazine was "among the top 60 magazines in beer advertising, fifth in drugs-proprietaries, eighth in cigarettes, tenth in liquor, 12th in canned goods and 16th in shoes and cosmetics."[71]

Each of the most advertised products listed by Johnson coincides with my findings that Black consumerism was being cultivated around appearance and entertainment, while White middle-class consumerism was driven primarily by homeownership. In the emancipation issue there was only one advertisement for a major appliance or a home good that could be tied to ownership. Interestingly, Johnson's Wax took out a four-page full color ad that frames the need for the company's products through the lens of homeownership and home life. The advertisement features "the Louis Jordan family" in their modern home. Louis is described as chairman of the Art Department of Chicago's Dunbar Vocational High School, while his wife, Cordelia, is "an accomplished sculptress."[72] The couple live with their nine-year-old daughter, Celeste. The featuring of this Black, middle-class family paints a picture of possibility. Far removed from the government policies that kept most Black Americans from attaining such ownership, the Jordan family fits within the paradigm of exceptionalism, proof that social mobility and access to the American Dream are indeed possible for those who work hard enough.

Despite the degree to which the advertisement emphasizes the Jordans' homeownership and lifestyle, the goods advertised (floor wax, cleaning products, bug spray, air freshener) have little to do with ownership itself. It would seem that these products, which were being marketed to a public with limited access to homeownership, were being sold via the reader's desire to partake in the dream embodied by the Jordan family in these ads.

The contradiction between the message conveyed about *Ebony* as a magazine focused on Black rights and social mobility, and its widespread embrace of exclusionary consumerism comes across visually in several striking ways. For one, just two pages after a section titled "Speaking of People" that highlights the achievements of Black professionals, there is a full-page ad for Nadinola Bleaching Cream. The equation of Whiteness with betterment is explicit: "Nadinola brightens your opportunities for romance. . . . Men take notice like never before."[73] It is worth noting that the majority of whitening cream advertisements in *Ebony* were geared toward women, suggesting a gendered narrative of Black social mobility that links women's futures to "lighter and brighter" skin.

This becomes particularly ironic when a similar full-page color ad for Artra skin tone cream appears alongside a multipage article titled "The Negro Woman." The article itself repeats a common narrative that Black women were socialized by slavery to be overly dominant, much to the detriment of Black men. What is most interesting, however, is that the article's author, Lerone Bennett Jr., warns parents to protect their children against "impossible beauty standards" driven by a desire for Whiteness. He laments that "a very large part of the family budget is spent on beauty preparations. Many women will keep a beauty appointment before they will keep a medical appointment."[74] This statement appears directly opposite the image depicted in figure 5.

The fact that Bennett, as an *Ebony* contributor, articulates the very narrative that, I argue, emerged from the targeted marketing embodied in this ad suggests that even as early as 1963, this stereotype of Black consumerism was already deeply ingrained both culturally and ideologically. The sociocultural construct of the streets had evolved to include narratives of flashy, superficial Black urban consumers—narratives that continue to shape perceptions of Blackness today.

The Consumer of the Streets

The connections between government housing policies and socioeconomic disparities discussed in the previous chapter tell only part of the story of how the streets came to exist as a distinct sociocultural entity. Although the physical space of the streets was created through government housing policy, its social and cultural meaning was constructed through other means. As I have illustrated in this chapter, these policies reached beyond their immediate economic and geographic spheres to facilitate a particular racial

FIGURE 5 Advertisement for Artra skin tone cream, *Ebony*, September 1963.

formation of Black urban identity. One example of this is the specific way Black consumerism is perceived in contrast to that of "all other Americans." As a result of dual marketing practices, there are radically divergent images of White and Black consumerism. In one, White Americans are understood as largely middle-class consumers who prioritize spending on long-lasting investments. In the other, Black Americans are perceived as poor urbanites who spend their money on ephemeral products such as clothes, cars, cosmetics, food, and liquor.

One of the key points I wish to make is that Black consumerism has been purposefully and distinctly shaped. Much like other aspects of Black urban life, Black consumerism is often codified and criminalized in overtly negative ways. As Naa Oyo A. Kwate notes, even today, Black consumers are seen as "combat consumers" and "mythologized as susceptible to commodity fetishism and are willing to kill, injure, or steal from others to satisfy their desires for expensive brand name goods."[75] However, when contemporary critics decry Black commodity fetishism—the perception that Black consumers extravagantly spend their income on status symbols when they could be saving and pulling themselves up out of poverty—they fail to acknowledge the way such spending habits have been carefully crafted by institutions over the past century. The so-called extravagance of Black urban life is not the result of some pathology, but rather the effect of the streets operating as they were intended to from the beginning.

CHAPTER THREE

From *The Street* to the Streets
Black Literary Production and Urban Space

In the opening lines of Between the World and Me, the narrator tells his son, "'Black-on-black crime' is jargon, violence to language, which vanishes the men who engineered the covenants, who fixed the loans, who planned the projects, who built the streets and sold red ink by the barrel."[1] By tracing the genealogy of a term like "black-on-black-crime" back to the politicians and government employees responsible for geographic segregation, Ta-Nehisi Coates signals the reach of the streets beyond physical space. Numerous Black authors have explored this theme of the streets as more than a geographic entity.[2] While government policies, economic rationales, and marketing campaigns historically worked to create a derogatory narrative around urban Blackness, Black American authors were simultaneously wrestling with the cultural and ideological impact of living in racialized urban spaces.

In this chapter, I examine how these authors use their work to theorize the streets in ways that are either counter to, or critical of, the way the streets exist in the broader White imaginary. Black authors often utilized literature as a means to assert power over how the streets were being defined socially and culturally. This cultural labor represents what George Lipsitz calls an effort to "construct discursive spaces as sites of agency, affiliation, and imagination" by "people who do not control physical places."[3] I argue that, beyond recording the oppressive nature of the streets, the discursive space created through Black literature depicts the alternative communities and geographies of belonging that coexist with the streets. This idea is reminiscent of sociologists St. Clair Drake and Horace Cayton's discussion of "Bronzeville" in *Black Metropolis*. "Bronzeville," a name given to Black urban Chicago by its inhabitants, expresses "the feeling that the people have about their own community."[4] Conceptually, Bronzeville challenges the notion that Black urban life is binary. Rather than seeing it as entirely good or bad, violent or peaceful, damning or inspiring, "Bronzeville" reflects the at times contradictory coexistence of these characteristics.[5]

Although I focus on twentieth-century and twenty-first-century literature, which coincides with the timeline of systemic housing segregation and increasing Black urbanization, it is important to acknowledge that Black authors had been writing about the city long before that time. Analyzing these earlier texts about the city reveals the drastic differences in how Black urban space was socially and culturally understood before and after the implementation of segregationist housing policies. W. E. B. DuBois, for instance, was the first Black American author to explore the issue of urban Blackness in a book. In his sociological study *The Philadelphia Negro*, DuBois identifies urban Black inhabitants as members of "a city within a city."[6] Like other Black intellectuals of the time, DuBois's discussion of the city focuses on its association with so-called high culture. His concerns reflect those of the Black middle class. Yet, even as DuBois argues that Black urban inhabitants are diverse in a number of ways (including his emphasis on the role of the cultural and intellectual elite), his text acknowledges the way urban Blackness has always existed apart from White urban experiences. This is a theme that also appears, albeit sometimes subtly, in works by Pauline Hopkins, James Weldon Johnson, and Charles Chesnutt.[7] While the city may present itself as a civilized space, the realities of anti-Blackness complicate this narrative.

During the Harlem Renaissance, Alain Locke's idea of the "New Negro" was distinctly tied to the city. Locke, who was born and raised in Philadelphia, saw Harlem as the epitome of Black urban space. His famous anthology, *The New Negro*, grew out of a special issue of *Survey Graphic* dedicated to life in Harlem. For Locke, Harlem was the center of a movement toward reshaping public perceptions of Blackness. As he explains, Harlem "is the home of the Negro's 'Zionism.' The pulse of the Negro world has begun to beat in Harlem."[8] When Locke envisioned the future of Black America through the "New Negro," he did so by localizing this future in Harlem. However, much like DuBois, Locke's view of the city used the Black elite to counter stereotypes, rather than focusing on the broader conditions of anti-Blackness in the city.

This is an idea that literary scholar Charles Scruggs discusses as he analyzes the portrayal of the city in African American literature, such as Richard Wright's *Native Son*, Ralph Ellison's *Invisible Man*, James Baldwin's *Go Tell It on the Mountain*, and Toni Morrison's *Beloved*.[9] Scruggs argues that the city in Black literature is represented as both dystopian and utopian. While, on the one hand, it reflects the harsh realities of American anti-Blackness, on the other it fosters a "beloved community." As he puts it, "The city as a symbol of community, of civilization, or home—this image lies beneath the city of brute fact in which blacks in the twentieth century have had to live."[10] Scruggs's work offers a point of departure for this chapter. I argue that this tension between Black urban community and isolation undergirds writing about the streets. Where Black American authors had previously seen the city as a site of potential and achievement, writings about the streets depict them as a space that actively restricts Black Americans from those dreams. Nevertheless, Black authors depict the streets as a space capable of fostering community and belonging.

In this chapter, I analyze Anne Petry's *The Street*, James Baldwin's *The Fire Next Time*, and Ta-Nehisi Coates's *Between the World and Me* to determine how the streets have been depicted and theorized in Black American literature throughout the twentieth and early twenty-first centuries. The three selected texts are products of pivotal cultural moments in the history of Black urban space. Petry's novel *The Street* came out of her experience living in Harlem after the so-called renaissance. A couple of decades later, Baldwin wrote *The Fire Next Time* within the context of the civil rights and Black Power movements. Finally, more than fifty years later, Coates reminds readers that the post–civil rights era has yet to address the legacy of housing segregation and the creation of Black space in America. In looking at these authors' works, I argue that, despite their disparate historical contexts, there is a continuity in the way each author describes the streets. Their writing demonstrates how the streets threaten Black life. However, this threat is not just physical, although that violence does exist. Petry, Baldwin, and Coates each illustrate that the streets also operate on a more pervasive, ideological level by enticing those who live there with the promise of wealth and achievement typically associated with the American Dream. As their stories illustrate, this promise is never fulfilled because those who live in the streets are prohibited by their racial and geographic belonging from ever attaining that level of power. In this way, these authors articulate the way power itself operates in the streets. However, each them also acknowledges how Black urban inhabitants challenge and subvert this power through both self-expression and communal expression. I argue that this literature reflects the fact that, while the streets may operate in oppressive ways that require large-scale change, this power is not totalizing. Black Americans resist and contest this power, carving out the space for meaningful existence in the streets.

116th in Harlem: *The Street* by Ann Petry

Ann Petry published *The Street* in 1946, just twelve years after the passage of the National Housing Act. Set in Harlem in 1944, it is arguably the best example of mid-twentieth-century Black American literature depicting the streets as more than a physical space. Petry's focus on the nature of life in

Harlem was influenced by her experience entering this space as an outsider. She was raised in a quiet town in Connecticut and lived a life of relative privilege for a Black person in early twentieth-century America. Petry was raised in a middle-class family and earned a degree from the Connecticut College of Pharmacy. She worked as a pharmacist in her family's drugstore for several years before marrying and moving to Harlem.[11]

Petry's upbringing undoubtedly shaped her perspective on Harlem. Hilary Holladay suggests that Petry "looked at Harlem with the dual vision of an outsider, who had not grown up with the problems endemic to ghetto life, and an insider, who identified with the people of her own race and wanted to put their struggle into words."[12] This is not to say that Petry was somehow an exceptional outsider. As Evie Shockley argues, Petry's focus on Harlem demonstrates an awareness that "it was less an individual exceptionality than it was her exceptional circumstances that had preserved her from the more common fate of African Americans."[13] Arguably, this realization makes Petry uniquely qualified to depict the nature of the streets as something that shapes and defines all Black life in one way or another.

Petry's novel follows the journey of the protagonist, Lutie Johnson, as she attempts to build a life for herself and her son. Lutie migrates to Harlem after her marriage falls apart. Determined to work her way up the social ladder, Lutie pursues a number of careers, all while her son, Bub, finds himself alone on the streets. The novel is a tragedy that highlights the specific impact the streets have on Black familial relationships and the pursuit of the American Dream. More relevant, however, is the way Petry's work narrates the transformation of a street, 116th Street in Harlem, from the figurative representation of everyday life in Black spaces into a menacing sociocultural entity—*the* street.

The first lines of the novel depict the transformation of 116th into the streets. Petry does this through detailed nature imagery and personification. The novel opens with a description of 116th as cold and weatherworn. The cold wind is described as having "rattled the tops of garbage cans, sucked window shades out through the top of open windows and set them flapping back against the windows."[14] As if this destruction were not enough, the wind begins "fingering its way along the curb" and "sets the bits of paper dancing high in the air, so that a barrage of paper swirled into the faces of the people on the street."[15] In this opening scene, the wind is personified as a violent menace. It is disruptive and antagonistic. If this "cold November wind" is to be understood as the proverbial winds of change, then the change it represents is a threatening one.

This impending threat becomes clearer in the paragraph that follows, where the wind is described as actively working to "discourage the people walking along the street. It found all the dirt and dust and grime on the sidewalk and lifted it up so that the dirt got into their noses, making it difficult to breathe; the dust got into their eyes and blinded them; and the grit stung their skins. It wrapped newspaper around their feet entangling them until the people cursed deep in their throats, stamped their feet, kicked at the paper."[16] Petry's opening description of dirt, dust, and grime is an all-too-familiar image of urban landscapes. The difference here, though, is the way such grime is portrayed as actively attempting to blind and choke the people. Likewise, the newspaper chains that entangle them signify inescapability. This is affirmed by the cyclical actions of the wind blowing and the people attempting to free themselves, only to find that "the wind blew it back again and again."[17] It is then, when the people are at their lowest point, that the wind delivers its final blow, sticking "its fingers inside their coat collars" and stripping them of the only remaining covering on their bodies.[18]

On the surface, the opening scene of Petry's novel reads as a description of the coldness and isolation of city life, but it also signals a certain predetermined pattern for the people who inhabit 116th Street. This opening scene is an important contrast to the seemingly eternal optimism and perseverance displayed by Lutie Johnson. By juxtaposing the harsh, overwhelming environment against the will of an individual, Petry establishes a central thematic question: Can individualism overcome the streets?

Petry's answer to this question is made clear by the end of the novel. Once again, she uses nature to frame the inevitable result of the story. The novel ends with Lutie fleeing town. As she considers what led her to this moment, she concludes: "It was that street. It was that god-damned street. The snow fell softly on the street. It muffled sound. It sent people scurrying homeward, so that the street was soon deserted, empty, quiet. And it could have been any street in the city, for the snow laid a delicate film over the sidewalk, over the brick of the tired, old buildings; gently obscuring the grime and the garbage and the ugliness."[19] By blaming the street, Lutie reveals that she is conscious of the fact that it represents more than a geographic place. It is a social force, one responsible for her tragedy. Petry uses the white snow to represent the sanitizing narratives that obscure Lutie's reality. Because Petry is writing at the precise moment when urban space is becoming synonymous with Blackness and suburbia is becoming synonymous with middle-class Whiteness, her framing of the city as a hidden source of tragedy and oppression is significant. It serves as a warning of what is to come if places like 116th continue to morph into the streets.

This danger becomes clearer as the streets are revealed as the novel's ultimate antagonist. Within the story, the most obvious antagonist is Jones, the superintendent at Lutie's apartment building. Jones has an unhealthy obsession with Lutie that results in him stalking her and her son and ultimately culminates in an attempt to rape her. However, despite the obvious grotesque nature of Jones, he is not the novel's primary villain. Rather, the street—which works slowly, methodically, and subtly to wear down the characters—becomes Lutie's greatest foe. Its effects are drastic: the physical scarring of Mrs. Hedges, Lutie's neighbor who was trapped in a fire in a slum building; the incarceration of young Bub; and the ultimate destruction of Lutie's American Dream.

One of the most interesting depictions of the street as a facilitator of these events is when Lutie's neighbor Mrs. Hedges starts operating a brothel in her apartment. After she is burned in a slum fire, Mrs. Hedges has a young woman, Mary, move in to help her with cooking and cleaning in exchange for room and board. One night, Mary has a young man come and visit. Mrs. Hedges realizes that she can take advantage of this situation and make money from their affair. This is a pivotal moment for her character as she moves from being a victim of the street to being its accomplice. She reflects in that moment, "The street would provide plenty of customers. For there were so many men just like him who knew vaguely that they hadn't got anything out of life and knew clearly that they never would get it . . . men who had to find escape from their hopes and fears."[20] The language of provision is interesting here. It suggests that the desperation that drives men to seek companionship in these circumstances is a direct product of living in the streets.

Soon after sending the young man in to see Mary, Mrs. Hedges has a moment of realization. It is not just the nature of city life, but something specific about her street that facilitates her hustle. She reflects: "She knew so much about this particular block that she came to regard it as slightly different from any other place. When she referred to it as 'the street,' her lips seemed to linger over the words as though her mind paused at the sound to write capital letters and then enclosed the words in quotation marks—thus setting it off and separating it from any other street in the city, giving it an identity, unmistakable and apart."[21] This moment, when 116th becomes The Street, is also the moment when Petry identifies the streets as more than urban geography. The specificity of Mrs. Hedges's context, living in a Black neighborhood where one can easily fall victim to slum fires, makes The Street unique. Its uniqueness is fleshed out through its repeated characterization as an entity that produces hopeless, fearful souls, ripe for exploitation. This characterization also illustrates The Street's role in the novel as the primary antagonist. Mrs. Hedges appears to realize this before any other character, perhaps due to her choice to become its accomplice. Yet, although she works with The Street, preying on its victims, she herself is a product of the same oppressive circumstances. As such, she occupies a contradictory role, perpetuating the very systems responsible for ravaging her body.

Although Mrs. Hedges is among the first to fully acknowledge The Street, Lutie becomes increasingly aware of its dangers throughout the novel. Despite her growing awareness, she is determined to overcome these obstacles. On the one hand, she recognizes that she is living in the very same circumstances that turned Mrs. Hedges into a madam and Jones into a violent drunk. On the other hand, even as she recognizes the depressing circumstances of everyone around her, Lutie denies that she could ever fall prey to the same force. She declares instead that "none of those things would happen to her . . . because she would fight back and never stop fighting back."[22] In many ways, Lutie embodies the sensibilities of American meritocracy and the belief that individuals can pull themselves up by their bootstraps. She sees the reality of the streets, but she refuses its logic.

Despite being able to work her way through night school to become a file clerk, Lutie struggles to reconcile her desire for social mobility with her concern for her son's upbringing. She laments the dangers that Bub faces after school while she is still at work. From the "dreary little rooms" of their apartment to "his playing in the street where the least of the dangers confronting him came from the stream of traffic which roared through 116th Street," Bub's environment is relentlessly dire. Moreover, as Lutie laments, Bub is too young to understand the larger threats of the streets, like the "gangs of young boys who were always on the lookout for small fry Bub's age, because they found young kids useful in getting in through narrow fire-escape windows, in distracting a storekeeper's attention while the gang light-heartedly helped itself to his stock."[23]

Petry's use of language here points the reader to the way the streets operate. Her use of pronouns is a minor but important detail. The threats of the streets are dehumanized—the traffic and the gangs. Even as Lutie describes the boys who make up the gang, their humanization stands apart from the entity that helps itself "light-heartedly" to food from the grocery store. The gangs Lutie worries about are not the product of Black pathology but of social circumstance. It is the streets, not Blackness, that represent a threat capable of consuming the humanity of a young boy like Bub. If we understand the streets as a product of U.S. policy, this is a radical claim. Petry uses her novel to push back against both genetic and cultural explanations for crime and violence in Black space. Instead, she points toward the streets, and indirectly, at their makers.

Lutie's preoccupation with the streets as a threat to her son comes to a head when she comes home from work one day and finds Bub working as a shoeshine boy. At first she does not notice him, ignoring the repeated question "Shine, Miss?" She even begins to lament the fact that boys are out on the street, stuck doing such work, until finally Bub gets her attention. Horrified by the fact that her own son is a shoeshine boy, Lutie slaps him three times and exclaims, "I'm working to look after you and you out here in the street shining shoes like the rest of these little niggers."[24] The fact that she calls her son the N-word is significant because it speaks to an understanding of how labor is racialized and classed.

As she berates Bub, she admits to herself that her anger is not so much a direct result of Bub's actions as it is caused by her frustration that her son is forced to be a shoeshine boy while the little Henry Chandlers of the world (the son of a wealthy family she once worked for) get to wear fine clothes, live in nice homes, and attend good schools. Petry uses this contrast between Lutie and White Americans throughout the novel to challenge the idea of U.S. meritocracy. For example, Lutie's experience of living in Black urban space while trying to pursue the American Dream is contrasted with her previous life as a domestic worker in Connecticut. Before Lutie's husband left her and she moved to the city, she sought her chance at the American Dream by working for the wealthy Chandler family. Interestingly, Petry uses both the Chandlers and Lutie's previous employers, the Pizzinis, to depict the contrast between urban Blackness and different types of midcentury Whiteness.

In order to secure her new job working for the Chandlers, Lutie has to get a reference from her former employer, Mrs. Pizzini. The Pizzinis are Italian immigrants who own the local grocery store. Despite their status as small-business owners, the Pizzinis are not well educated. In fact, Mrs. Pizzini has to have her daughter write the reference letter because she and her husband "don't write so good."[25] Yet, this couple owns not only a small business but also a nice home. The Pizzinis are representative of the White-adjacent families that benefited from housing segregation policies. Although they are not White, Anglo-Saxon Protestants, they were eventually allowed to move into American Whiteness, homeownership, and social mobility. The same cannot be said of Lutie.

Wishing to better understand the secret to the American Dream, Lutie turns herself into a disciple of her next employers, the Chandlers. Mrs. Chandler is young, rich, and blonde, but not much older than Lutie. In contrast to her perplexity over the Pizzinis, Lutie is enamored with the Chandlers. Their massive home is described as having four large bedrooms and bathrooms, a nursery, servants' quarters, a library, a living room, a dining room, and a laundry room.[26] Despite the Chandlers' many character flaws, Lutie hangs on their every word: "After a year of listening to their talk, she absorbed some of the same spirit. The belief that anybody could be rich if he wanted to and worked hard enough and figured it out carefully enough. Apparently that's what the Pizzinis had done."[27]

This belief continues to drive Lutie, even after she leaves the Chandlers. It leads her to rent the apartment on 116th, which she believes will lead to social mobility. The fact that this is a clear fallacy, given that renting produces no equity, does not stop Lutie. Her desire for even the appearance of ownership reflects the way this issue was as much a cultural one as it was economic. This is made clear as Lutie daydreams about owning a home while looking at an advertisement for home goods. The ad is described as having "a girl with incredible blond hair" leaning "close to a dark-haired, smiling man in a navy uniform . . . in front of a kitchen sink—a sink whose white porcelain surface gleamed."[28] This short descriptive sentence reveals a lot about how homeownership was culturally and ideologically engendered. First, the woman's "incredible blond hair" signifies not only her Whiteness but also her embodiment of ideal White feminine beauty standards. Her counterpart is not only tall, dark, and handsome but also patriotic. The racialized characterization of homeownership within the advertising world of Petry's novel is far from fictitious. As I discussed in chapter 2, advertisements like this one defined homeownership, suburban identity, and American belonging along racial lines throughout the mid-twentieth century.

The ad Lutie admires goes on to describe how "the linoleum floor of the kitchen was a crisp black-and-white pattern that pointed up the sparkle of the room. Casement windows. Red geraniums in yellow pots. It was, she thought, a miracle of a kitchen. Completely different from the kitchen of the 116th Street apartment she had moved into just two weeks ago."[29] In contrast to her Harlem apartment, the couple lives with new appliances, flooring, and landscaping. The parallel goes beyond that of home decor and signifies a contrast in the nature of the spaces each party inhabits. The couple from the ad can claim ownership over a space of cultural and monetary value. Lutie, at least by mainstream standards, can do neither. Yet her persistent desire for a nice apartment illustrates the way the appearance of ownership and middle-class membership, even if rented, was sold as something just as meaningful as actual ownership. Eventually, Lutie begins to accept these facts, so when she encounters Bub outside of her apartment shining shoes, she is enraged by what this means for Bub's future. She realizes that she lives in an area without playgrounds or after-school activities.[30] As a result, Bub is left without anything to do after school and finds himself searching for something with which he can occupy his time. The space they inhabit is set up in such a way as to lead him to the streets.

When working as a clerk fails to move Lutie up the social ladder, she tries her hand as a singer. Nevertheless, her attempts to work her way up fail, and while she is out pursuing the American Dream, her son gets tricked into performing mail fraud for the building superintendent. After Bub is arrested and sent to a juvenile center, Lutie is in desperate need of money for a lawyer. She goes to see Boots, her former band leader, who is another male character who wants to bed her. While she is asking for the money, Boots attempts to rape her. Overwhelmed by her circumstances, Lutie snaps and murders him. What is particularly interesting about this scene is the fact that, just prior to killing Boots, Lutie had noted, "As she stared at him, she felt she was gazing straight at the street with its rows of old houses, its piles of garbage, its swarms of children."[31] Even as she is committing the act of murder, her vision is obstructed and she never really sees Boots. Rather, the act is transformed into a violent uprising against the street—the cause of all her troubles. Despite her attempt to assert her own power, in the end the street wins. Realizing the gravity of what she has just done, Lutie decides to flee town, abandoning young Bub.

As all of her dreams come crashing down, "her thoughts were like a chorus chanting inside her head. The men stood around and the women worked. The men left the women and the women went on working and the kids were left alone. . . . Alone. Always alone. . . . And the street reached out and sucked them up."[32] She continues this line of thought, laying out the logical outcomes of living in racialized spaces such as 116th Street, and tells herself: "Go on. . . . Go all the way. Finish it. And the little Henry Chandlers go to YalePrincetonHarvard and the Bub Johnsons graduate from reform school into DannemoraSingSing. And you helped push him because you talked to him about money. All the time money. . . . Only you forgot. You forgot you were black and you underestimated the street outside."[33] Of all of the dramatic events that take place in the novel—Jones's sexual harassment of Lutie, Boots's murder, Bub's arrest—this one is the most pivotal for

Lutie's development as a character. Up until this moment, Lutie was resolved to be the exception. She wholeheartedly believed that individual hard work would allow her to escape the violence of the streets. However, as her life unravels, she realizes the error of underestimating them. As a whole, this moment communicates the brutality of the streets with respect to their impact on Black life. Petry paints a tragic picture of inescapability, violence to family structure, and risk of imprisonment. Lutie's fears about the streets and their effect on Bub are heartbreakingly realized by the novel's end. The separation of Lutie and Bub harkens back to the pattern of natal alienation that was commonplace during slavery.[34] By ending the text in such a heart-wrenching way, Petry effectively communicates the gravity of the streets.

While much of *The Street* details the threat the streets pose to Black life, Petry is careful to juxtapose this with the imagined threat of Black space within the White imaginary. Toward the end of the novel, the reader is privy to Bub's teacher's perception of Harlem. Through her reflections, the reader is introduced to the way urban Blackness is being constructed as a pathological threat to middle-class White America. In chapter 14, for example, the teacher, Miss Rinner, reflects on "the unpleasant sight of these ever-moving, brown young faces."[35] As she counts down the time left at work, her narration reveals the level of her disdain: "She came to think of the accumulation of scents in her classroom with hate as 'the colored people's smell,' and then finally the smell of Harlem itself—bold, strong, lusty, frightening."[36]

Despite feeling like this odor "assailed her," Miss Rinner cannot keep the windows open because they will let in the cold air, and she does not want to see the children's shabby coats. If she was forced to look at them, "she felt as though she were suffocating, because any contact with their rubbishy garments was unbearable."[37] Petry's use of diction in these lines reveals the way both Blackness and Black space were being pathologized at the time. The notion of unbearable contact alludes to Blackness as a contagion, a narrative that defined public discourse of the streets throughout the twentieth century. Likewise, "lusty" and "frightening" are stereotypical perceptions of American Blackness. When combined with Miss Rinner's reaction, "the hysterical desire to scream," one is reminded of the perceptions of Blackness depicted in *The Birth of a Nation*.

Even when Miss Rinner leaves the confines of the school, on the streets "she thought of every person she passed as a threat to her safety."[38] The irony in these last lines is that they directly follow Miss Rinner's confession of using physical violence as a means of controlling the children. Yet it is Harlem and its occupants that are ultimately seen as violent and frightening to the teacher. Overall, Miss Rinner's view of Black urbanites demonstrates both the continuity of anti-Blackness and the emerging views tied specifically to the streets. Moreover, while her reaction to Harlem may seem hyperbolic, it is in fact a poignant representation of how the racialization of space impacts social relationships and institutions such as the public education system. Petry's novel highlights how the sociocultural construct of the streets impacted everything from housing to educational quality.

In contrast to Miss Rinner's White imaginary, Harlem itself is depicted in the novel as a safe space for Black people who seek a reprieve from White supremacy. When Lutie returns home to Harlem after work, she reflects that "she never felt really human until she reached Harlem and thus got away from the hostility in the eyes of the white women who stared at her on the downtown streets. . . . These other folks feel the same way . . . once they are freed from the contempt in the eyes of the downtown world, they instantly become individuals."[39] Lutie's narration of Harlem as a humanizing space is an important intervention. While Petry details the real threat of the streets, as well as the imagined threat they pose in the broader White American imaginary, she also takes the time to narrate how a space designed for isolation and subjugation can be reclaimed for another purpose.

The Sin of the Innocents: Black Space in James Baldwin's *The Fire Next Time*

Whereas Ann Petry's novel depicts a protagonist witnessing the emergence of the streets, James Baldwin's *The Fire Next Time* combines the intimate genre of a familial letter with a nonfictional essay to create a text that examines the streets from the perspective of deep familiarity as well as intellectual distance. Baldwin's letter to his nephew creates the kind of discursive space articulated by Lipsitz. On the one hand, the letter to his nephew provides instruction on how to navigate America's racial landscape. On the other hand, the letter offers Baldwin the space to subvert racial power dynamics through language and rhetorical strategy. A prime example of this is when he tells his nephew: "These innocent and well-meaning people, your countrymen, have caused you to be born under conditions not very far removed from those described for us by Charles Dickens in the London of more than a hundred years ago. (I hear the chorus of the innocents screaming, 'No! This is not true! How *bitter* you are!'—but I am writing this letter to *you*, to try to tell you something about how to handle *them*. . . . I *know* the conditions under which you were born, for I was there . . .)."[40] Within this passage, Baldwin uses parentheses and italics to delineate belonging and understanding. Rather than use the parentheses to insert a personal opinion or counter a dominant discourse, Baldwin begins with a countercultural conversation and only allows the dominant view to exist within the bounds of the parentheses. By confining anti-Black discourse this way, Baldwin uses language to exercise power in a way that parallels and challenges the power that created the streets.

Baldwin uses italics in a similar way to differentiate between us—those who have lived the realities of the streets—and them, the rest of America. Moreover, by comparing the streets to the setting of a Dickens novel, Baldwin draws attention to the specific ways poverty is racialized in the United States. Whereas Dickens's poor protagonists solicit empathy, those who inhabit the streets are accused of bitterness when they complain about their circumstances. Rather than acknowledge the systematic way these conditions were produced through public policy, "the innocents," Baldwin's take on Americans who ignore this history, dismiss Black Americans as irrational and emotional.

Baldwin continues his counternarrative of the streets when he describes the extent of their influence on Black life to his nephew. He tells his nephew, the fact that "this innocent country set you down in a ghetto . . . that you should perish" is "the root of my dispute with my country."[41] For Baldwin, the injustice of American anti-Blackness lies not only in geographic segregation but also in the way that segregation is tied to life outcomes and possibilities. He poignantly expresses this to his nephew when he says, "You were born into a society which spelled out with brutal clarity, and in as many ways as possible, that you were a worthless human being. You were not expected to aspire to excellence: you were expected to make peace with mediocrity."[42] The way Baldwin combines the tender intimacy of a letter with the harsh exposition of American anti-Blackness personalizes the realities of the streets as policy and history alone cannot.

In contrast to this personal letter, the rest of *The Fire Next Time* consists of an essay titled "Down at the Cross," which is primarily an autobiographical account of Baldwin's religious experience. Baldwin grew up in a deeply religious (Black Baptist) household. In fact, his adoptive father, David, was a preacher whom he described as angry and bitter.[43] As an adolescent, Baldwin worked as a youth preacher at a Pentecostal church. Eventually, Baldwin left the church at seventeen, but these experiences greatly informed his analysis of Black Christianity in relation to the streets.[44] Ultimately, Baldwin sees the streets and Black Christianity as products of White supremacy, mirrored attempts to subjugate Black Americans. As such, he rejects their hold on him. Still, Baldwin's autobiographical accounts of religious practice illustrate the way those who live in the streets fashion a sense of belonging and power through religion.

Early on, Baldwin recounts how his teenage years were marked by an increased awareness of how both he and the ills of the streets were "produced by the same circumstances."[45] His discomfort with this proximity and what it might mean for him led him to throw himself into church life. He paints this as one of the few paths Black youth are offered when childhood innocence fades and the desperate realities of life in the ghetto become clear. Because Baldwin's youth coincided with World War II, he describes friends who enlisted only to be changed or die. "Others fled to other states and cities—that is, to other ghettos. Some went on wine or whiskey or the needle. . . . And others, like me, fled into the church."[46] In many ways, his story reflects a familiar dichotomy between the so-called secular life of the streets and the holy life of the church. It is a fascinating expression of how religion in particular plays a role in creating space that is both within and apart from the streets.

In Baldwin's case, life in the church was just another "thing" or "gimmick, to lift him out, to start him on his way."[47] The parallels between seemingly divergent paths such as ministry and prostitution are made clear through the way Baldwin is inducted into church life. When he is first introduced to his school friend's pastor (Baldwin did not join his father's church), she asks him, "Whose little boy are you?" As he explains, this is the same phrase used by pimps and prostitutes out on the avenue when they attempt to lure him. Yet, despite what that may have signaled, Baldwin confesses, "I unquestionably wanted to be *somebody's* little boy. I was so frightened, and at the mercy of so many conundrums, that inevitably, that summer, *someone* would have taken me over; one doesn't, in Harlem, long remain standing on any auction block."[48] Fear of succumbing to the conditions of life in the ghetto produced such a desperate longing in Baldwin that he was willing to ignore his suspicions in order to find some semblance of belonging.

Baldwin's introduction to the church makes it abundantly clear that his relationship to religion was one born more of necessity than piety. Yet, as much as he was driven to the church by fear of his social circumstance, he was also driven by a self-loathing produced by White supremacy and Christian legalism. His religious motivation helps frame one of the most pivotal passages in "Down at the Cross." At the height of his religious experience, Baldwin recounts falling down at the foot of the altar. However, rather than narrating a Pentecostal encounter with God, Baldwin describes a deep sense of pain and abandonment: "All I really remember is the pain; it was as though I were yelling up to Heaven and Heaven would not hear me. And if Heaven would not hear me, if love could not descend from Heaven—to wash me, to make me clean—then utter disaster was my portion."[49]

At the very same time that these thoughts are running through his head, the churchgoers around Baldwin are celebrating his salvation. Yet he concludes: "And if one despairs—as who has not?—of human love, God's love alone is left. But God—and I felt this even then, so long ago, on that tremendous floor, unwillingly—is white. And if His love was so great, and if He loved all His children, why were we, the blacks, cast down so far? Why? In spite of all I said thereafter, I found no answer on the floor."[50] Despite the pain and abandonment he feels here, Baldwin remained in the church and took on the role of a young minister. By embracing this role, and performing it well, Baldwin further compares the way Black people are socially coerced into performing certain roles in broader society, both literally and figuratively.

For Baldwin, however, the fact that Black Christianity failed to truly challenge White supremacy or, at the very least, speak more directly to the material needs of Black people living in the streets, was proof of God's disinterest in him. He questions the logic of a Black Christianity that proclaims that silent suffering is the way to respond to oppression. He wonders, "Were only Negroes to gain this crown? Was Heaven, then, to be merely another ghetto?"[51] The idea of heaven as a ghetto points to Baldwin's understanding of the streets as not just a way of enforcing physical and social segregation, but also a hegemonic understanding of Blackness as inferior to Whiteness. It was not just the hypocrisy of preachers who profited from poor parishioners, or division within the church that turned Baldwin off to Christianity; rather, it was the way he saw Christianity as intimately connected to White supremacy in America. For this reason, Baldwin and his brother believed "if Harlem didn't have so many churches and junkies, there'd be blood flowing in the streets."[52] This blood is not the product of internal violence, but rather a collective revolt against the systems responsible for creating the streets.

While Baldwin's criticism of Black Christianity could be taken at face value as a personal response to religious experience, I argue that his discussion of Black religion is part of a broader condemnation of the sociocultural systems that restrict Black life. When Baldwin states that he turned to the church because "the wages of sin were visible everywhere," he is using religious rhetoric to describe social ills. He sees sin in "every scar on the faces of the pimps and their whores, in every helpless, newborn baby being brought into this danger, in every knife and pistol fight on the Avenue, and every disastrous bulletin."[53] Prostitution, single-parent households, and physical violence are the fundamental characteristics ascribed to the streets. However, contrary to the obvious Christian logic, the sin is not the actions of the pimps, prostitutes, or drug dealers. Rather, the sin is the system that produced such stifling and cyclical conditions.

This view of sin explains Baldwin's declaration, "I was icily determined . . . never to make my peace with the ghetto but to die and go to Hell before I would let any white man spit on me, before I would accept my 'place' in this republic."[54] Baldwin situates the streets as part and parcel of the broader history of Black subjugation within the American republic. Despite his powerful declaration, Baldwin admits, "Of course, at the same time, I *was* being spat on and defined and described and limited, and could have been polished off with no effort whatever."[55] This contrast illustrates how even carving out discursive space, through the declaration of a counterpurpose, is a struggle in and of itself. In this way, he articulates the ideological work of the streets. It is not just the physical isolation and violence nor the evident social ills that threaten Black life, but how Blackness is defined and limited in such a way as to seep into the very souls and self-knowledge of those who live in the ghetto.

In addition to connecting Black Christianity to the streets, Baldwin also addresses the role of the Nation of Islam (NOI). While he often publicly defended and rationalized the NOI to White liberals, Baldwin had his qualms with the religion. Yet he understood its appeal. As he puts it, the NOI provided "divine corroboration" of the experience of being Black in America.[56] The problem for Baldwin was that the NOI placed racial boundaries on love and power. Despite his issues with the NOI, Baldwin recounts somewhat fondly being invited to dinner with Elijah Muhammad, an event that frames Baldwin's understanding of the NOI's relationship to the streets.

After an evening of conversation and debate on the South Side of Chicago, Baldwin feels slightly embarrassed to give Elijah Muhammad's driver the address of the place he is staying. He explains that it was "the kind of address that in Chicago, as in all American cities, identified itself as a white address by virtue of its location." In that moment, when physical spaces reveal the fluidity of Baldwin's social belonging, he realizes the real reason he cannot support the NOI. He explains: "It was very strange to stand with Elijah for those few moments, facing those vivid, violent, so problematic streets. I felt very close to him, and really wished to be able to love and honor him. . . .

Yet precisely because of the reality and the nature of those streets—because of what he conceived as his responsibility and what I took to be mine—we would always be strangers, and possibly, one day, enemies."[57] For Baldwin, he and Elijah Muhammad shared a concern for the reality of the streets and how they negatively affect Black life. This is a reality Baldwin was intimately familiar with. Yet Baldwin's social location as Black, queer, and working class lent itself to an understanding of the world that refused the isolationist logic of the NOI. For Baldwin, the answer to the streets was in their transcendence. This does not mean that he overlooked the material realities of urban Blackness, but rather that he refused to respond to them with racial essentialism.

Baldwin's ability to capture not only the cultural and ideological implications of Black urbanization but also the emotional and visceral experience of living in the streets continues to impact Black authors, activists, and intellectuals. Black activist Assata Shakur, for example, credits Baldwin with awakening her to the political realities of Black life in the city. In her autobiography she recounts reading Baldwin: "Anguished voices scream and moan from the pages. Compressed ghettos threaten to explode. Poverty and fire and brimstone boil over into a deadly stew."[58] Likewise, Ta-Nehisi Coates has been repeatedly compared to Baldwin. While both Shakur and Coates know the streets through personal experience, they do not rely on this alone in their writing. Rather, they build on Baldwin's artistic expression of the streets. Baldwin's influence speaks to the way the streets exist not only as a physical space but also as an imagined one that, when expressed in certain ways, gives rise to new thought, expression, and activism.

The Streets and the Dream in Ta-Nehisi Coates's *Between the World and Me*

As I mentioned in the introduction, of all the authors and artists whose work I discuss, Ta-Nehisi Coates makes the most explicit connection between government housing policies and the creation of the streets as a physical and sociocultural entity. Like James Baldwin, Coates frames his text as a letter to a younger Black family member. In Coates's case, he writes to his son in the aftermath of Trayvon Martin's murder and the acquittal of his killer, George Zimmerman. The visceral reality of anti-Blackness is the central theme of *Between the World and Me*. While Coates spends time addressing more obvious facets of this, such as police brutality, he also indicts the education system, the American Dream, and the streets as central sites of anti-Blackness.

One of the most compelling examples Coates provides of how the streets continue to shape Black life is that of fear. Coates recounts his father's methods of discipline as a prime example of this fear: "I felt it in the sting of his black leather belt, which he applied with more anxiety than anger, my father who beat me as if someone might steal me away, because that is exactly what was happening all around us. Everyone had lost a child, somehow, to the streets."[59] Coates discusses the fear of losing one's loved one to the streets, whether through police brutality or other types of violence, as "ancestral fear." In many ways, Coates's description echoes the theme of resignation present throughout Petry's novel *The Street*. His language of "ancestral fear" functions as a meaningful way to convey the generational legacy of anti-Blackness, but it also signals a particular kind of sociocultural inheritance tied to the streets. This is something James Baldwin also discusses when he recounts how anti-Black violence shapes Black parenting. He speaks of the fear in his father's voice when he realized that, as a child, Baldwin thought he could do anything a White child could as a primary example of how intergenerational violence is tied to broader power dynamics.[60]

This becomes all the clearer when, despite his objections to his father's parenting style, Coates finds himself considering the same actions. After the death of his college friend Prince Jones, he confesses to his son that he finally understood his father's mantra: "Either I can beat him or the police."[61] He reframes the physical discipline he grew up with by stating, "Black people love their children with a kind of obsession. You are all we have, and you come to us endangered. I think we would like to kill you ourselves before seeing you killed by the streets that America made."[62]

In *The Political Sublime*, political scientist Michael J. Shapiro theorizes on the seemingly contradictory use of violence as a survival mechanism. He suggests that "given the seemingly unpunishable violence that makes the white world's law enforcement agents uninhibited in their use of weapons . . . Coates infers that the violence 'within' the African American house (administered in his case by his father) was connected with that violence 'without.'"[63] Rather than see the father's style of punishment as a stand-alone act of violence, Shapiro suggests that we contextualize it and see it as a response to the wider pattern of anti-Black violence in America.

By framing his father's seemingly violent act of discipline as one driven by fear and anxiety, Coates resists the conclusion that these acts are solely the product of individual or cultural practices. Instead, he suggests that these actions arise out of what he calls "the philosophy of the disembodied."[64] This philosophy is a result of being socialized to fear violence within Black spaces, from police and community members alike. This fear, according to Coates, is not individual, nor is it dependent on being a parent. In fact, the narrator shares with his son, "I was afraid long before you, and in this I was unoriginal."[65]

Shortly after confessing his own history of fear, the narrator describes how he has seen it manifest in the streets he grew up in: "The fear was there in the extravagant boys of my neighborhood, in their large rings and medallions, their big puffy coats and full-length fur-collared leathers, which was their armor against the world. . . . The fear lived on in their practiced bop, their slouching denim, their big T-shirts, the calculated angle of their baseball caps, a catalog of behaviors and garments enlisted to inspire the belief that these boys were in firm possession of everything they desired."[66] In this passage, Coates theorizes the fear of anti-Black violence as much more than an emotion. Rather, it is a coercive force that solicits a specific performance of Black masculinity.[67] This performance of hypermasculinity is akin to the zoot suits of the early twentieth century.[68] However, in addition to asserting Black humanity through extravagance, this clothing provides a certain invulnerability meant to counter the ever-present threat of violence on the streets.

This fear also manifests itself in the performance of physical power, which extends to how one carries oneself in order to exude power and resist the inevitable vulnerability of being a Black body in an urban space. In *We Were Eight Years in Power*, Coates describes this performance as the effort of "those who knew what they were not but had no power to declare what they were."[69] This attempt to declare one's personhood manifests itself through specific language, movements, and phrases meant to convey belonging and control. In *Between the World and Me*, the narrator tells his son that mastering this performance was as fundamental as learning one's shapes and colors as a child. These behaviors were the only means of securing one's body.

Not unlike his father's use of violence when disciplining him, Coates theorizes that the violence that is so prevalent in the streets is, at least in part, about demonstrating invulnerability and control within a social context that is the result of a complete lack of either. Coates acknowledges the grand irony in Black youth proclaiming to run the streets. As he puts it, "We did not design the streets. We do not fund them. We do not preserve them."[70] Regardless of this truth, the performance of power becomes missional: "prove the inviolability of their block, of their bodies, through their power to crack knees, ribs, and arms."[71]

However violent, however seemingly brash these actions are, Coates reframes them as a product of a systemic fear. The narrator continues to challenge the reader to see this fear in the same places he does by cataloging the places it manifests:

> I saw it in their customs of war. . . . I knew that there was a ritual to a street fight, bylaws and codes that, in their very need, attested to all the vulnerability of the black teenage bodies. I heard the fear in the first music I ever knew, the music that pumped from boom boxes full of grand boast and bluster. The boys who stood out on Garrison and Liberty up on Park Heights loved this music because it told them, against all evidence and odds, that they were masters of their own lives, their own streets, and their own bodies.[72]

Once again, Coates describes the behavior and music of Black urban youth as a means of constructing a sense of security and futurity in the face of material threats. Furthermore, the music that tells these youth that they are "masters of their own lives, . . . streets, and . . . bodies" is about creating a sense of autonomy among what seem like harsh, predetermined social conditions. This is not unlike the way Black revolutionary groups such as the Black Panthers used clothing and weapons to perform power and ward off police. As cultural theorist Nikhil Pal Singh explains: "Rather than seeing the Panthers as the vanguard of a visible, guerilla insurgency in the country, they might better be understood as practitioners of an insurgent form of visibility, a literal-minded and deadly serious kind of guerilla theatre, in which militant sloganeering, bodily display, and spectacular actions simultaneously signified their possession and yet real lack of power."[73] Although the political basis of these actions differs, these performances of power are both aimed at the same kinds of anti-Black violence. The narrator confirms this when, speaking of the Black teenagers in his neighborhood, he states that their "guns seemed to address this country, which invented the streets that secured them with despotic police, in its primary language—violence."[74]

By interpreting the clothing, culture, and actions of Black urban youth for the reader, Coates breaks the barrier of performative illegibility. He illustrates that what is often labeled as a product of pathological violence, or poor moral fiber, is in fact the result of the living fear of anti-Blackness. All his talk of fear points to the way the streets operate on an ideological and psychological level to control and police Black communities. By bringing these concerns back to the security of the body, Coates reminds readers that the ideologies that govern Black urban life are not abstractions. They have material, life-and-death consequences. This is perhaps Coates's greatest accomplishment in *Between the World and Me*: his ability to convey the visceral experience and high stakes of trying to survive the streets in a Black body.

Like Baldwin and others before him, Coates also links the system of the streets to that of education. As the narrator continues to tell his son about his childhood, he explains, "If the streets shackled my right leg, the schools shackled my left."[75] The particular imagery of slave shackles is more than a metaphor. Rather, Coates is making an important connection between the practices of racialized slavery, the current systems of neoslavery (i.e., mass incarceration), and the dual function of the streets and urban education systems. He describes these as "two arms in relation—those who failed in the schools justified their destruction in the streets. The society could say, 'He should have stayed in school,' and then wash its hands of him."[76] Coates points to the ways in which the streets coerce Black behavior to either embrace the social practices of the streets previously outlined or buy into the belief that education and assimilation will provide a way out. If one does not embrace the schools as a means of social mobility (and frequently even if one does), the alternative is often physical death or imprisonment. By juxtaposing the harsh realities of physical, social, and civil death as the alternative to behaving in these prescribed ways, Coates's work demonstrates how the streets govern both the minds and the bodies of those who live in them.[77]

Coates's discussion of urban education in connection with the streets also calls into question the nature of freedom for Black Americans. His analysis of the streets aligns with that of Black intellectuals like Malcolm X who famously declared, "If you're black, you were born in jail."[78] Malcom X's words speak to the way Blackness is policed in America, whether or not one is physically imprisoned. Similarly, in her autobiography, Assata Shakur suggests "The only difference between [Rikers] and the streets is that one is maximum security and the other is minimum security. The police patrol our communities just like the guards patrol here. I don't have the faintest idea how it feels to be free."[79] This comment, which was made to Shakur by a fellow inmate, reflects a critical awareness of how the streets police Black life. Coates, Malcolm X, and Shakur recognize that the streets create a permanent state of unfreedom for Black Americans, albeit to varying degrees. Whether one is being coerced into unquestioning assimilation, imprisoned, or murdered, the streets exert their influence over Black life in one way or another.

In addition to depicting the streets as a policing force for Black life, Coates discusses the streets in relation to the wider American imaginary. For Coates, the streets and the dream, as he calls them, are complementary pieces of the same puzzle. The American Dream continues to fuel belief and investment in hegemonic ideals, while the streets continue to stifle Black life. By linking the streets to the American Dream, Coates highlights the centrality of the streets to the American way of life.

Coates also uses this connection to identify the influence of the streets on those who manage to "escape." The primary example of this is the narrator's son, who has benefited from his father's success and ability to raise him beyond the direct threats of the streets. Yet, despite this, the streets still influence him. This becomes clear as the narrator laments the fact that his son, like all others who manage to escape the physical confines of the streets, is still forced to live by the "the rules designed to protect you from [the violence of the world], the rules that would have you contort your body to address the block, and contort again to be taken seriously by colleagues, and contort again so as not to give the police a reason."[80] Regardless of social mobility and individual success, his son's Blackness signifies his belonging to the streets. Coates's lament for his son is an example of my claim that the streets govern all Black life in America to some extent. While one might escape the bounds of racialized geographic locations, the ideologies and practices that govern Black life continue to follow them. The narrator's friend, Prince, is a prime example of this. He was educated and raised in a well-off Black family. He was a "good Christian" and a family man. He ticked every box of Black respectability. Yet his Blackness, and its perceived connection to the streets, defined him as a threat. As a result, he was murdered by a police officer. Coates's *Between the World and Me* does an exceptional job of tracing out the quotidian ways in which the streets shape all Black life, as well as their stakes.

The Streets in the Black Imaginary

Each of the texts I analyze in this chapter reveals the complex reality of the streets, as well as the ways in which those who inhabit these spaces cope with this reality. While Petry, Baldwin, and Coates acknowledge the existence of violence and poverty within Black urban space, each author frames these as the product of systemic anti-Blackness. Furthermore, their experiential narratives of the streets provide a nuanced contrast to the one-dimensional view of urban Blackness that has permeated political discourse since the early twentieth century. Petry's novel *The Street*, in particular, serves as a stark contrast to narratives of the broken Black family that would come to dominate the public discourse on the streets in the late twentieth century. Lutie's belief in American meritocracy and equal opportunity, however naive, challenge the notion that urban Black inhabitants suffer poverty and violence because of their cultural and moral deficiencies. Yet, her ultimate failure deconstructs these ideologies and points to the systems that prevent individuals like her from succeeding.

James Baldwin challenges the relational limitations of the streets. Baldwin's social location as a working-class, Black, queer man forced him to move beyond the use of religion or respectable Black masculinity as a means of coping with the streets. His interactions with the NOI are a primary example of how Black intellectuals can simultaneously acknowledge the specific context of the streets and their impact on Black life, while also attempting to broaden conceptions of Blackness itself.

Like Petry, Coates also deconstructs another key myth around urban Blackness. Through his philosophy of the disembodied, Coates prompts the reader to reinterpret the spectacle of young Black masculine extravagance. In an era in which children such as Jordan Davis are murdered for playing loud music, this understanding of urban Blackness is an intervention with very real, material implications.[81] Overall, these authors are examples of the ways in which Black intellectuals continue to carve out discursive space that challenges and contests the meaning of urban Blackness as imagined by White America.

CHAPTER FOUR

Music Born of the Streets
Hip-Hop's Articulations of Urban Life and Identity

In the summer of 2017, I had the pleasure of hearing Kendrick Lamar perform live. A friend from graduate school was in town, and she had an extra ticket to the concert. It had been years since I had attended a concert. While I still loved music, hip-hop especially, the experience of live music had changed as I had gotten older. I was more aware of the age gap between other concertgoers and me and even more aware of our racial differences. These differences seemed especially heightened when I went to see Lamar. I did not expect to be surrounded by a predominantly White audience that was ten to fifteen years my junior. What felt particularly unsettling was the disconnect I felt when the song "m.A.A.d. City" came on. "m.A.A.d. City" is a personal narrative about navigating survival on the streets of Compton. While catchy, the line "YAWK! YAWK! YAWK!" is meant to be jarring. It is the verbalization of gun violence. Yet, when that song came on, all I saw was a sea of White teenagers joyfully screaming that lyric, smiling and dancing, completely disconnected from the reality of the streets.

My experience at Kendrick Lamar's concert is a reminder of how vast the divide is between those who see hip-hop as a manifestation of Black spatial experience and those who consume it as an abstract art form that exists primarily for their entertainment and indulgence. While today hip-hop is a widely consumed mainstream musical genre, it emerged as a mode of expression distinctly tied to the streets and the specific experiences of the Black youth who inhabited them. I argue that hip-hop remains a unique artistic expression of the streets that allows Black youth to theorize their sense of self-identity and belonging. Much like the literature analyzed in the previous chapter, hip-hop is a medium through which Black artists create discursive space and exercise power within the streets.

The connection between hip-hop, the streets, and the identity of Black youth has been articulated by many Black authors and intellectuals. In his memoir, *The Beautiful Struggle*, Coates describes hip-hop as "the music of city . . . something that spoke to our chaotic, disfigured, and gorgeous world."[1] What Coates narrates through personal experience, scholar Murray Forman theorizes on a broader scale, arguing that in hip-hop, more than any other genre, space is a prominent concern.² According to Forman, "In the rhythm and lyrics, the city is an audible presence, explicitly cited and sonically sampled in the reproduction of the aural textures of the urban environment."³ Forman connects the spatial concern of hip-hop to the history of geographic segregation, as well as radio DJing practices that segregate Black and White music. As Forman astutely points out, "The segregation of the airwaves . . . parallels the cultural and geographical ghettoization of black communities in American cities."⁴

The way hip-hop is consumed and analyzed is a prime example of the "ghettoization" of Black art. Even today, when the majority of hip-hop listeners are not urban or Black, and when artists such as Kendrick Lamar are winning Pulitzer Prizes, hip-hop remains tied to the streets. While the positive result of this is that hip-hop remains connected to its sociocultural roots, it also means that the genre is rarely analyzed as an artistic means of negotiating spatial power.⁵ Much like the Black authors I discussed in chapter 3, the hip-hop artists I examine in this chapter demonstrate a hyperawareness of this fact, as well as a resistance to such racialization.⁶ Moreover, like the inhabitants of Drake and Cayton's "Bronzeville," these musical artists depict a complex community, blurring the lines between stereotype and reality. By examining the ways in which artists make theoretical contributions to how the streets are understood by those living within and outside of Black urban spaces, I hope to meet Murray Forman's call to see hip-hop as "crucial in the redefinition of the American urban environment and, more pointedly, the redefinition of the relationships between minority youth and the American metropolis."⁷

There are a number of artists and albums I could have selected for close analysis in this chapter. For instance, N.W.A.'s album *Straight Outta Compton* (1988) is well known for its articulation of Black urban life and the threat of police violence. Likewise, Nas's *Illmatic* (1994) provides a personalized account of life in the streets, as well as a detailed critique of gang violence and urban poverty. However, I am not concerned with chronicling every instance of hip-hop's articulation of the streets. Instead, I am interested in music that reflects a unique perspective or theory of what the streets are and what they mean for Black life and/or personhood. For this reason, I selected three albums for analysis: the Fugees' *The Score* (1998), Lupe Fiasco's *The Cool* (2007), and Kendrick Lamar's *Good Kid, M.A.A.D. City* (2012). *The Score* represents a transnational articulation of the streets by focusing on the shared themes and experiences of members of the Black diaspora from the United States and the Caribbean. In doing so, the Fugees depict the way the streets shape a common Black experience for African Americans and Black immigrants. In *The Cool*, Lupe Fiasco draws from the Black radical tradition to connect the anti-Blackness that governs the streets to U.S. colonialism. Finally, in *Good Kid, M.A.A.D. City*, Kendrick Lamar uses his teenage persona to provide a personal narrative of life in Compton that reveals the conflicts and internal thought processes of those who live in such spaces. Overall, these artists challenge the one-dimensional depiction of Black urban youth as violent, unambitious gangsters by asserting a sense of individual power and identity, as well as broader solidarity with victims of U.S. power across the globe.

A Street Genre: The History of Hip-Hop

To say that hip-hop is connected to the streets is an understatement. In *Rap Music and Street Consciousness*, Cheryl L. Keyes explains that hip-hop is *the* definitive musical expression of the streets because "the streets nurture, shape, and embody the hip-hop music aesthetic, creating a genre distinct from other forms of Black popular music that evolved after World War II."[8] The popularization of hip-hop in the mid-1970s literally took place in the streets at local block parties. Moreover, the conditions that produced the genre were the direct result of government housing policies in the South Bronx. When the Cross Bronx Expressway was built under the direction of Robert Moses in 1953, it displaced the existing community of color (mostly African American, Puerto Rican, and Jewish inhabitants). The rationale for building the expressway was that it would provide a direct route between the increasingly wealthy and cosmopolitan space of Manhattan, the suburbs of New Jersey, and Queens—spaces that were being built up with the aid of FHA housing loans. However, the environmental and sound pollution caused by the project, combined with the physical disruption of city space, effectively destroyed the neighborhood in the name of progress and urban renewal. Where there was once a racially diverse neighborhood in the South Bronx with decent apartments and single-family homes, there was now an increased number of public housing projects. These new towers were designed to confine poor people of color to manageable spaces that would not interfere with business development.[9] Unsurprisingly, most of the White residents who formerly inhabited these spaces moved to the suburbs.

In addition to funneling people of color into the projects, the construction of the Cross Bronx Expressway depressed the local economy. In *Can't Stop, Won't Stop*, Jeff Chang breaks down the impact of these policies through clear statistics. Around 600,000 manufacturing jobs were lost, and the local average per capita income dropped to $2,340—half the city's average. The economic impact of these policies was not confined to neighborhood inhabitants. As slumlords took over many of the remaining private buildings, they increasingly turned to arson, insurance fraud, or tax evasion as a means to greater economic gain. Between 1973 and 1977, there were around 30,000 fires in the South Bronx. As Chang so poignantly states, "These were not the fires of purifying rage that had ignited in Watts. . . . These were the fires of abandonment."[10]

In addition to these economic losses, youth unemployment increased to 60 percent after the creation of the Cross Bronx Expressway, resulting in a prevalence of young people of color confined to urban spaces with nothing to do.[11] Although political organizations such as the Black Panther Party and the Young Lords Party were actively engaged in recruiting these youth, so too were newly emerging gangs.[12] These conditions became the basis for a narrative around Black and Brown youth that purported they were self-destructive and undeserving of help or support.

This narrative was most infamously expressed in a memo Daniel Patrick Moynihan wrote to President Richard Nixon. Moynihan, then a Democratic senator for New York, had previously argued that "people in the South Bronx don't want housing or they wouldn't burn it down."[13] What Moynihan neglected to mention was that most of the people responsible for the burning of the Bronx were building owners, not the people they employed to start the fires, who were just trying to earn enough money to get by. In the memo to Nixon, Moynihan suggested the "benign neglect" of "race issues"—in other words, a decrease in social and political support for the people of color who occupied urban spaces.[14] With this simple statement, Moynihan spun a dangerous narrative with disastrous effects. Nixon replied with an enthusiastic, "I agree!"[15] Thus began the systematic neglect of the inner city. In the decades that followed, Nixon, and later Reagan, turned this narrative into a set of policies that reduced social services and educational funding for the city as well as increasing the policing and incarceration of Black and Brown youth.

It is within this context that the youth culture of the Bronx produced hip-hop pioneers such as Afrika Bambaataa (Kevin Donovan) and DJ Kool Herc (Clive Campbell). It is worth noting that, despite how male-centric the origin story of hip-hop is, many early pioneers of the genre were women. MC Lyte, Queen Latifah, Roxanne Shanté, and Monie Love, for example, spoke to many of the prominent themes of hip-hop while also addressing their unique experiences as Black women. Still, the narrative of hip-hop's emergence is tied most closely to DJ Herc and Afrika Bambaataa. In fact, most scholars and historians agree that hip-hop's origins can be traced back to a party hosted by DJ Kool Herc on August 11, 1973.[16] The eighteen-year-old Herc got his start in music by playing for high school parties. His style was heavily influenced by the music of his home country, Jamaica. When he moved to the Bronx from Kingston in 1967, he brought with him the practice of "toasting," or speaking over instrumental records (often the dub/B side of records). This eventually evolved into rapping over musical tracks that were already well-known songs (Herc did not necessarily rap, but he paved the way for regular MCs to take up the mantle). Eventually, DJ Herc's parties became popular places for break-dancers, or B-boys, as they were known colloquially.[17]

Herc had made a name for himself as a DJ by the time he decided to host the now famous community party one summer evening in an apartment recreation room in the West Bronx. His sister had rented the room and decided to cohost with her popular brother as a way to make extra money. By the day of the party, around a hundred people had responded to the hand-drawn flyers and decided to come for a good time. As Herc DJed, his friend Coke La Rock would hype the crowd during "breaks," or instrumental sections. This was the beginning of hip-hop.[18] By the next summer, Herc was hosting these events outside as block parties. Siphoning electricity from city streetlights, Herc set up his sound system in the street.[19] In his words, "After the block party . . . we couldn't go back to the rec room."[20]

Although DJ Herc is credited with creating hip-hop, its consolidation as a Black cultural entity was heavily led by Afrika Bambaataa. Bambaataa's origin story has its own mythic narrative. A former gang leader, he is said to have changed his name and reoriented his leadership efforts around hip-hop after watching the film *Zulu* (1964) and taking a trip to Africa.[21] After this redefining moment, he embraced hip-hop with a vision for its potential to unite Black people. Bambaataa made his debut as a DJ on November 12, 1976, and founded the Zulu Nation, a group that took its cue from Pan-Africanism.[22]

In a way, Bambaataa's origins have become the equivalent of a spiritual conversion narrative. This story serves a purpose, framing the next stage of hip-hop as one concerned with Black unity and futurity. However, to fully understand the weight of Bambaataa's significance to hip-hop, one must consider some of the finer points of his origin story. Like DJ Herc, Bambaataa made his name by throwing community parties. Also like Herc, Bambaataa grew up in the Bronx. More specifically, he grew up in the Bronx River Houses, a public housing project that became increasingly synonymous with poverty and urban decay throughout the middle and late twentieth century.²³ Journalist Steven Hager describes the Bronx River Project as "a cluster of unadorned, fifteen-story brick buildings circling two small playgrounds. . . . It looks like this neighborhood once had a reputation for violence that was unequaled in New York."²⁴

Hager's bleak description of the Bronx River Houses frames Bambaataa's response to his environment, which was to join the Black Spades, more understandable. However, what is interesting about Hager's narration of Bambaataa's preconversion life is the rhetoric, as well as the common tropes associated with Black urban youth. For one, when Hager recounts the origins of the Black Spades, he describes them as "terrorizing" the neighborhood. He goes on to frame Bambaataa's participation: "Without a gang affiliation, a young boy was vulnerable to beatings, robbery and general day-to-day harassment."²⁵ On the one hand, given that Hager's story was published in the 1980s, this could be read as a generous explanation of the social factors responsible for gang affiliation. Hager challenges dominant narratives around the gangs that existed in the 1970s. He points out that the gangs worked directly against the drug dealers, attempting to push them out of the neighborhood. He even interviews Bambaataa, who explains that the "Black Spades was also helping out in the community, raising money for sickle-cell anemia and gettin' people to register to vote."²⁶

On the other hand, the narrative that follows Bambaataa serves as a way of divorcing hip-hop from the more uncomfortable realities of Black urban life. This is perhaps made most evident when Hager claims that hip-hop replaced the gangs of the early 1970s and saved the neighborhood from their terror.²⁷ Much of the narrative around Bambaataa and his role in hip-hop, as exemplified by writers like Hager, is that he is the "exceptional Negro" among a band of violent gang members who "understood only three basic concepts: 'crush, kill, and destroy.'"²⁸ His exceptional nature is often credited to his love for and knowledge of music. He also became known as a moral leader in the community, who frequently told young people to stay in school.

While it is true that Bambaataa stands out as a pioneering figure for the morality and political identity of hip-hop, I resist the tendency to reduce his influence to antigang, "stay in school" messages. Yes, Bambaataa was an early advocate for an expanded definition of hip-hop that included knowledge of self as its fifth element.²⁹ He also sought to unite people from competing gangs and crews, at least when they were in the spaces devoted to hip-hop (parties, dance battles, etc.). However, he also defined hip-hop in a way that left room for other interpretations. His belief was that hip-hop was about "survival, economics, and keeping our people moving on."[30] More than a musical expression of respectability politics, Bambaataa's contribution to hip-hop was his insistence that it was an art form that spoke to the reality of Black urban life in the wake of the policies of Nixon and Reagan. Afrika Bambaataa solidified the connections between the experience of the streets and their articulation through music.

While Bambaattaa's legacy can be seen in the emphasis on self-expression and critical consciousness throughout hip-hop's golden era, many scholars argue that this ended in the 1990s when the genre became highly commercialized. For instance, scholars of hip-hop such as Tayannah Lee McQuillar, J. Brother, Eithne Quinn, and Tricia Rose have all suggested that the commercialization of hip-hop in the early 1990s (in particular the period that coincides with the rise of artists such as Snoop Dogg) signifies the turn from the genre's primary focus on questions of Black life and well-being to the neoliberal commercialization of hip-hop via the rise of West Coast gangster rap. As Tricia Rose puts it, "the extraordinary commercial penetration of hip hop" has turned a "black cultural form designed not only to liberate but to create critical consciousness and turned it into the cultural arm of predatory capitalism."[31] Rose's criticism contextualizes views on post–golden era hip-hop as a mode of making profit rather than an art form. Because all the artists I examine in this chapter come from this era, her criticism is worth a closer look.

While it is true that hip-hop produced in the 1990s and beyond saw a greater emphasis on commercial success, the genre remained a complex expression of the streets in several ways. In her brilliant study of hip-hop as a complex artistic form, Imani Perry speaks to this quality, explaining that while the 1990s saw a divergence between West Coast gangster rap, in which the gangster "mimicked a stereotype, thus becoming a survivalist hero," and East Coast "cultural nationalist" hip-hop, which emphasized Afrocentrism, Black beauty, and Black excellence, both of these new subgenres continued to challenge White supremacy.[32] Yet, because gangster rap is less legible to the mainstream, it is often cast as a lesser art form. However, the violent imagery and language of gangster rap serves different purposes for different listeners. As Perry explains, for "a mainstream audience, rap may indulge voyeuristic fantasies of black sociopathy and otherness, while for an oppressed community, these images might engage fantasies of masculine power in people who feel powerless."[33] This history of simultaneously affirming the dominant discourse of the streets as a violent space while also asserting the power of the person exercising this violence is reminiscent of

Coates's discussion of how power operates in the streets. Much like the clothing and behaviors Coates depicts in *Between the World and Me*, gangster rap is about performing power, even when it is systematically denied.

Still, while gangster rap may challenge the racialized power dynamics of the streets, it also reinforces a number of troubling ideologies, although scholars such as Michael Eric Dyson argue that this is not a valid reason for dismissing the genre as a whole. Dyson, a public intellectual who has a personal connection to the streets as a former gang member turned minister from Detroit, offers a unique perspective on this debate. He argues that while hip-hop may be full of "problematic expressions," including materialism, stereotypes, and hedonism, this is not unique to hip-hop. Literature, art, and music from numerous races and cultures reflect similar problems, yet it is often the work produced by Black youth that is disregarded.[34]

I agree with Dyson that much of the criticism directed at hip-hop fails to acknowledge its complexity as an art form, or the fact that Black life is heterogeneous. The problematic aspects of hip-hop, namely, the conspicuous themes of misogyny, Black essentialism, violence, materialism, and homophobia, are not easily swept under the rug. However, I would argue that these problematic aspects are fundamental parts of the streets as a cultural entity and can be linked to the design of government policy. Dyson gets at this when he writes, "When black people come up with forms of cultural expression that are narrow and rigid—essentialist—they're often in response to the attempt to impose vicious, or racist, or stereotypical views of black life from outside our culture. Essentialism is often conjured by bigotry and attack."[35] Misogyny, materialism, and homophobia are not unique to Black urban communities. Rather, they are merely more explicit articulations of ideologies that have been fundamental to American identity for centuries. The themes debated by Perry, Rose, and Dyson, among others, are precisely why I chose hip-hop as the subject for this chapter. Hip-hop is a musical genre that emerged from the streets as a direct response to the way the streets were shaping Black life. Perry and Dyson offer an important reminder that artistic expression does not have to be a pristine mode of protest in order to challenge power.

When the Streets Become Transnational: The Fugees' *The Score*

As a transnational musical trio, the Fugees used their cultural backgrounds and music to challenge narratives of the streets that relied on a homogeneous depiction of depraved Black life. Their name, for one, acknowledges the belonging of Black refugees and reappropriates a derogatory term that was used to separate Haitian Americans from other Black Americans in the 1980s and 1990s. The group members, Lauryn Hill, Wyclef Jean, and Pras (Samuel Prakazrel Michel), also represent the heterogeneous, transnational nature of urban Blackness. Lauryn Hill and Pras are both African Americans who were raised primarily in New Jersey, although Pras lived in Brooklyn until 1984. Wyclef is a Haitian native who was raised in Brooklyn before moving to New Jersey, where he met the other group members. Known for his fluid movement between languages, Wyclef earned the nickname "Rap Translator" long before he joined the Fugees.[36] In addition to their personal backgrounds, the Fugees incorporate musical and cultural elements from Black American and Caribbean traditions throughout their work, drawing from genres such as soul, reggae, and rock. Their lyrics are chock-full of diasporic allusions to Haile Selassie and Rastafarianism, and yet their most famous album, *The Score*, is definitively about Black life in urban America.

The Score, which was their second and final studio album, was released in 1996 by Columbia Records. Lauryn Hill describes it as "an audio film" that "tells a story, and there are cuts and breaks in the music."[37] This theme is made clear by the album's cover, which mimics the font and imagery of *The Godfather*. If this album is to be considered a story, the imagery associated with it tells us this is a story about family, violence, loyalty, success, and survival. The opening track introduces it as such, with a framing of the album by DJ Red Alert as a "feature presentation."[38] This introduction sets up the following stories, imagery, and sounds as part of a larger narrative worthy of the same kind of critical attention extended to a film such as *The Godfather*. Thus, when the intro track segues into what may appear to be a chaotic recollection of violent encounters, the listener is alerted to the deeper meaning. This is the beginning of a larger story of the streets, which is abundantly clear if one recognizes the many references to specific album tracks made in the introduction. Overall, this opening track establishes the album as a work that balances its grounding in lived reality, through language and events, with its broader theorizing, through historical references, biblical allusions, and complex intertextuality.

In terms of its themes, Wyclef describes the album as "three kids from an urban background expressing ourselves."[39] On the one hand, this is the crux of the album; it is an expression of their experience growing up in the streets. On the other hand, there is something unique about the way these "three kids" express themselves through the lens of transnational Blackness. This is something of which the artists themselves are aware.

Wyclef has explained that he credits much of their success to the perfect blending of divergent styles. While he draws heavily from his Caribbean heritage, Hill is credited with bringing soul music to the table. Pras brought a background in rock music, as well as "the roughness and a little flash" that was missing from the equation.[40]

Of all the tracks on the album, "Fu-Gee-La" best exemplifies the group's transnational politics. One of the ways this song embraces a transnational view of Blackness is through the music video's filming location and aesthetic inspiration. The Fugees originally wanted to film the video in Wyclef's native country of Haiti. However, due to the political climate at the time, they decided it was too risky and used Jamaica as the setting instead. Once they decided to record the video in Jamaica, they also opted to model it after the Jamaican crime film *The Harder They Come* (1972), which depicts the protagonist's trials as he tries to make it in the city of Kingston.[41] In many ways, the film represents a parallel to the expressions of street violence and survival depicted in *The Score*.

Another way "Fu-Gee-La" expresses transnational Blackness is through the promotional image that accompanied the single (figure 6). In the photo the nationality of each group member is listed on their passport. By invoking national belonging and reminding listeners of each artist's own sense of identity, the image presents a richer, more heterogeneous picture of Blackness. This idea is carried through into the various remixes of the song. Although each remix is almost identical lyrically, the base rhythm, intonation, and language all shift. The "Refugee Camp Remix," for instance, embraces a smoother R & B rhythm. In the "Sly & Robbie Remix," the song is set to a dancehall rhythm; this version also features Akon, a Senegalese American rapper. Finally, in the "Refugee Camp Global Mix," the artists move fluidly between languages such as Haitian Creole, French, and Spanish. Because these remixes utilize much of the same lyrical content, their primary difference becomes the expression of these concepts through music, tone, and language. As such, much like the promotional photo, these remixes highlight the plurality of transnational Blackness while simultaneously grounding it in the similar thematic experience of urban Black life.

The notion of blending cultures and styles to give perfect expression to the streets permeates the rest of the album. "Ready or Not" is a prime example of this. The song samples from both the Delfonics, a 1960s soul group, and Enya, an Irish singer-songwriter, in the hook. Adding another layer of reference, Wyclef alludes to the film *Sleepwalkers* in the first verse, which is the soundtrack from which Enya's sample comes. This practice of encoding

FIGURE 6 Cover image for "Fu-Gee-La" single from the Fugees' album *The Score*.

multiple meanings, whether through allusions or themes, is one of the Fugees' strengths. It allows them to make a series of critiques at once, such as when Wyclef raps, "Jail bars ain't golden gates, those who fake, they break," he simultaneously critiques the glorification of jail time as a currency of street credibility and the system of mass incarceration as a whole.[42]

Despite the fact that songs like "Ready or Not" are laced with layered cultural critique, the artists avoid a holier-than-thou tone through their narrative point of view. Right after Wyclef makes his prison critique, his narrative voice goes on to list his own "sins": robbery, gun violence, and so on. Rather than fall into the trap of casting street life as a binary of good and evil, he uses a narrative self-framing as a "born again hooligan" to suggest that the view of street life is much more complex from the perspective of those living it.[43]

Still, much like other 1990s hip-hop, *The Score* also includes more explicit cultural critiques. "The Beast" represents the somewhat requisite track on any semi-socially conscious album that addresses police brutality. What is particularly interesting, however, is that when speaking about this song, Wyclef explains, "I didn't get any extra hassle from [the police] because I was Haitian—just because I was black."[44] Wyclef's comments point to the way Blackness operates in the contemporary United States, regardless of ethnicity. Just as Coates's *Between the World and Me* illustrates the futility of relying on social mobility to escape the streets, "The Beast" suggests that cultural and ethnic difference will not provide a reprieve either.

While the "The Beast" condemns police brutality, it does so in a unique way by using biblical language to frame the forces that govern the streets as pseudosupernatural powers. The police are named as "the beast," the biblical end-times name for Satan, and the government politicians who cut WIC (the Special Supplemental Nutrition Program for Women, Infants, and Children) are named the 666. Amid this, Wyclef uses his narrative voice to frame the system responsible for shaping ghetto life as a temptation. Alluding to Christ's last temptation by the devil, he puts himself in the messianic figure's place. This time he is offered Manhattan instead of the world. Rather than succumb, he calls out to God, or "Jah Jah," for help. All of these allusions work to subvert the normative use of biblical narratives in the service of Whiteness by recasting U.S. hegemony as Babylon and drawing from the theology of Rastafarianism.[45] Arguably, by using biblical narrative in this way, Wyclef casts the young, Black urban protagonist as the ultimate heroic power.

As a whole, *The Score* is like many other hip-hop albums made in the 1990s. It critiques police brutality and the systems responsible for the violence and poverty of the streets. What distinguishes the Fugees, and this album in particular, is the way they reframe the Blackness of the streets through the lens of transnational solidarity. As the album constructs a broader narrative about life in the streets, this narrative is connected to that of Black urban centers outside of the United States. For instance, in "No Woman, No Cry," Wyclef takes Bob Marley's well-known track and transports the second part of the narrative to New Jersey. Where there were once only references to Trenchtown, there is now also a description of projects in New Jersey.[46] This adaptation is representative of the many ways the album draws from various Black traditions in order to tell a story of the streets that transcends the geographic boundaries of cities and nations.

Engaging the Black Radical Tradition: *Lupe Fiasco's The Cool*

At times polemical, Lupe Fiasco's emphasis on framing the streets through the lens of Black radicalism provides a unique analysis of how U.S. hegemony operates in similar ways in Black urban space and abroad. Today, Lupe Fiasco is somewhat of an outlier among hip-hop artists who have increasingly moved toward the mainstream. Yet, just a decade ago he was one of the genre's most well-known artists, with hits such as "Superstar" and "The Show Goes On." He found mainstream success at a young age after connecting with hip-hop mogul Jay-Z in the first decade of the 2000s. He signed with Atlantic Records and released his debut album, *Lupe Fiasco's Food & Liquor*, in 2006. When his 2007 album, *Lupe Fiasco's The Cool*, was released, he was at the height of his game. He had successfully broken away from his association with Jay-Z and Kanye West in order to carve out his own distinctive brand of socially conscious rap lyrics, known for references to anime, robots, and sci-fi. He was the child of Black radicalism, a Chicago rapper who rejected the materialism and overt misogyny that permeates much of hip-hop.

Lupe Fiasco's mainstream downfall came when he released *Lasers* in 2011, an album in which he critiques American imperialism more directly than in any previous work. It was his song "Words I Never Said" and the commentary he made regarding President Obama that outed him, so to speak, as a Black radical. The actual lyrics focus on U.S. support for Israel and Obama's failure to condemn the bombing of Gaza.[47] This criticism of Obama, who was perceived at the time as evidence of racial progress and the power of American liberalism, led to a series of interviews. In perhaps the most infamous of these, Lupe Fiasco explained to the hosts of CBS's *What's Trending*: "My fight against terrorism, to me, the biggest terrorist is Obama and the United States of America. . . . You know, the root cause of terrorism is the stuff the U.S. government allows to happen. The foreign policies that we have in place in different countries that inspire people to become terrorists."[48]

Whereas Lupe Fiasco's previous music could be interpreted as a progressive criticism of gang violence and racial essentialism, this song connected internal critiques of racial inequality to U.S. foreign policy. The public response to these comments and the inability to see their connection reflect the unique way Lupe Fiasco approaches his music politically. For the most part, Lupe Fiasco has not publicly defined his politics, but if one pieces together his statements, his politics become much clearer. When he says that he does not vote, he is invoking a version of Black radicalism that takes issue with state power, whether it is in the hands of Republicans or Democrats. He almost said as much in an interview with Steven Colbert in which he described his political views as being about the "critique of power, even power one agrees with."[49] In addition to challenging state power, Lupe Fiasco frames his role as being one who intervenes into narratives for the sake of critical attention and change.

Lupe Fiasco's role as a cultural critic who targets American imperialism, as well as issues internal to Black communities, is not surprising if one considers his personal and intellectual history. Born in 1982 as Wasalu Muhammad Jaco, the Chicago native spent his early childhood living in the Madison Terrace housing project. His parents played a significant role in his cultural and political formation. His father was an engineer, Black Muslim, martial artist, and former member of the Black Panther Party. His mother, who was also a Black Muslim, was a gourmet chef.[50] His upbringing reflects an interesting juxtaposition. On the one hand, his childhood reflects some of the harsh realities of growing up in Chicago. As he describes it, there were "prostitutes on the corner, gangs, drive-bys, [and] blood stains in the hallway."[51] On the other hand, Lupe Fiasco had the rich experience of being raised by racially and socially conscious parents who invested time in their child's emotional, mental, and social development. He developed an early love for music and martial arts. He passed out pamphlets for the Black Panther Party. Lupe Fiasco's childhood is a personal reflection of the nuanced experience of growing up in the streets.[52]

Out of all of Lupe Fiasco's work, his second album is the best articulation of the streets and their connection to broader patterns of U.S. power and hegemony. The album includes his reflections on fame and his role as a musician, as well as the diasporic fate of Black and Third World people. This album has a decidedly darker tone than his previous work, not only musically but also thematically, due, at least in part, to the circumstances surrounding Lupe Fiasco's life at the time. During the recording of the album his father died from type II diabetes, and his friend and business partner, Charles "Chilly" Patton, was arrested and sentenced to forty-four years in prison on drug charges.[53] These events and their impact on Lupe Fiasco undoubtedly contributed to the album's tone.

Beyond this self-reflection, *Lupe Fiasco's The Cool* is a concept album that blends the genres of music and graphic arts to create an intricate story that personifies the streets through three main characters: The Cool, The Streets, and The Game. He describes the main premise of the album as a story about "a hustler who dies and comes back to life, only to get robbed by two little kids with the same gun that killed him."[54] This concept emerged from the songs "He Say/She Say" and "The Cool" from Lupe Fiasco's previous album, *Lupe Fiasco's Food & Liquor*. In "He Say/She Say," a young mother speaks to her partner about their son, asking him to stay and be a part of the child's life. The father, whose absence is signaled in the song by a list of the son's increasingly worrying behaviors, refuses his parental responsibility. After the little boy from "He Say/She Say" grows up without a father, he becomes the subject of "The Cool." As Lupe Fiasco explains, "The people that step in to raise him are the Streets and the Game, like how people also say, 'The streets raised me.' It's an answer to that."[55]

In both *The Cool* and his previous album, Lupe Fiasco uses fantasy to characterize the inescapability of the streets. In the original song "The Cool," the character, whose full name is Michael Young History, is described as a zombie-like figure who digs his way out of a Hennessey-filled casket buried six feet underground. The motivation for his desperate escape from death's clutches is signaled in the hook: he is "chasing the cool." Despite his awareness of his grotesque physical state, which includes a fleshless hand, his only concern is finding "something to slang." Instead, he is robbed by two young boys with the same gun used to kill him. Yet, in the last lines of his story, The Cool promises to keep hustling.[56] Not even death is greater than the call of the streets.

The elaborate conceptual framework for *The Cool* also manifests itself in the album's artwork. Nathan Cabrera created several pieces that detail the three main characters. For instance, the album cover includes three cryptographic images, one for each of the album's main characters. The Cool is symbolized by his skeletal hand; The Streets and The Game are symbolized by a heart-shaped locket and a venomous skull, respectively. In an interview with *Pitchfork*, Lupe Fiasco explains the imagery and symbolism in detail:

> The Cool, his right hand is rotted away. . . . It represents the rotting away of his righteousness, of his good. And the Streets and the Cool kind of have a love affair going on. So she's represented by this locket. And the locket has a key and it's on fire. And as a gift to the Cool on his rise to fame, she gave him the key. And the key represents the key to the Streets. . . . The Game, he's represented by a stripped-down skull, a skull with dice in his eyes and smoke coming out of his mouth. The billowing smoke is actually crack smoke.[57]

The images he describes fill the album's booklet. In one particularly striking image, The Streets, The Cool, and The Game appear on the left, staring menacingly toward the right. On the right, Lupe Fiasco stands with his finger raised to his mouth as if to silence them. In this way, he inserts himself into both the album's story and the narrative about the streets.

Each character of *The Cool* has a corresponding song that demonstrates their role or connection to the streets. In "The Coolest," a resurrected Michael Young History narrates the desire The Streets elicits and how that desire traps him. Spoken from The Cool's perspective, the song sets up a series of paradoxes to define his mindset. He raps about competing devotion to things such as God and self, peace and war.[58] This dichotomous struggle is then juxtaposed with his definitive declaration of love for The Streets. He professes to love her with more than all his heart. He loves her with every vein and vessel of his being. He even loves the destruction she has inflicted on his body, every bullet hole and scar.[59] Where God and peace could not successfully claim him, The Streets does. The Cool goes on to explain his devotion to her. She is described as a queen, one he dreams of ruling alongside. Her beauty is described in terms of financial capital. Her eyes "glow green with the logo of our dreams."[60] For Michael Young History, The Streets represents access to the money, power, and status denied to people like him. She can turn him into The Cool, the ultimate embodiment of his desire. What Lupe Fiasco achieves through this narrative of devotion to The Streets is a personalized expression of what it is like to internalize and be governed by the power and cultural constructs of the streets.

While The Streets is described in terms of desirability in "The Coolest," she is characterized as a pathogen in "Streets on Fire." The hook, which is sung by Matthew Santos, describes The Streets as carrying death on her tongue and danger on her fingers.[61] Yet, this hook is sung in such a slow melody and soothing tone that one could easily miss the warning issued about The Streets. In contrast, each verse is rapped at a quick pace, almost jolting the listener into a state of panic.

By framing the streets as an illness, Lupe Fiasco challenges narratives that pathologize Blackness itself. If the streets are the disease and not the people who inhabit them, the question becomes, who is responsible for creating this disease? The song answers this question by naming all of the people blamed for the pathology of the streets. From the rich to the poor, the religious to the conspiracy theorists, the blame for the streets is passed from one group to another.[62] By frantically vocalizing the circular way this blame is passed around, he suggests that we are so caught up in arguing over who is responsible that we forget to ask other, equally important questions, such as what to do about the streets. This becomes abundantly clear through the parallelism between the first and second verses. The final three lines of both verses focus on the explanations given by the little boy, the preacher, and a street figure (a bum in verse 1 and a dope boy in verse 2). In both verses, the final line suggests the streets pose a danger to "the whole wide world," an idea that is present throughout the album. Between the hyperbolic descriptions of desire tied to the streets in "The Cool" and global panic about them in "Streets on Fire," Lupe Fiasco frames the streets as an entity that is ultimately about power and who holds it. While the streets reflect the specific exercise of power over Black Americans, Lupe Fiasco connects the local site of this injustice to global struggle.

While Lupe Fiasco elevates the power of the streets, he does not frame them as insurmountable. On the contrary, he uses his characterization of The Streets to demystify their power. Toward the end of "Streets on Fire," Lupe Fiasco describes The Streets as a "fraudulent angel." Instead of an omnipotent, supernatural being, she powers her halo with batteries and wears store-bought wings.[63] Everything about The Streets can be rationally explained. By the end of the song, she goes from a global threat causing worldwide panic to an exposed imposter. Between "The Cool" and "Streets on Fire," Lupe Fiasco questions the basis of the streets' power over Black life and suggests that their real power lies in their ability to govern Black desire.

While the streets and coolness are familiar concepts to most, the game may be less legible to those who are unfamiliar with urban culture. Discussing its use in hip-hop, rapper KRS-One defines the game as "the readiness in the creation of a business venture that brings about grassroots business practices. . . . Its practitioners are known as *hustlers* and *self-starters*."[64] KRS-One's definition highlights the fact that, despite its association with urban Blackness, the game is essentially about embracing a capitalist entrepreneurial spirit. What differentiates the game from other capitalist endeavors is its frequent overlap with underground economies and extralegal activities.

While the game is used widely to refer to everything from a life of hustling to drug dealing, the concept is theorized in a much more complex way in Lupe Fiasco's song "Put You On Game." Through a first-person narrative perspective, The Game reveals his nature to the listener. The complexity of The Game and the difficulty of fully understanding its connection to other nameable force, are expressed as the song's speaker taunts that artists, poets, and intellectuals have fruitlessly tried to articulate his role in the streets. In contrast to their confusion, The Game's deep voice inserts itself rhythmically throughout the song, promising to put the listener on game.[65] As the song continues, The Game takes credit not only for the social order of the streets but also for the internalized desire to pursue the lifestyle of the streets.

In contrast to The Cool and The Streets, The Game is more than a personified character. He is described as ancient and omniscient, with his role in urban space connected to historical and transnational forces of oppression. He describes himself as the sum of the American Dream, African colonization, hypercapitalism, urban crime, and gun violence. The negative current of these forces is described in vivid imagery as the "blood . . . gas, water, and electricity" of the city.[66] In this way, The Game's reach and impact liken him more to a god than a man.

Still, while the song draws on epic, religious language to convey The Game's magnitude, its metaphors and imagery ground The Game in material reality. The Game is not some metaphysical force but rather a complex combination of cultural ideologies (the American Dream, colonialism, and cultural representation), violent social practices (crime and gun violence), systems and structures (the Oval Office, crack houses and apartments), and dysfunctional social relationships (absent, drug-addicted parents and abandoned children).

Of all the characters depicted in *Lupe Fiasco's The Cool*, The Game is the most comprehensive, as well as the most dehumanizing. This is most poignantly conveyed when he tells a baby who has been discarded in a trash can, "All I hear when you're crying is laughs."[67] Through this graphic imagery and off-putting language, Lupe Fiasco conveys the totalizing violence of The Game. This culminates at the end of the song when, after The Game proclaims his hope that bullet wounds will sing his praise, we hear the single echoing sound of a gunshot.[68]

In many ways, what Lupe Fiasco names The Game is closer to what I am calling the streets: a complex set of interpolated practices, structures, and ideologies that violently stifle Black life and futurity. However, Lupe Fiasco also points toward the driving forces that sustain the streets. Racialized capitalist desire, personified through The Streets, and the desire for power, status, and recognition, embodied by The Cool, explain how the streets continue to operate generation after generation. Lupe Fiasco's album illustrates the way these forces are tied to the broader ideologies inherent in U.S. hegemony, yet tailored in such a way as to pigeonhole urban Blackness into one specific manifestation of them.

Good Kid, M.A.A.D. City: Kendrick Lamar's Personalization of the Streets

Much of the critical praise for Kendrick Lamar, Pulitzer Prize and twelve-time Grammy winner, focuses on his musical talent and engagement with complex themes, such as racism and American belonging. His song "Alright" has become an anthem for the Black Lives Matter movement, and many of his other songs speak to his experience growing up in Compton, California. In fact, it was his neighborhood ties that led him to fame. Eventually, after releasing a series of mixtapes and making a name for himself as a teenager, Lamar gained the attention of West Coast veterans The Game, Dr. Dre, and Snoop Dogg, who gave him a platform that helped launch his career.[69] What sets Kendrick Lamar apart from other artists, though, is the way he uses musical composition and lyrics to express the kind of complex emotional identity often denied to Black urban Americans. Whether expressing extreme loss or joy, his songs insist on the personhood of those represented and explicitly tie that personhood to urban belonging.

A primary example of how Kendrick Lamar uses personalized, vulnerable expression to humanize the streets is the song "XXX" from his Pulitzer Prize-winning album, *DAMN*. The track, which features U2 and was released in 2017, incorporates many of the elements seen in Lamar's debut album—religious imagery, the personalization of urban life, and contradictory desires. Before ever broaching the topic of violence, the song starts with a series of biblical references whose framing alludes to a conversation between God and the devil in the book of Job. In the biblical story, Satan questions Job's loyalty to God. To prove his unwavering devotion, God allows Job to be put through a series of trials. Similarly, an unknown speaker, presumably God, commands that Lamar be left in the wilderness with an enemy to be tested. This stacked allusion, first to Job and then to Jesus's temptation in the wilderness, seems to affirm Lamar's religious devotion. However, the following lines contest this by suggesting that if pushed far enough, he would show his unfaithfulness.[70]

As the song continues, the "wilderness" where Lamar is tested is revealed to be the streets. This becomes clearest in the second verse, which involves a personal narrative in which Lamar is asked for advice by a friend whose only son was just murdered. However, instead of giving the expected advice on how to overcome the situation, Lamar responds with arguably the most human of emotions, anger. His desire for vengeance is expressed through the melody as well. While the rest of the song is slow and sultry, this verse is fast-paced and laced with the sound of sirens. After explaining that his spirit knows it is better to forgive, he tells his friend that his emotions favor the Old Testament approach to vengeance, "an eye for an eye." His desperation for payback is exemplified by his admission that he would get revenge as the killer was leaving church, if that was his only means.

While the raw, vulnerable admission that he would respond in this way speaks to Kendrick Lamar's tendency to paint the streets through the lens of realism and personal experience, his questioning of the listener's own potential actions also points to a more universal human experience. Instead of depicting his friend's loss as a casualty of urban violence, he frames it as a personal loss of love, loyalty, and memories.[71] In a climate where Black youth are killed daily by police and gang violence, this line reveals the kind of humanization that is missing from public discourse.

In addition to critiquing dominant narratives around urban Blackness, part of Lamar's brand of new West Coast hip-hop is the embrace of contradictions. For example, Lamar is a self-proclaimed Christian who credits God for his success and artistic purpose.[72] Yet, in songs like "Bitch Don't Kill My Vibe," he reflects on his nature as a sinner "who is probably gonna sin again." Likewise, he displays elements of conscious hip-hop, discussing issues such as police and gang violence while also expressing desires for things such as fame and materialism. Lamar also often nods toward the need to affirm Black women's natural beauty, yet his lyrics and videos are often full of misogynistic imagery.

Lamar's embrace of complexity and contradiction suggests that he is far less interested in being the latest and greatest conscious hip-hop star than he is in being an artist from Compton whose work mirrors the complex, often contradictory realities of his life. In many ways, Lamar's style reflects Michael Eric Dyson's observation that "hip hop is neither sociological commentary nor political criticism," but "an art form that traffics in hyperbole, parody, kitsch, dramatic license, double-entendres, signification, and other literary and artistic conventions to get its point across."[73] Dyson points to the fact that in categorizing hip-hop performers as either conscious or not, or religious or not, we often fail to understand them as artists above all. It is through this lens that I wish to examine Lamar's debut album, *Good Kid, M.A.A.D. City* (2012), as a text that engages in the techniques listed earlier in order to express and humanize the emotional reality of the streets.

As the title suggests, *Good Kid, M.A.A.D. City* tells the story of a good kid, K-Dot, growing up in the streets of Compton. Much like *Lupe Fiasco's The Cool*,

Good Kid, M.A.A.D. City is a concept album. It follows K-Dot as he rides down Rosecrans Avenue with friends, attends local parties, and tries to escape gang violence. The fact that the album was released about a month before Trayvon Martin was murdered, an event that arguably served as a tipping point for widespread activism against anti-Black violence, is significant because it illustrates that the realities reflected in the album are not a response to social trends or a renewed public interest in Black life on the part of progressives. Rather, they are primarily the expressions of a kid from Compton who grew up to be an artist.

While on one hand the concept for *Good Kid, M.A.A.D. City* is a version of Kendrick Lamar's own origin story, on the other hand it is an album about the city itself. This latter element and its relationship to the personal development and experience of the protagonist are what interests me most. What Lamar's album accomplishes that other albums do not is a clear articulation of the complex ways in which the environment of the streets socializes the protagonist and fosters the internalization of particular ideologies and practices. As Bettina Love explains in her analysis of the album, Lamar seems to articulate his realization that the city is "a co-conspirator in gang violence and drugs."[74] This realization does not take the form of more radical or Black Nationalist rhetoric. It does not necessarily present a clear alternative, but rather an acute recognition that the reason Black life exists as it does in these spaces is bigger than the will of gang leaders. It has to do with the cities themselves and the way they operate on sociocultural and ideological levels. The result is a complex narrative that reveals the extent to which one must struggle against these forces for survival and selfhood.

The theme of the streets as a site of complex personal struggle is exemplified in the album's seventh track, "good kid," which was produced by Pharrell Williams. This song, whose slower rhythm and pace contrast with the album's other tracks, takes on a jazzy melody with understated drumbeats. The tone suggests this is a much more reflective track. Lyrically, the song narrates a series of threats to the album's protagonist, with each threat (gang violence, police brutality and drugs) having its own dedicated verse. The personal impact of these threats is articulated through the song's hook, which describes the experience of growing up in the streets as a "mass hallucination," where education fails and escapism and resignation prevail.[75] Neither school nor church are enough to protect K-Dot. The only thing that ensures his survival is a belief that one day he will be respected and recognized as a good kid from a mad city.[76]

In contrast to "good kid," "m.A.A.d. City" has one of the album's most aggressive beats. Yet, instead of being a gangster rap anthem, the song provides both a personal and a communal history of Compton. The album's protagonist, K-Dot, recounts seeing his first murder victim at age nine. Likewise, he speaks of the failed 1992 truce between the Bloods and the Crips. Rather than frame these events as merely adjacent to the protagonist's life experience, the hook contextualizes them and their direct impact on his livelihood. When K-Dot runs into the hook's speaker, he is hit with a barrage of questions about belonging. The angry demand to know where he is from, and the disregard for who he knows, is a reminder that geographic belonging supersedes all.[77] Safety and survival are inscribed onto the city's very geography.

In addition to narrating these experiences, K-Dot speaks of the psychological impact of navigating such a "mad city" at a young age. He raps about internalized trauma and pain too difficult to process. The weight of the pressure felt by K-Dot leads him to conclude that the whole city is against him.[78] In many ways, the song narrates the isolation and adversity one faces if one chooses to go against the established order of life in the streets.

While Lamar juxtaposes the competing elements of the streets in "good kid" and "m.A.A.d. City," it is worth noting that on the album he also takes time to capture the mundane adventures of teenage life. On the one hand, songs such as "The Art of Peer Pressure" frame the creeping threat of criminality that lurks in the streets and the way this threat can easily consume young Black boys. On the other hand, songs such as "Backseat Freestyle" serve as a necessary pause and reminder that this is not *all* that the streets are. "Backseat Freestyle" is framed as a skit where K-Dot has just jumped into a car with his friends and begins rapping. Comically, the song starts off by referencing the political dreams of Martin Luther King Jr. before jumping to the protagonist's own dreams for money and power. The rest of the song is full of imagery about cars, money, sex, partying, and respect. Unexpectedly, the music video for the song does not really draw upon this imagery. Instead, the majority of the video is set in Compton and chronicles mundane activities such as playing dominoes and getting a haircut. This seems to solidify the point that this is a song more about K-Dot's life in Compton than it is about the list of things he dreams about.

It would be easy to dismiss "Backseat Freestyle" as a nonsensical reflection of the ills that permeate hip-hop culture. However, given the placement of the song within the album's narrative, it represents more than this. I would argue against the temptation to decontextualize this song, which is meant to be a representation of teenage thought and ambition. While these desires are arguably fostered by the culture of the streets, they should not be reduced to their ideological components. Taken as a whole, this song makes a simple point. Sometimes life in the streets just means talking a big game about your dreams to become a star while driving around with your friends. "Backseat Freestyle" revels in these moments without trying to make sense of them or offer any particular social commentary. Lamar affirms this in an interview, saying, "That is just me capturing the moment and being 16 and saying the most outlandish shit when you are around your homeboys or you are around whoever. You know, you really don't care what you're talking about. That is the type of way we used to talk. That is dope because that was me going as ignorant as possible, and they are still analyzing it as ignorant as possible and putting national stats behind it. That is funny."[79] These moments humanize the protagonist by capturing the universal experience of teenage revelry. Yet, because this revelry takes the form of gendered bragging, it is easy to dismiss. Still, even more than capturing a moment of teenage fun, Lamar offers listeners a complex picture of Black boy joy. Whereas most images of Black boy joy are sanitized by respectability politics, Lamar seems unconcerned with such measures. Intentional or not, he makes a case against the racialization of Black adolescence as somehow more devious, angry, or violent than others. Given the recent history of cases such as that of Jordan Davis, I would argue this intervention is a necessary one.

Although the album's lead single, "Swimming Pools (Drank)," is not overtly about the streets, it still speaks to the larger success of Kendrick Lamar's work as an artist concerned with expressing his life experience. Likewise, it captures the way he is able to take something that is specific and personal, the peer pressure to use alcohol as a vehicle of escape on the streets, and turn it into something that is also universally understood. The commercial success of this song highlights how Lamar is able to foster a wider consideration of what the streets are and how they impact people like him in very real, tangible ways.

On the surface, "Swimming Pools" could easily be interpreted as an anthem about partying and binge drinking. The catchy bridge is a series of instructions on how to get "faded," while the hook is a direct questioning of the listener/protagonist as to why he is not drinking more heavily. However, the verses of this song challenge this interpretation. The first verse narrates the speaker's experience with peer pressure and an alcoholic grandfather. Similarly, the second verse is a conversation between the speaker's conscience and himself. His conscience warns him that this path will lead to his end, but the speaker can only think of the pleasures associated with drinking, namely, sex and acceptance. These verses serve as a personalized narrative of the dangers of surrendering to the peer pressure voiced in the hook and bridge.

The music video that accompanies this song complicates this alternate interpretation. It starts with images of smashed bottles and scantily clad models as the bridge repeats instructions for getting blackout drunk.[80] During the first verse, Lamar is pictured dressed all in white, sitting in what appears to be a condemned house. A few pictures remain on the walls, but missing sheet rock and windows convey that this is a dilapidated space. While posing next to various liquor bottles, Lamar raps his confessions about peer pressure and the effects of misusing alcohol. All of this culminates in the imagery of him falling into dark space while the song's hook is played. However, during the second verse Lamar is shown struggling and intoxicated at a party. This is juxtaposed with images of a dancing woman in a swimsuit and Lamar rapping while the camera circles him as he stands in the center of crown-shaped light. After that, the sequence of Lamar drowning in darkness is less stark. It is interspersed with red-light party scenes, images of Lamar dressed in street clothes, coyly smiling and enjoying the party vibe as he raps. The final images of alcohol are more playful than those at the beginning. Unbroken bottles and supermodels splash into the swimming pool in a full-color sequence. At the end, when the Lamar who was previously drowning in darkness lands in the swimming pool, he is helped up by a partially hidden figure.

Despite the fact that close attention to the song reveals its critique of binge drinking, the song ended up being a college party anthem of sorts. I remember working as a graduate student when this was a Top 40 hit and hearing the song play on campus as I walked by fraternity and sorority parties. The song's ambiguity and its ability to serve as both cultural critique and commercial hit represent the unique quality of Kendrick Lamar's music overall. Because his music is about artistic and personal expression, rooted in the complex and contradictory experiences of a Black man from Compton, it is interpreted as more fun and accessible than other clear-cut versions of conscious hip-hop. He allows listeners both to be convicted and to continue on living, as is best reflected in his analogy of the sinner who cannot help but sin again. Lamar's album is not necessarily an attempt to change anything. Rather, it aims to reflect the experience of being young and living in the streets in a way that is intellectual, artistic, and personal. Kendrick Lamar uses personalized narratives to walk listeners through the experience of living with street violence, poverty, and gang violence on a daily basis. He reminds listeners that the people who live in the streets are just that, people.

They are rambunctious teenagers who brag about their dreams, young couples in love, people who enjoy a good party, and good kids in school.

What the Streets Are Still Saying Today

What the Fugees, Lupe Fiasco, and Kendrick Lamar seem to collectively suggest is that the streets are an entity that shapes Black life in positive and negative ways across the boundaries of ethnic and national belonging. In this way, they foster a sense of communal Blackness based on shared space, while also acknowledging the heterogeneous experiences of Haitian transplants, Black radicals, and teenagers. Despite the obvious threats of police violence, gang violence, and drug addiction that appear in each artist's work, the streets are also capable of producing the universal experiences of communal belonging, love, and adolescent irreverence. Lamar captures this particularly well through his personalized narratives of Compton. All of these artists seem to suggest that hip-hop is worth greater attention as a genre with unique proximity to the streets. If, as Michael Eric Dyson suggests, we approach hip-hop as an art form, we are likely to find a host of complex expressions that will complicate the monolithic narratives about the streets, and Black youth in particular. Given the current dangers these narratives pose to young Black lives, the stakes for doing so are high.

CHAPTER FIVE

A Hood Genre
Visualizing the Streets in TV and Film

While I was revising this book, director John Singleton passed away at the young age of fifty-one. While Singleton was known for films such as *Boyz n the Hood* (1991) and *Poetic Justice* (1993), his significance as a cultural icon extends far beyond his cinematic work. In the wake of his death, Black celebrities and public intellectuals such as Ava DuVernay, Barry Jenkins, and Michael Eric Dyson flooded social media with Singleton's praise. He was called a visionary who centered Black experience within America's cinematic landscape. In addition to these accolades, pictures of Singleton with rappers Tupac and Ice Cube circulated online. Singleton was a contemporary of these artists, attempting to do through film what they achieved through music.

The celebration of Singleton's life, relationships, and work signals the importance of Singleton and others who carved out space in America's cultural imaginary through so-called hood genre films. In this chapter, I analyze the hood genre films *Boyz n the Hood* (1991) and *Just Another Girl on the I.R.T.* (1992) as examples of how Black filmmakers in the 1990s challenged the way the streets existed in the White American imaginary. I also argue that, over time, this genre has been reimagined in films like *Moonlight* (2016), which take up the legacy of depicting urban Black youth in nuanced ways by moving beyond the boundaries of heteronormative Black urban masculinity. Finally, I examine how television has played a similar role in fostering competing visions of the streets. Despite the critical praise *The Wire* received, I argue that it falls into the trap of depicting the streets through the White gaze. In contrast, a show like *The Chi* insists that audiences see urban space through the Black gaze. The films and television shows about the streets produced by Black creators illustrate how community and joy exist alongside threats of violence, providing a powerful counternarrative to the one-dimensional stereotype of Black urban identity often perpetuated through public and political discourse.

The Emergence of Hood Genre Films

One of the ways the policies and political discourse surrounding the streets became solidified in the wider American imaginary was through film and television. As America's geography became increasingly racialized, television and film filled the chasm between Black and White, often determining how Black urbanites were seen and understood by their White, suburban counterparts. As some scholars have argued, "Into this void contemporary television, film, and popular culture entered, creating the most poignantly sordid fantasies of inner-city degeneracy and moral decrepitude. These representations of urban life would serve as markers of the distance the suburban dweller had traveled away from perdition."[1]

While at times countercultural in their depiction of Black agency, the blaxploitation films of the 1970s are an example of the cinematic "sordid fantasies" of the streets. Blaxploitation films were, in some respects, a step forward for Black representation. The films featured Black leads in urban spaces. They also capitalized on perceptions of urban Blackness through images of Black fashion and natural hairstyles, as well as an emphasis on Black vernacular and popular music. Films such as *Sweet Sweetback's Baadasssss Song* (1971), *Shaft* (1971), and *Foxy Brown* (1974) featured a lone Black hero fighting "the man," often by drawing on Marxist and/or Black nationalist politics.[2] In fact, Huey Newton called *Sweet Sweetback's Baadasssss Song* "the first truly revolutionary Black film made."[3]

In terms of cinematography, blaxploitation films utilized handheld cameras, location shooting, and synchronized sound to create a gritty sense of Black urban realism.[4] Yet, despite the fact that these films featured Black actors who were actively fighting White supremacy, they also often relied on a caricature of Black radicalism that undermined their political groundings. They also reaffirmed stereotypes of Black men as pimps, Black women as prostitutes, and urban space as rife with crime, poverty, and drugs. Furthermore, these films were almost exclusively created and produced by White Americans.[5] The way Black radicalism and urban space were used by these filmmakers to increase their profits is what led Junius Griffin, then head of the Los Angeles NAACP office, to coin the term "blaxploitation film."[6]

In contrast to the often one-dimensional depiction of the streets in blaxploitation movies, films produced by Black directors in the 1980s and 1990s portrayed urban Black identity and experience in more nuanced ways. In the mid-1980s, for instance, Spike Lee emerged as one of the few filmmakers to create works about Black urban protagonists for mainstream audiences. Two of his most well-known movies from this time are *She's Gotta Have It* (1986) and *Do the Right Thing* (1989). While *She's Gotta Have It* is largely a film about women's sexual liberation, Timothy Edwards points out that one of the main character's lovers, Mars Blackmon, is an early archetype of the "B-boy" characters who appear throughout hood genre films in the 1990s.[7] Lee's *Do the Right Thing*, in contrast, is a clear setup for the hood film genre by focusing on issues such as racism and police brutality within urban spaces like New York.

Just a few years after *Do the Right Thing* was released, several other urban-centric films came out, signaling the beginning of the hood genre film boom. S. Craig Watkins suggests that these films were a response by the film industry to three developments: the rise of the "postindustrial ghetto," the emergence of a marketplace centered on youth and popular culture, and the commercialization of hip-hop.[8] These social factors make it easy to assume that hood genre films are nothing more than a reincarnation of early blaxploitation films, which is true to some extent. However, a number of things distinguish hood genre films from their 1970s predecessors. First, they are often written and directed by Black Americans. Second, whereas 1970s films focused on a lone Black hero who challenges the cultural norms of the hood, these films focus on communal dynamics and collective belonging. Finally, hood genre films typically feature urban youth, as opposed to older adult figures, and in this way are a visual counterpart to hip-hop, challenging the way Black urban youth in particular are stereotyped.

Because hood genre films revolve around young Black identity, they tend to follow the pattern of most coming-of-age stories. Unlike in mainstream coming-of-age tales, however, knowledge of the streets is a fundamental component of each protagonist's growth and survival.[9] Furthermore, the streets shape the actions and behaviors of the films' characters, sometimes to a stereotypical extent. Set in major cities like New York or Los Angeles, these films are characterized by the presence of armed young Black men who often deal drugs and murder each other. They also tend to include the figure of the so-called welfare queen.[10] In addition to these settings and themes, hood genre films are known for utilizing filming techniques that contribute to a new Black realism.[11] For example, synchronized sound recording, handheld cameras, and grainy film stock create a greater sense of authenticity and urban realism. The films also often include dialogue in Black vernacular, as well as hip-hop-inspired clothing and music.[12] Many of the movies feature rappers, who also contribute to the film's soundtrack. For instance, Ice Cube both stars in and provides the music for *Boyz n the Hood*. Likewise, films such as *Juice* and *Poetic Justice* feature Tupac as an actor and performer.

The emphasis on urban realism frames hood genre films as a form of self-expression for Black urban youth. While this is certainly true, film scholar Michael Boyce Gillespie makes a compelling argument that Black film, including blaxploitation and hood genre movies, should not be viewed as a singular entity, the merit of which is determined by so-called authentic representation. Rather, Black film should be untethered from the restrictiveness of embodiment and "identitarian fantasies of black ontology."[13] I agree that the kind of analysis Gillespie condemns represents unimaginative configurations of Blackness. However, hood genre films set out precisely to speak to questions of authenticity and ontology. I would argue that this intention set by Black creators is not mutually exclusive from the freedom to imagine and depict Blackness in new ways. In fact, as I will discuss later in this chapter, the hood genre films laid the foundation for such work, paving the way for films like *Moonlight*, which simultaneously engage the hood genre film tradition while also deconstructing it.

Gillespie's criticism points to the way Black film, and hood genre films in particular, can be interpreted by the public as a confirmation of stereotypes and one-dimensional Black identity. When hood genre films debuted, critics and politicians claimed that the movies would inspire greater real-world violence perpetrated by Black men.[14] Today, some cultural critics see the themes in these films as nothing more than a racialized manifestation of the middle class's obsession with sensational stories about sex, drugs, and violence.[15] Media studies scholar S. Craig Watkins argues that "Hollywood's decisive turn to ghetto-theme action pictures was symptomatic of a broader shift in post–civil rights era racial discourse: the fantastic and wildly distorted notion that poor Black youth constitute the core of America's social, economic, and moral crisis."[16] In other words, while Black filmmakers were using the medium as a mode of self-fashioning, Hollywood studios and White moviegoers perceived the genre as an affirmation of urban Black otherness.

To the White gaze, much of what is depicted in hood genre films is a direct reflection of how White middle-class suburban culture was defining itself against Black urban America at the time. This is even clearer when one considers a subset of this genre, what Robert C. Bulman calls "the urban-high-school genre." In these films, the hood is presented as a space of redemption, but this only takes place through the hard work of an (often White) teacher-outsider. In films such as *Lean on Me* (1989) and *Dangerous Minds* (1995), a middle-class teacher-outsider comes to teach at a dysfunctional inner-city school. This teacher-outsider often finds him- or herself in front of a class of one-dimensional, impoverished student characters. By instilling in them a sense of personal responsibility and hard work, the teacher-outsider somehow manages to save the students from their troubles. However heartwarming and satisfying this redemption may be to viewers, it is ultimately a middle-class fantasy that relies on the sensibilities of meritocracy and individualism to avoid facing the complex social and systemic issues responsible for urban students' difficulties.[17]

How hood genre films, and the streets by proxy, are interpreted through the lens of middle-class desire and sensibilities demonstrates the contentious nature of the public imaginary. For Black filmmakers, hood genre films allowed them to assert their own vision of the streets, challenging the way they exist in the broader White imaginary. Yet, they could not control how that expression was consumed and reinterpreted by the public. Regardless, these films inserted powerful counternarratives into popular culture. Films like *Boyz n the Hood* (1991), *Straight Out of Brooklyn* (1991), *New Jack City* (1991), *Juice* (1992), and *Menace II Society* (1993) focus on how young Black male protagonists navigate the threats of poverty and gang violence through familial and/or communal relationships. By framing the hood as a repressive space these protagonists must fight against or try to escape, these films offer a cultural critique of the policies responsible for creating the streets. This ultimately suggests that the difference between poor Black urbanites and White middle-class suburbanites is not a matter of work ethic or predisposition, but rather spatial belonging and sociocultural predetermination.

Still, the progressive nature of this depiction of the streets does not nullify criticisms of stereotypical representation. At times the characters in hood genre films seem more like archetypes than people. One of the most troubling examples of this is in the portrayal of Black women. As film studies professor Paula Massood argues in "Street Girls with No Future?," "At their worst, hood films featured black women as nothing more than the bane of the black man's existence—as 'bitches' or 'hos'—and, most egregiously . . . as the cause of the majority of the problems in the African American community."[18] As bell hooks observes in *Black Looks*, this depiction of Black women as nagging and/or secondary characters who exist solely to aid the development of Black male characters is not new. Historically, Black women characters have been used to soften the image of Black men and make them appear more "vulnerable, easygoing, funny, and unthreatening to a white audience."[19] In fact, these representations of Black women in film and television became so prominent in the twentieth century that they gave rise to a new stereotype, the sapphire. Named after Sapphire Stevens from *The Amos 'n Andy Show*, this trope took the stereotype of the domineering, masculine Black woman and heightened it. Sapphire was angrier and more of a nag than her predecessors, and much of her negative attention is directed toward the Black man. In many ways, these depictions of Black women reinforce Daniel Moynihan's 1965 assertion that overly dominant Black women are the source of Black men's stunted development.[20] The presence of these stereotypes in hood genre films is a prime example of how Black art can be used to express the unique humanity of some, in this case Black men, while failing to do so for others.

Despite their inherent misogyny, the fact that hood genre films focused on Black male protagonists' inner struggles to adapt to and survive the streets was an important cultural intervention in the 1990s. At the time, young Black men were being increasingly dehumanized in the mainstream political discourse. A prime example of this is John J. Dilulio Jr.'s superpredator thesis, which popularized the view of young Black men as violent threats to themselves and White America.[21] By narrating the complex interior life of young Black men, hood genre films contributed to an important counter discourse. Moreover, they paved the way for early twenty-first-century film and television to continue this work.

Black Masculinity in Hood Genre Films

Boyz n the Hood, written and directed by John Singleton, is arguably the quintessential Hollywood hood drama. The film stars Cuba Gooding Jr., Ice Cube, Morris Chestnut, and Laurence Fishburne. Like many hood genre films, it is a coming-of-age tale about Tre Styles (Gooding), who moves in with his father after having trouble at school. His father, Furious Styles (Fishburne), is a veteran and small-business owner who spends the majority of the film teaching his son how to "be a man" and survive the threats he faces as a young Black man living in South Central Los Angeles.

The film was inspired in part by Singleton's childhood growing up in South Central. After he graduated from high school, Singleton attended the University of Southern California (USC), where he graduated with a degree in film. Singleton drew from his life experiences to write and direct *Boyz n the Hood*, which was released just one year after he graduated from college. With the success of the film, Singleton became the first African American, and the youngest person, to be nominated for Best Director by the Academy Awards. Despite his successes, Singleton articulates a critical perspective of American society, something that plays out in his work. As he puts it, "You are told to believe in the system—a system that was not created to serve you and your own. Sometimes you believe in the dream; other times you catch reality."[22]

Coming to terms with reality is something Singleton attempts to capture in *Boyz n the Hood*. Still, despite its use of urban realism, the film feels somewhat like a covert public service announcement. In addition to the sentimental music, touching father-son scenes, and one-dimensional portrayals of gang members and drug dealers, the film is visually framed in such a way as to make its social message extremely clear. The movie's opening scene is a prime example of this. The first thing viewers see is a Black screen. However, in the background one can hear screeching tires, gunshots, and men arguing, all of which signal a drive-by shooting. Shortly after this auditory opening, the title screen appears and the camera zooms in. The next image is a typewritten statement: One out of every twenty-one Black men will be murdered, most at the hands of another Black man. As this fact appears on-screen, the audio of a 911 call plays in the background. A young boy cries out, "They shot my brother!" This dramatic opening sets up the film's themes of inner-city violence and Black-on-Black crime. At the end of the film, after the audience learns, again through written on-screen narrative, that Doughboy was murdered two weeks later, the title screen appears again. This time, though, the words "increase the peace" are written directly below it. This last image bookends the film and reinforces the idea that it is aimed at urban Black youth.

Like sound effects, visual cues throughout the film reinforce the concept of the streets as a confining space. For instance, in the first few minutes, viewers are shown an image of a stop sign with a plane flying overhead. The juxtaposition of these two divergent symbols reflects the contrast between the confines of life in South Central and the wealth and freedom typically associated with Los Angeles. This is reinforced minutes later with an image of a Reagan-Bush political poster with bullet holes in it. Again, Singleton contrasts the promise of neoliberal social mobility with the visceral threat of gun violence. Likewise, "Do Not Enter" and "One Way" signs appear in shots throughout the film. All of these work as visual reminders of the limitations the streets place on the film's protagonist.

Beyond these visual reminders of how the streets govern Black life, the film at times relies on heavy-handed plotlines. For instance, in a party celebrating Doughboy's release from prison, he and some other young men are playing dominoes. As they discuss their sex lives, they end up talking about AIDS. Doughboy informs one of his confused friends that one can contract the disease in numerous ways. While the colloquial language and Ice Cube's acting almost make the conversation seem like a natural one, it still comes across as an intentionally placed scene to inform Black youth about the dangers of unprotected sex.

Even less subtle messages include the appearance of a crack addict named Cheryl, who literally lets her child run around in the street. The viewer is introduced to Cheryl after Tre finds her baby in the road and stops her from being run over by a car. He knocks on Cheryl's door, and as she nonchalantly takes the baby from him, she asks desperately for drugs, even offering sexual favors in exchange. Her disheveled appearance and complete lack of maternal care may have some grounding in reality, but the random insertion of this encounter and the stereotypical interactions between her and Tre seem more like an antidrug skit than a movie scene.

In contrast to this overt social commentary, in some moments the characters engage in dialogue about their daily lives, hopes, and fears, which frame the social issues they face in a more subtle light. For example, when a college recruiter from USC visits Ricky, the high school football star and martyr of the film, he urges Ricky to use college as a more secure avenue to a better future than his NFL prospects. This encounter challenges the belief that urban Black men can only escape the streets as entertainers or athletes. More important, it does so by speaking to the young Black men who internalize these beliefs rather than to the people who stereotype them.

Another successful example of how the film engages with Black youth directly takes place after Tre and Ricky take the SATs. When they decide to go visit Tre's father at work, he takes them on a field trip to a billboard advertising cash for houses. There, Tre's father explains gentrification. As a crowd forms around him, he encourages community members to keep property and ownership in Black hands. He also takes the opportunity to discuss the systemic issues that are responsible for drugs and violence and encourages the crowd not to give in to the system. While still somewhat clichéd, this scene diverges from the typical antidrug or safe-sex public service announcement. Here, Singleton is drawing on the Black nationalist tradition to encourage a sense of Black collectivism and shared responsibility for change. By discussing the external forces responsible for social ills in the streets, he also resists the notion that Black urban inhabitants are solely at fault for the conditions in which they live.

While *Boyz n the Hood* relies heavily on plot, it also uses sound to convey a specific sense of Black urban space. The sound of police helicopters, for one, can be heard throughout the film. Even when the film falls into conventional tropes of coming of age, such as when Tre finally convinces his girlfriend, Brandi (Nia Long), that they should have sex, the sound of helicopters patrolling the neighborhood remains a constant presence. Similarly, characters like Tre's girlfriend are plagued by the persistent sound of car tires screeching and gunshots in the background. These sounds remind viewers that the streets are a violent space under constant surveillance. Yet, within that space we witness such quotidian activities as teenagers doing homework and falling in love. Through this juxtaposition, Singleton offers a picture of Black youth that is both specific and universal.

While the film's aesthetic properties contribute to an overall message about Black life in the streets, and Black youth specifically, the film is also highly concerned with the role of Black masculinity in creating resilience to the streets. The scene in which Laurence Fishburne's character discusses gentrification gives some insight into how we might interpret the film's central argument about Black masculinity. From the beginning, the film suggests that a strong Black father is the key to stemming urban crime and violence. As young Tre begins to have trouble at school, his mother sends him to live with his father. When she drops Tre off at his father's house, she tells the dad that only he can teach Tre how to be a man. This is a responsibility Furious Styles embraces. He tells young Tre that it is his job to teach him responsibility so that he does not end up like Doughboy across the street.

Throughout the film, Tre's relationship with his father moves back and forth between that of a normative father-son relationship to that of a specific relationship between a Black father and a Black son. For instance, Furious teaches his son that Black men have no place in the army. Having gone to Vietnam, he realizes this and encourages his son to avoid being a pawn in an army for a government that has yet to fully recognize his humanity. Likewise, after they call the cops to report an attempted robbery, the father-son duo encounters a Black cop who has it in for Black urban inhabitants. When the cop makes a remark about it being too bad that Furious missed the robber when he shot at him, because then there would have been "one less nigger out here in the streets we have to worry about," Furious does not let the comment slide. Instead, he makes his disdain clear. After sending Tre inside, he makes a subtle critique of the Black cop's paradoxically racist attitude. By teaching Tre about the various threats to his life, not just the so-called urban ones, Furious Styles embodies the specificity of Black fatherhood.

Despite the politically conscious nature of Furious's fathering, the film cannot help but sentimentalize the father-son relationship. Early on, there is a montage of the duo spending time together. They go fishing, Furious teaches his son life lessons, and the two even sing songs from the radio together. The significance of Black fatherhood is made abundantly clear when this scene ends precisely as the two get home in time to see a young Doughboy and his friend Chris being arrested for stealing. The viewer knows that Tre, who was hanging out with Doughboy and Chris earlier, only escaped this fate because he was spending time with his father. While they were learning to steal, Tre was learning to "be a man."

The film's principal message seems to be that there is a lack of strong Black male leadership and that Black people need to come together to resist the social and systemic forces bent on eliminating them. The theme of Black fatherhood and teaching Black youth to be men is not unique to *Boyz n the Hood*. Part of this message is revolutionary, drawing clearly from the Black nationalist tradition. However, not unlike the practice of Black nationalism in the mid-twentieth century, the other part of this message is regressive in its treatment of women. While I understand that these films are trying to speak to how the community can make positive changes, this narrow focus on Black fatherhood plays into some of Moynihan's arguments about the Black family structure being the root of urban social ills. This becomes even clearer when one considers how Black women are portrayed in films such as *Boyz n the Hood*.

Admittedly, the film does challenge certain stereotypes about the Black family. For example, Angela Bassett's character, Reva (Tre's mother), is portrayed as highly educated and professional. When Tre's teacher calls to report his issues at school and assumes it is due to Tre being raised in a poor, single-mother household, Reva retorts that she is getting a master's degree and has a job and that Tre has a healthy relationship with his father. Additionally, she and Tre's father have a rather healthy relationship themselves. Overall, the film's central family resists stereotypes. However, with the exception of Tre's teenage love interest (Nia Long), this is the extent of the film's humanizing depictions of women. In addition to the aforementioned crack addict, Cheryl, Doughboy's mom is characterized as a stereotypically overbearing mother. While she nurtures her son who loves football, she berates Doughboy and tells him frequently that he will never amount to anything. Likewise, most of the women in the film are nameless "hoochies, hos and bitches" who serve little purpose other than to be the object of Black male desire.

Despite its shortcomings, *Boyz n the Hood* is groundbreaking in a number of ways. For one, it challenges conventional images of Black youth by simultaneously depicting the threats of the streets and challenging the idea that these unilaterally produce violent gangbangers. Moreover, the film humanizes characters like Doughboy, offering a nuanced view of those who may participate in the violence of the streets. Second, the film is aimed at members of the Black community. By making Black urban Americans the target audience, Singleton devotes much-needed attention to them. In many ways, Ice Cube's character, who is intelligent, receptive, and socially aware, represents the intended audience's place within the film. He represents the kind of viewer who might just be persuaded to change through the film's logos and pathos.

Despite the clear attention to the Black urban community as an audience, Singleton also seems to be aware that the film will be consumed by those outside the Black community. In fact, Frank Price, who was the president of Columbia Pictures at the time of the film's release, was clear that while the target audience for *Boyz n the Hood* was Black youth, the secondary audience was White youth who were consumers of the wildly popular hip-hop culture.[23] Singleton capitalizes on this reality by offering a critique of mainstream America. For one, he avoids the temptation of providing numerous scenes of Black death for the viewer's consumption. Sheril Antonio points out that one of Singleton's strengths is his use of these omissions. For instance, neither Doughboy's death nor the violence he discusses with Tre at the end of the film is ever shown. In this way, the violence that drives the narrative takes place off-screen.[24]

In addition to his strategic use of violence, Singleton uses Doughboy's last words to critique White audience members. At the end of the film, after Doughboy and his friends exact revenge on Ricky's killers, Doughboy goes over to visit Tre. He says that he turned on the news hoping to hear something about his brother but instead saw only coverage of foreign violence. He concludes, "Either they don't know, don't show, or don't care about what's going on in the hood. They had all this foreign shit. They didn't have shit on my brother, man."[25] Despite the fact that Doughboy is the film's cautionary character, he is also portrayed as particularly insightful. Earlier in the film he talks about his Malcolm X–esque moment of learning about the world by reading in prison. He makes his intellectualism clear at various points throughout the film when he discusses religion and society. As such, his final remarks are meant to solicit deeper reflection from the viewer. He leaves the White audience to ponder the question, Why is there so little concern for anti-Black violence in America? This, together with the earlier image of a Reagan-Bush poster, offers a subtle sociopolitical critique for members outside of the Black community to consider.

While *Boyz n the Hood* opened the door for future hood genre films, not everyone was pleased with the movie, nor did everyone appreciate its take on Black urban life. Reportedly, Allen and Albert Hughes, directors known for *Menace II Society* (1993), *Dead Presidents* (1995), and *The Book of Eli* (2010), were appalled by "the Hollywood sentimentality" of *Boyz n the Hood*.[26] As a result, they set out to direct their own, grittier version of a hood genre film. Their version of urban realism, *Menace II Society*, blurs the line between cultural intervention and blaxploitation. The film features explicit imagery of violence and drug use. Although both Allen and Albert Hughes are African American, some of their character depictions are arguably stereotypical. The character O-Dog (Larenz Tate), for instance, is described as "America's Nightmare" and performs this threat of Black hypermasculine violence throughout the film. Like the male protagonists of most hood genre films, the film's lead, Caine (Tyrin Turner), is presented with a choice: to be like O-Dog or to live a better life. He can leave the city with his love interest, Ronnie (Jada Pinkett), or remain and continue on the path that leads to a life of crime. Despite interventions by his grandfather, Mr. Butler, and his friend Sharif, Caine eventually makes the wrong choice and pays for this with his life. While this plotline is reflective of the broader morality of these films, *Menace II Society* portrays the violence, drugs, and crime that pervade the streets as inescapable entities.

While the popularity of hood genre films declined after the 1990s, their influence on contemporary depictions of the streets is undeniable. Although produced twenty-five years after *Boyz n the Hood*, Barry Jenkins's film *Moonlight* takes up a similar project of redefining Black urban masculinity. An adaptation of Tarell Alvin McCraney's unpublished play, *In Moonlight Black Boys Look Blue*, *Moonlight* was the 2017 Academy Award winner for Best Picture. The film was infamously almost denied this award. In a moment that can only be described as cringeworthy, *La La Land* producers Fred Berger and Jordan Horowitz were in the middle of their thank-you speeches when a stagehand notified them that *Moonlight*, not *La La Land*, had actually won Best Picture. Ultimately chalked up to an envelope mix-up, this awkward moment, and the tension it produced, highlights the social and cultural implications of *Moonlight* as a film about Black space and life. *La La Land* is a predominantly White-led musical romantic comedy that follows the lives of two struggling performing artists (an actress and a musician) as they look for love and success in Los Angeles. While the film reflects the difficulty young artists face, it ultimately reinforces the idea that Los Angeles is a magical land where dreams eventually come true for those who are deeply passionate and committed to their craft. This depiction of Los Angeles stands in stark contrast to Kendrick Lamar's narrative of Compton or John Singleton's depiction of South Central.

In contrast, *Moonlight* takes place in Liberty City, Miami, Florida, outside of the safe, magical space of Hollywood. Like most hood genre films, *Moonlight* is ultimately a coming-of-age story about a young Black boy. Unlike *La La Land*, *Moonlight* is a film about a Black boy who is struggling for self-realization, rather than one about achieving an occupational dream. Moreover, it focuses entirely on historically underrepresented people. The protagonist, Chiron, is a queer Black man, a clear departure from earlier protagonists of hood genre films.[27] His family, friends, enemies, and schoolmates are all Black and, for the most part, working class. *Moonlight* also diverges from traditional hood genre films through its setting. Unlike the majority of hood genre films, which are set in Los Angeles or New York, this film takes place in Barry Jenkins's hometown.

While earlier hood genre films seem to rely on the trope of authenticity, *Moonlight* focuses on something more akin to sincerity. Building on John Jackson's work, Michael Boyce Gillespie explains that "questions of sincerity imply social interlocutors who presume one another's humanity, interiority, and subjectivity. It is a subject-subject interaction, not the subject-object model that authenticity assumes."[28] In addition to this departure, the film is unique in terms of its sound and cinematography. For example, the film rarely features hip-hop, which stands in stark contrast to early hood genre films that relied on hip-hop as a demonstration of authenticity. Instead, the film's composer, Nicholas Britell, created a series of instrumental tracks that were then "chopped and screwed" in a southern hip-hop style.[29] In doing so, he manages to simultaneously depart from the commodification of hip-hop and honor its original purpose of intercommunal sincerity.

Another key difference between *Moonlight* and the hood genre films of the 1990s is that, rather than rely on urban realism, *Moonlight* embraces vivid imagery and lighting to characterize the streets and their inhabitants. *New York Times* film critic A. O. Scott describes *Moonlight* as "a poem written in light," arguably because light is the lens through which viewers are led to interpret the film's characters.[30] Cinematographer James Laxton seems to suggest as much, arguing that light in the film complicates the face-value interactions of the characters.[31] This is evident in the way purple, pink, and blue lights often amplify the characters' emotional state. The characters' ability to take on these different colors creates a visual of their internal complexity and, much like the hood genre films, deconstructs the notion of one-dimensional Blackness.

Another key difference between *Moonlight* and hood genre films like *Boyz n the Hood* is that Jenkins substitutes overt sentimentality and morality for the vulnerability of human connection. The beach scene in part one is a clear change from what one might expect from two Black men on-screen. The camera lens is positioned so that the waves flow to the top of the screen and then recede, making the viewer feel submerged in the water with Juan (Mahershala Ali) and Chiron. Rather than giving Chiron a list of rules to live by, his mentor, Juan, cradles him in his arms as he floats carefree on the water. In that moment, Juan provides Chiron with a freedom from fear or worry that he is rarely afforded.

While *Moonlight*'s aesthetic techniques differentiate it from most hood genre films, it still continues the tradition of framing the streets through a coming-of-age story. The film is set in three parts, each one depicting a stage in Chiron's life. These parts work together to narrate Chiron's coming of age, but they also present the protagonist as three distinct versions of himself. The result is a representation of Black masculinity that is complex and, at times, even contradictory. In "i. Little," the viewer is introduced to Chiron (Alex Hibbert), or Little as he is called then, as a child. He lives with his mother (Naomie Harris), who struggles with drug addiction, and he is constantly harassed by the school bullies who sense his divergence from traditional heteromasculinity.

The second part of the film, "ii. Chiron," depicts a pivotal moment for the protagonist. The viewer learns that Juan is dead, but that Chiron (Ashton Sanders) continues to spend time with Juan's longtime partner, Teresa (Janelle Monáe). He is still bullied, but he gets by. The most significant aspect of this part is his developing relationship with Kevin, who is first introduced as a school friend. Their ambiguous relationship becomes clearer one evening when Chiron encounters Kevin on the beach. While smoking marijuana, the two engage in an open, vulnerable dialogue about life, sadness, and hopelessness. Slowly their intimacy turns physical. After a brief sexual encounter, Kevin cradles Chiron, a scene that is mirrored at the end of the film. The intimacy in both scenes transcends the physical, as the film resists the tendency of collapsing their identities into singular or stereotypical depictions of queer sexuality. Instead, Chiron and Kevin are allowed to experience the universality of human connection, as well as the specificity of queer love.

Much like his trips to the beach with Juan in part one, the setting of Chiron and Kevin's love scene signals another turning point in Chiron's development as a person. It uses spatial separation to highlight the constraints of Black urban space. On the beach, Little can experience the tenderness of mentorship and love. Likewise, it is there that he connects with his school crush as a young, Black queer boy. Back in the city, however, these things are more challenging. These spaces demand that one embrace heteromasculinity as a mode of survival. This becomes extremely evident in the scene that follows their encounter, when Kevin is peer-pressured into beating Chiron up at school. More than his physical bruises, Chiron is visibly hurt by the betrayal.

There is a moment where he breaks into vulnerability with a school principal who is attempting to get him to press charges. However, this moment is brief. Considering his love for Kevin and the seemingly insurmountable circumstances that surround him, Chiron instead retreats into himself and resolves to get revenge. The next day he goes to school and beats the bully responsible with a chair. As he is being arrested and placed into a police car, Chiron's eyes meet Kevin's. The moment of tension between them subverts the trope of young, star-crossed lovers. They are prevented from being together not by fate but by the sociocultural expectations of young, Black men. Realizing this, Chiron essentially chooses to embrace and perform the traditional Black heteromasculinity required to navigate the streets unscathed.

The final part of the film, "iii. Black," picks up after Chiron (Trevante Rhodes) has been released from prison. Chiron seems to personify stereotypical Black urban masculinity. The film shows him working out, talking with other men about women, and driving around in a souped-up car while wearing a gold grill. There are, however, hints of the parts of Chiron seen earlier in the film. For instance, he now goes by the name Black, the nickname Kevin gave to him. Likewise, despite his external bravado, he remains deeply lonely and isolated. These cracks in his performance of Black heteromasculinity are made even clearer when he receives a phone call from Kevin out of the blue. Kevin calls Chiron to apologize for everything that happened when they were teenagers. As Chiron listens, the camera focuses on his face as he fights to hold back tears and maintain a stern expression.

Kevin's apology and invitation to come visit him open the door for Chiron to reconcile with his past. He makes a trip to see his mother, who is now in a rehab center. It becomes clear through their conversation that the two are estranged and that she disapproves of his current lifestyle. She tries to talk to him about dealing drugs, but Chiron calls out her hypocrisy. In many ways, this scene mirrors an encounter the mother has with Juan in part one. Just as she called Juan a hypocrite for selling drugs to her and then turning around to judge her for her poor parenting, Chiron calls out his mother for judging him after years of addiction and abuse. More than a moral lesson, these scenes humanize the addicts and drug dealers who are often so synonymous with the streets. This representation is an important aspect of the film for both Naomie Harris, who was hesitant to play a drug addict, and Barry Jenkins, who was raised by a mother much like Chiron's.[32] Their concern over representation can be seen in the fact that no character is singular; the characters change, grow, and regress. In depicting this complexity, the film also demonstrates the limitations of addressing social problems, such as drug dealing and addiction, from the perspective of moral superiority.

Despite their initial confrontation, Chiron accepts his mother's earnest apology. His next stop is to confront his past with Kevin. As he drives up to the restaurant where Kevin is a chef, a distorted version of Jidenna's "Classic Man" plays in the background. The song and its distortion seem to highlight the augmented form of classic masculinity embodied by Black. The way the film presents nuanced forms of Black masculinity can be seen not only through Chiron but also in his desire for Kevin. For instance, when Chiron watches longingly as Kevin walks to the kitchen, his gaze is directed toward what viewers would consider conventional Black urban swagger. Thus, instead of playing into the stereotype that all nonheterosexual men are feminine and flamboyant, the film deconstructs the false dichotomy of queerness and Black urban masculinity.

The film ultimately concludes with Kevin and Chiron slowly moving past their external personas to connect once again in a vulnerable way. Chiron confesses to Kevin that he is the only man he has ever been with. However, rather than concluding with the image of the two embracing, the film closes with young Chiron at the beach. This circular imagery forces the viewer to reconcile each piece of Chiron. Rather than presenting the story as the loss of vulnerability and innocence due to the harsh realities of the streets, the film's framing causes the viewer to consider the contradictions of Chiron's life and personality as part of one, continuous story. He is a tender soul, a drug dealer, a Black urban man, a queer man, and much more. As such, Jenkins presents the viewer with a story about coming of age in the streets that does not revolve around escaping urban forces but around finding ways to realize and love oneself within them.

In addition to the way it subverts the traditional Black heteromasculinity associated with the streets, *Moonlight* challenges how the streets themselves are viewed as a racialized space. For instance, the film opens with Juan, the head of a drug syndicate, checking in on one of his stash houses. As he chats with one of the men who deals for him, he notices young Chiron being chased by bullies. Later, he finds Chiron hiding within an abandoned house, and thus begins their mentor-mentee relationship. While acknowledging the realities of drugs and violence, *Moonlight* depicts the streets as a space that can also nurture. The same block that lends itself to drug dealing also creates an opportunity for a young, vulnerable boy to be mentored. The film continues to disrupt our expectations of which spaces Black people belong in by placing Chiron's life-changing moments at parks, on beaches, and in happy domestic spaces (Juan and Teresa's home in particular). Although there are plenty of images of urban poverty and drug addiction, the film spends much more time on where and how Chiron finds joy.

Beyond Chiron's spatial movements, his relationship with Juan allows *Moonlight* to engage in the discourse about the role of Black fatherhood in the streets that is prevalent in films like *Boyz n the Hood*. The film never makes Juan's motive for taking Chiron under his wing explicit. It could be guilt over selling the drugs that prevent Chiron's mother from taking care of him or just a general sense of benevolence. Whatever the reason, Juan ends up fulfilling the role of father-mentor. He and Teresa often let Chiron stay at their house, where they have family dinners and reassure Chiron that there is nothing wrong with his queerness. When Juan takes Chiron to the beach one day, he teaches him how to swim and shares his perspective on life. This scene is very similar to the day Tre and Furious spend at the beach in *Boyz n the Hood*. Juan tells Chiron that there are Black people all over the world and that he should remember that they were the first ones here, and there is no place where they are not.

While this exchange is reminiscent of the kind of Black nationalist fathering that takes place in *Boyz n the Hood*, *Moonlight* moves beyond these themes with regard to sexuality and how masculinity is performed and internalized. This is made clear when Juan's greatest lesson for Chiron is that "at some point you gotta decide for yourself who you gonna be. Can't let nobody make that decision for you."[33] Unlike in earlier hood genre films, Juan is not teaching Chiron to "be a man." Rather, he is teaching him to be himself. He reassures Chiron that being a Black man can look many different ways. This affirmation of a complex Black masculinity is just one of the ways the film builds on hood genre films' attempt to deconstruct the homogeneous characterization of those who live in the streets. Moreover, where hood genre films often verged on pathologizing the streets in their depiction of fatherhood as the solution, *Moonlight* deconstructs this notion altogether. Juan is a loving, nurturing drug dealer. He is a part of the streets, and his characterization suggests that the streets are not a problem to be solved.

Recharacterizing the Black Urban Protagonist: *Just Another Girl on the I. R. T.*

While the majority of hood genre films focus on the lives of young Black men, Leslie Harris's *Just Another Girl on the I. R. T.* uses the genre to challenge stereotypes of urban Black women. Harris herself called the film "a low-budget, Brooklyn-based Girlz N the Hood."[34] In contrast to the blockbuster hood genre films with Black male protagonists (many of whom were already famous actors or musicians), *Just Another Girl* was made for $130,000 and featured relatively unknown actors.[35] Perhaps this is the reason that, unlike *Boyz n the Hood*, which had a budget of $6.5 million and was produced by Columbia Pictures, *Just Another Girl* was not picked up by a studio until postproduction.

The film follows the life of Chantel (Ariyan A. Johnson), a teenager from Brooklyn, as she deals with the ramifications of teen pregnancy and life in the inner city. Beyond just featuring a Black woman protagonist, the film focuses on how Chantel is perceived by others in contrast to her self-perception. While she appears brash and careless, a series of direct addresses to the viewer reveal that Chantel is an intelligent young woman with plans to graduate from high school early and eventually become a doctor. This seeming contradiction is the film's key theme. The viewer is treated to the external view of a "Brooklyn girl" like Chantel, as well as the more intimate knowledge of her aspirations and home life. Despite these dreams, Chantel allows herself to be distracted by a love interest with a car and decides to have sex, which results in her pregnancy. The latter half of the film follows her as she attempts to reconcile the reality of her pregnancy with her dreams for the future. However, rather than frame Chantel's story as a cautionary tale, *Just Another Girl* uses urban realism to depict both the explicit struggles she faces and her response to them. Chantel ends up keeping the baby and raising it along with her now ex-boyfriend, Ty (Kevin Thigpen). Although she may not be able to pursue her original dreams, she does attend community college. As she tells the viewer at the end, "We're getting our shit together."[36]

From the opening scene, *Just Another Girl* sets itself up as an exercise in deconstructing stereotypes. The movie begins, much like *Boyz n the Hood*, with images of urban buildings and trash lining the streets. The viewer later learns, however, that this opening image is also of Chantel's baby wrapped in a garbage bag. Immediately after giving birth at her boyfriend's apartment, Chantel panics and tells Ty to get rid of the baby. While this opening scene frames the streets through the lens of decay and moral deficiency, the rest of the film works to slowly deconstruct this by contextualizing Chantel's actions.

Similarly, the film attempts to deconstruct stereotypes through shifts in narrative point of view. At first, it shows Chantel riding the train, flirting with a young man, and talking loudly in slang. Just as the viewer is forming an opinion of Chantel, she turns to the camera and abruptly addresses the viewer directly. She proclaims, "I'm a Brooklyn girl. Lots of folks think Brooklyn girls are real tough. I guess that's true. I don't let nobody mess with me, and I do what I want when I want."[37] Her words assert a sense of agency and independence that challenges the viewer's initial assumptions.

Chantel continues to break the fourth wall in this way throughout the film. In another scene, after loudly goofing off with a couple of friends on the train, Chantel pauses to explain to the viewer she is aware that people stare at her and her friends "like we was some sort of street girls with no future."[38] She goes on to explain that she enjoys these carefree moments, but that she is also serious at other times. She gets As and Bs in school and has great plans for her future. In another scene, the viewer sees Chantel's parents arguing about their living conditions, the difficulty of finding work while Black, and the dangers of gun violence in their neighborhood. As they argue, the camera shifts to Chantel in her room, listening at the door. She then addresses the viewer to explain that she does not want to struggle and live paycheck to paycheck like her parents.

In some ways, these interventions are progressive. They assert Black women's unique sense of identity and desire. Still, as in other hood genre films, the characterization of Chantel as a good student who longs for social mobility tends to frame her self-realization as incompatible with the streets. Moreover, the strategy of shifting points of view comes across as a bit manufactured and jarring. One moment the film is following the carefree life of a teenager, and the next, the protagonist is explaining things to the viewer. Furthermore, some of the statements Chantel makes, and their contrast to the way she acts throughout the film, seem a bit exaggerated. It is almost as if the film wants Chantel to fit a stereotype within the main narrative, but also wants to complicate that stereotype through a secondary narrative of self-explanation. On the one hand, there is value in this approach. The film does not attempt to deconstruct Black female stereotypes altogether, but instead complicates and contextualizes them. As such, it does not play into respectability politics by pretending that loud, brash Black women do not exist. Rather, it urges the viewer to consider that these characteristics are not *all* that Black women are.

This rejection of respectability politics with regard to Black urban femininity is the film's strongest challenge to how the streets are depicted on film. In the political discourse of the 1980s and 1990s, and even in other hood genre films, Black women were depicted as loud, angry, and domineering. These behaviors were tied to the streets through their perceived impact on Black men and Black Americans' desire to work and succeed. In the moments when Chantel refuses to tone down her persona or separate it from her intelligence or ambition, the film deconstructs this notion. A primary example of this is when Chantel gets into trouble for challenging her history teacher. While he is teaching a predominantly Black class about the Holocaust, Chantel repeatedly interrupts his lesson to draw a parallel between the Holocaust and contemporary causes of premature Black death. For her intervention, Chantel is sent to the principal's office. The principal, Mr. Moore, tells Chantel that in order to follow her dream of becoming a doctor she needs to learn how to behave like a lady and "tone that mouth of yours down."[39] She challenges this logic, though, by questioning what her attitude has to do with her intelligence. In essence, Chantel rejects the notion that she must perform a certain type of femininity in order to succeed.

Chantel's questions are not well received, and when her argument with the principal leads to her swearing, he yells at her to never curse at him. This is a line said throughout the film by three different male authority figures: her White teacher, her Black principal, and her father. Each man seems infuriated by the fact that Chantel has the audacity to swear at them. Through scenes like these, the film provides the viewer with an important counter to other hood genre films. Whereas Black women are often depicted in those films as domineering, *Just Another Girl* reframes this as confidence, intelligence, and an unwillingness to perform submissiveness for the sake of male fragility.

In many ways, the lack of critical and commercial success of *Just Another Girl* demonstrates how difficult it is to critique gendered narratives of urban Black identity. Despite its uniqueness within the genre, *Just Another Girl* received mostly negative reviews. Some of these focused on the poor filming quality.[40] However, unsurprisingly, many of the negative reviews critiqued Chantel's characterization as too irreverent and unsympathetic. Terrence Rafferty's review in the *New Yorker*, for example, criticized Chantel for being too "brash" and "self-absorbed."[41] Film scholar Amy Taubin argues that "the reaction to Chantel as a character suggests the kind of unconscious racism that refuses to acknowledge that a girl from the hood could be intelligent, ambitious and vulnerable."[42] In response to these criticisms, Harris explains Chantel's characterization by saying, "This is just a portrait of one young woman, and I didn't want her character to speak for everybody. But at the same time, I think she has a right to be who she is."[43] Harris frames Chantel as a unique character, rather than a representative figure. As such, she questions whether the criticism of Chantel is an issue of writing or one of rejecting on-screen Black individuality.

In addition to the pushback Harris received for Chantel's characterization, she was frequently questioned by studio executives about the lack of common hood genre elements, such as gang violence and drugs. In response to this questioning, Harris has been clear. Although she was creating a female-centered hood genre film, she was not interested in telling the same story these other films told.[44] Black women have different experiences, ideas, and relationships to urban space; as a result, their stories may also be different. In many ways, Harris's film, particularly with its focus on reproductive rights, embraces Black feminist politics and presents the streets from the perspective of intersectionality.

While *Just Another Girl* may not have been as successful as other hood genre films, it is unique in its attempt not only to depict the streets in a nuanced way but to do so with specific attention to how Black women have been stereotyped in relation to Black urban space. The film's final image, a quote by Leslie Harris, suggests, this is "A Film Hollywood Dared Not to Do." This final commentary by the director highlights the ways popular culture and White American interest shaped the hood film genre. While these films allowed Black filmmakers to project their own views of the streets into the popular cinematic imaginary, their impact on that imaginary was largely dictated by public desire. Often, films that, however unintentionally, affirmed stereotypes about the streets found the most success. Still, the existence of films like *Just Another Girl* and, eventually, *Moonlight* demonstrates the importance of this genre for creating the space to see the streets through the lens of the people who live there.

From the Big Screen to the Small Screen: Urban Space in *The Wire* and *The Chi*

In the first few years of the 2000s, as hood genre films were on the decline, shows such as *The Wire* took up their mantle, so to speak, by attempting to present the American public with a gritty, morally gray picture of urban life. This complex depiction of urban Black life is often praised as countercultural.[45] On the one hand, shows like *The Wire* signify a continued public interest in understanding the complexity of streets. On the other hand, as Henry Louis Gates Jr. suggests, they reinforce the notion that "'authentic' African-American culture is to be found only on the streets of inner cities."[46] I argue that, while *The Wire* is successful at soliciting an empathetic view of the streets and those who inhabit them, it is limited by its emphasis on seeing the streets from the perspective of White America. In contrast, Lena Waithe's show, *The Chi*, focuses on the reality of the streets as a space that is home not only to complex people but also to complex ways of being.

Created by David Simon, *The Wire* ran from 2002 to 2008 and began filming shortly after 9/11. The post-9/11 world is a central theme in the show, as detectives lament the fact that the new focus on the War on Terror comes at the cost of policing the streets. The reality of a post–civil rights, post–War on Drugs, post-9/11 urban landscape is the show's main premise. Each of the show's five seasons focuses on a different aspect of urban corruption in Baltimore (the drug trade, shipping, city government, education, and the media) but keeps the same central characters to create a sense of continuity. Much like the hood genre films of the 1990s, the show is rife with urban realism. Gritty urban landscapes, Black vernacular, and hip-hop music create the perception of authenticity.

Like hood genre films, this perception of authenticity creates a sense of appeal to mainstream audiences. When I told colleagues I would be writing about this show, I was greeted with enthusiastic approval. In fact, several colleagues, all White progressives, shared with me that *The Wire* played an integral role in reshaping their perceptions of Black urban life. They found the characters to be nuanced and complex. For them, this was new. Seeing people who were involved in selling drugs, but who also demonstrated a great sense of morality, intelligence, and loyalty, among other characteristics, forced them to confront and deconstruct the stereotypes they had accepted about the streets. My colleagues are not alone in this view. Critics have repeatedly praised *The Wire* because it "blows apart the traditional limits in depicting African Americans on television."[47] This critical praise, along with my colleagues' comments, demonstrates the cultural phenomenon that the show represents. For many Americans, White middle-class ones in particular, *The Wire* serves as a portal to a complex world of hope, corruption, violence, joy, pain, and love. In short, it reveals the humanity of those who live in streets to White America.

A prime example of how *The Wire* humanizes the people who live in the streets is the characterization of Stringer Bell (Idris Elba) and Omar Little (Michael K. Williams). Stringer Bell is introduced in the very first episode as a highly intelligent and menacing member of a local drug syndicate run by Avon Barksdale (Wood Harris). For the three seasons he is a part of the show, Bell serves as the main adversary for Detective Jimmy McNulty (Dominic West). Interestingly, it is not McNulty who ultimately catches and kills Bell. Rather, it is another highly praised character, Omar. Throughout the show, it is clear that Bell has a great aptitude for business. He is shown taking night classes at a community college. He reads Adam Smith's *The Wealth of Nations*. He even works toward legitimacy through real estate purchases. His effectiveness is evidence of both intellectual capacity and the nature of the drug trade as a business like any other. Bell aspires to be a true American capitalist, who just happens to work for a drug syndicate. As such, his character works to challenge a number of stereotypes. Still, his characterization is somewhat of a double-edged sword.

For Idris Elba, the actor who portrayed Bell, the role continues to shadow his career and shade public perceptions of his Blackness. In one notable instance, *James Bond* author Anthony Horowitz called Elba "too street" to play the secret agent when his name generated significant buzz online as a potential candidate for the role.[48] As Ta-Nehisi Coates accurately points out, "too street" is merely code for "too Black."[49] However, I would argue that in addition to the British actor being seen as wrong for the role of James Bond due to his Blackness alone, his role on *The Wire* plays into a particular interpretation of his Blackness. It is not just that Elba is a Black British man, but rather that he conjures up the image of an urban drug dealer in the public imaginary. This is not to blame the role itself, but rather the cultural work a show such as *The Wire* does to solidify the link between the streets and unacceptable Blackness. However intelligent or ambitious Stringer Bell is—however much he challenges viewers' perceptions—he is still confined to the safe space of the on-screen city. Viewers are happy to get a humanizing glimpse of Black urban space, but that does not mean they want those characters, those people, making their way into other parts of their lives.

Along with Stringer Bell, Omar Little is often praised as a countercultural character for his portrayal of Black queerness. Throughout all five seasons of the show, Omar is seen with a number of male lovers. His queerness, however, is never characterized in opposition to his masculinity or his reputation on the street. He is called derogatory names behind his back, but this does not detract from the real threat he poses to the very same people who talk about him in such a way. He is known for strolling confidently with his shotgun in hand while whistling "A-Hunting We Will Go." He is so infamous that when he is seen making his way through the streets, people shout "Omar comin'!" If his cool confidence and reputation were not enough, Omar has a scar that runs across his face. He is in every way the embodiment of Black masculinity. Thankfully, the show resists the notion that Omar's masculinity is in contradiction with his sexual orientation. Instead, his masculinity is tied to his cunning and his ability to remain "hard" in opposition to the drug dealers he steals from.[50]

Omar is not the show's only character who diverges from traditional heteromasculinity. Bubbles (Andre Royo), the recovering addict/informant, has a consistent tendency to form intense male relationships throughout the show. Although we never see Bubbles engage in any sexual behavior with these men, his sexuality is left intentionally ambiguous, and his relationships make it impossible to categorize him as entirely heterosexual. Yet, even as characters such as Omar and Bubbles offer a progressive representation of Black male sexuality, the bigger picture of how Black men are eroticized and consumed by the viewer is troubling. As James S. Williams points out in "The Lost Boys of Baltimore," the show's visual display of Black masculinity functions as part of a broader "eroticization of the hood."[51] Between the show's own visuals and the viewing of police surveillance footage within the show, *The Wire* offers viewers "*tableaux vivants* of corner boys, hoppers, drug slingers, and hustlers."[52] While Williams is concerned with the show's use of homoeroticism and the theme of male intimacy, I would argue that the way the Black male body is portrayed, even in the progressive spaces of Black queer relationships, ultimately reinforces the hypersexualization and objectification of Black men.

This view of the Black male body is made abundantly clear from the beginning of the show. The first image one sees when watching *The Wire* is a stream of red blood on concrete, lit by flashing blue police lights. It would be easy to gloss over this opening image, but it is significant for how it frames the show as a whole. If *The Wire* is a show about the streets, as I argue it is, then this image introduces the streets as a violent space shadowed by police presence. In the first thirty seconds the viewer sees a Black body gunned down on the street, three Black children sitting on a bench, and a White male police officer taking inventory of the crime scene. Before anyone speaks, the sounds of sirens and police radios are heard. The very first person to speak is Jimmy McNulty, a White male police officer. While the show includes numerous characters and experiences, its opening episode elevates McNulty's as the main narrative perspective. McNulty is also the logical character, asking questions about the murder. There is an apparent intelligence gap between him and the young Black man he questions. Right before the introductory sequence, the camera pans Jimmy's face. His smirk seems to convey a playful fascination with the streets, one arguably shared by the viewer. For all the work the show does to move across class, race, gender, sexuality, and station, the opening and closing of the show solidify Detective McNulty's place as its antihero and principal character. Although McNulty faces off with a number of intelligent Black adversaries, such as Stringer Bell and Omar Little, he is ultimately the only one who remains alive and free at the show's close.

While *The Wire* may be progressive in its portrayal of Black urban identity, its broader depiction of the streets is mixed at best. Like its protagonists, the show manages to depict the streets in their full complexity. In fact, cultural studies scholar Caroline Levine argues that this is the show's greatest accomplishment. She suggests that what is significant about *The Wire* is the way "a great many social, political, natural, and aesthetic forms encounter one another" in the show.[53] Its structure, moving from a gritty cop drama in season one to an examination of education, politics, and journalism in other seasons, reflects a complex overlapping of different social experiences and forms rarely seen or studied elsewhere. Moreover, as Levine argues, each season contains its own set of "bounded wholes," such as apartment towers, prison cells, and foster homes, as well as shifting rhythms (the rate at which the show moves).[54] If, as Levine argues, despite being a work of fiction, *The Wire* "seeks to track the plausible unfolding of events as forms collide," then what does the way this collision and unfolding takes place say about the streets?[55] If one reads *The Wire* as Levine does, one can interpret it as revealing "institutional rhythms of replication and substitution that stretch forward and backward in time."[56] In other words, the show reflects the larger construct of the streets as something more than a place, or the people who inhabit it.

Still, while *The Wire* portrays the larger sociocultural construct of the streets, its characterization of this construct is less than gracious. This is not surprising when one considers that, unlike hood genre films that were produced by Black artists who grew up in the streets, *The Wire* emerged from David Simon's experience shadowing police. This origin shows in the fact that while *The Wire* is a show about the streets on one hand, it is decidedly a police drama on the other. Despite the shifting emphasis on different local systems, the police continue to play a central role in combating crime throughout all five seasons. The show's emphasis on the police is not surprising given Simon's previous work. A former *Baltimore Sun* reporter, Simon moved on from journalism to publish books and, eventually, create television. His earlier television credits include *Homicide: Life on the Street* (1993–1999), a series based on his 1991 book of a similar name. Film studies scholar Linda Williams argues that, unlike in his work for the *Baltimore Sun*, in *The Wire* Simon trades an "op-ed" voice that speaks for urban inhabitants for a show that allows them to speak for themselves.[57] According to Williams, *The Wire* is exceptional because it centers the Black spatial imaginary. I question how this can be true, though.

With the rare exception of Joy Fusco cowriting one episode or teleplay per season, all five seasons of *The Wire* were written almost exclusively by White men.[58] Moreover, Simon's previous work, and arguably *The Wire* as well, emerged from the perspective of policing the streets rather than living in them. What is more, the depiction of the streets in *The Wire* has been filtered through several levels of perspective. The first is that of the real-life police in Baltimore, whom Simon shadowed for a year; the second is that of Simon, who relayed this perspective of the streets in his earlier work; and the third is the input of producers, editors, and contributing writers. All of this compounds to create several layers of outsider perspectives on urban Blackness. In essence, *The Wire* is a show created and produced by White writers but performed by Black bodies. Can one really claim that the Black embodiment of White thought on the streets is genuinely groundbreaking?

To be fair, despite his historical alignment with the Baltimore police, Simon's show diverges significantly from most crime dramas by addressing police corruption and the flawed nature of those working on the police force. The lead detective and the show's main character, Jimmy McNulty, does more than bend the law for the sake of making arrests. He is also an addict with a deeply dysfunctional personal life. McNulty is very clearly the show's antihero, yet he still manages to err on the side of being an amiable character. Thus, despite the complex depiction of detectives such as McNulty, the show is still centrally about a core group of dedicated detectives fighting corruption at different levels. In the end, these detectives, and the people who fight alongside them, fail. Corrupt figures carry on with their rise to power, and each of the systems examined continues to run smoothly. The city, with all its chaos and corruption, wins the battle against these would-be do-gooders. Framing the ending in this light is essential for analyzing its depiction of Blackness and urban space because, while *The Wire* spends many seasons deconstructing both positive and negative stereotypes of drug dealers, cops, criminals, politicians, and a host of other figures, it ultimately paints the streets as a Black space that cannot be tamed, changed, or redeemed.

Whether one believes *The Wire* brought about a significant shift in the way White Americans perceive urban Blackness, or that it ultimately reinforces geographic segregation by making urban Black spaces a spectacle for White consumption, the show is inarguably a major cultural phenomenon—so much so that it prompted a conversation about U.S. urban spaces, mass incarceration, and other issues between series creator David Simon and President Barack Obama.[59] Yet, for all the praise the show has garnered for bringing attention to Black urban plight, it fails to do one essential thing: contextualize its themes. As George Lipsitz articulates so well, "*The Wire* increased the visibility of a few Black actors. Yet it did so by strategically evading the history of predatory lending, redlining, blockbusting, and urban renewal in Baltimore."[60]

In *On the Wire*, film studies scholar Linda Williams suggests that Lipsitz's critique of *The Wire* fails to recognize how the show purposely avoids the genre of the American racial melodrama. Williams argues that if the show addressed the history of geographic segregation, it would merely continue the pattern of American racial melodramas by pitting the real history of Black disenfranchisement against the fictitious narrative of White injury. She argues that "playing the race card" in this way is regressive because it furthers animosity.[61] While Williams makes a compelling point about the show's genre, she falsely concludes that because our neoliberal era will not accept the kinds of solutions necessary to redress these histories, revisiting them is not worthwhile. Even without specifically telling the history of geographic segregation, *The Wire* could have done more to surpass dominant narratives of the streets. Ultimately, the show is limited by the White gaze of those who created it.

Unlike *The Wire*, *The Chi* frames the streets through the lens of the Black gaze. The show was created by South Side Chicago native Lena Waithe, an Emmy Award–winning actress, writer, producer, and comedian. With *The Chi*, Waithe set out to create a counternarrative of her hometown. Discussing its creation, she explains that people "sort of assume Chicago is just one big jungle, and that little black boys are born with a gun in their right hand and a pile of drugs in their left, and that's just not true."[62] She goes on to clarify that she is not necessarily avoiding the harsh realities of the streets, but rather that she wants to humanize the people within these spaces and "show that their lives are valid."[63]

One of the ways Waithe accomplishes her goal is by saturating the show, from production to on-screen representation, with native Chicago perspectives. For instance, hip-hop artist Common, another South Side native, co-produces and stars in the show. The film crew is composed of mostly local workers. Moreover, the show's soundtrack heavily features artists from Chicago, such as Chance the Rapper and Kanye West. Even those who are not from Chicago, like the show's first-season star Brandon Mitchell, have personal experience in similar contexts. A native of New Orleans, Mitchell explains that the show's themes resonate with his own experience of losing loved ones to gun violence. In fact, he explains that working on the show is "one of those times where it's more therapy than acting."[64]

Still, despite the unprecedented control Waithe and other Chicago natives have on the show, it is still subject to studio approval and guidance. In one interview, Waithe explains this as the reason for certain choices that have been criticized by the *Chicago Tribune*, such as the lack of female character development.[65] There are some countercultural nods to female representation, such as Kevin's two moms, who raise him in a loving home equipped with a swear jar, but there are also a number of overbearing female characters, such as Brandon's mother and Ronnie's ex, who verge on being stereotypically domineering. Waithe explains that she is aware of these issues; however, they were the price of bringing the show into existence. Now that the show has established itself, she plans to rectify these mistakes, starting with the input of a new Black female showrunner, Ayanna Floyd Davis.

Waithe's desire to humanize the streets while also depicting them as a complex space full of joy, tragedy, violence, life, and much more comes across clearly in the show's plot. Season one of *The Chi* focuses on Brandon Johnson (Jason Mitchell) as he deals with the death of his younger brother, Coogie (Jahking Guillory). The plot largely revolves around Coogie's unjust death at the hands of Ronnie (Ntare Guma Mbaho Mwine), who mistakenly thought the boy was responsible for his own son's death. While the plot is set up as a murder mystery of sorts, where a host of characters attempt to get at the truth behind a star basketball player's death, the show's essence is really about a diverse set of people who live in the city and just so happen to be connected by a tragedy.

Despite the tragic story line, the show opens with a much different tone and imagery than those of *The Wire*. Whereas *The Wire* immediately immerses the viewer in violence, death, and policing, *The Chi* opens with what can only be described as an image of Black boy joy. Charles Frederick "Coogie" Johnson rides through the streets of Chicago on his bicycle. As he listens to Chance the Rapper's "We Back" with a wide grin on his face, long curly hair blowing in the wind, the viewer sees Coogie interact with locals. He stops to shoot hoops, feeds a local dog, and rides joyfully past kids playing in the street. In one scene, Coogie uses his business acumen to talk a local store owner into giving him a discount on soda pop and beef jerky. In another, he encourages a local police officer to buy some Timberland shoes so he looks cooler. He is smart, funny, and endearing. While this could be interpreted simply as a way to solicit viewer sympathy before his death, it also represents Waithe's attempt to depict a young Black man as more than just a victim or a statistic. Coogie is more than his fate. Moreover, this joyful, carefree teenager is not running scared, but rather seems at peace in the streets. He belongs on the South Side, yet he pushes back against viewers' expectations of what that belonging looks like.

Like *The Wire*, *The Chi* relies on characterization to challenge stereotypes about the people who live in the streets. In addition to the brief way Coogie is characterized, most of the other main characters either counter or complicate stereotypical views of Black urbanites. For example, the show's main character, Brandon, might easily be interpreted as the familiar Black urban male who wants to escape the confines of his circumstances. Brandon is an aspiring chef who dreams of opening his own restaurant. The viewer learns that he works as a sous chef at an upscale restaurant run by a White couple. He lives with his girlfriend, Jerrika (Tiffany Boone), who comes from the "right side of the tracks" and works as a realtor. However, Brandon also has an alcoholic mother. He suffers loss due to gun violence. He even contemplates murder after finding out who killed his brother. Brandon speaks in Black vernacular, and he is covered in tattoos. He has enough connections to purchase an unregistered gun. By all accounts, Brandon is not the out-of-place exceptional Black man trying to escape the hood. He is a comfortable member of the South Side who has dreams and aspirations that exceed most viewers' expectations.

Another lead character, Emmett (Jacob Latimore), similarly transcends viewer expectations. For the most part, Emmett spends season one coping with the fact that one of his ex-girlfriends dropped his son off to live with him. We learn that he has other children. On paper, he fits the stereotype of the absentee young Black father. He is obsessed with shoes and works a minimum wage job. However, the show chronicles his growing bond with his son and the way this inspires him to seek a better income and become more responsible.

Even less amiable characters are given the luxury of complexity and nuance in *The Chi*. Ronnie, for example, is shown in the first episode to have murdered Coogie, yet the show takes time to flesh out Ronnie's personal struggles, his motive for killing Coogie, and, ultimately, his repentance.

Even characters who play gangsters manage to blur the lines between stereotype and reality. Jake's older brother, Reg (Barton Fitzpatrick), and his superior, Trice (Tosin Morohunfola), are drug-dealing gangsters on the show. While Reg spends much of his time trying to toughen up his younger brother, and eventually inducts him into the gang, he also cares deeply for him (so much so that he betrays his boss). Likewise, Trice is shown to be a ruthless, greedy drug kingpin. However, he also enjoys yoga and wearing preppy clothes. These two characters, among others, are examples of how *The Chi* humanizes those in the streets without trying to sanitize them. The show does not appeal to respectability politics. Rather, it shows people as they are.

The show also relies on plotlines to challenge stereotypical views of the streets. For instance, a community block party highlights tensions around gun violence. The party includes people of all ages having fun while eating, dancing, and sporting Black Lives Matter T-shirts. This scene, which immediately follows a confrontation between competing drug dealers, reminds viewers that despite such violent realities, the South Side is still a community space where people live and enjoy their lives. This becomes even more apparent when the party is interrupted by two gunshots. Rather than run, the community members pause while the DJ responds, "We ain't going to let that end the night. This is our city, our community. We stopping the violence tonight. Put the guns down, Chicago. Put the guns down. Respect life."[66] Despite the fact that the DJ's message sounds a little like a public service announcement, the scene comes across as more authentic and nuanced than the forced interventions seen in early hood genre films. More than any other scene in the first season, this one demonstrates how someone intimately familiar with Black urban spaces such as Chicago can depict it complexly, while still asserting a clear social message about gun violence.

The very strategy that creates a complex image of the streets is also the source of major criticism of *The Chi*. One reviewer claims that *The Chi* feels like four different shows: a "gritty inner-city drama that looks at the choices Black men are forced to make under corrupt systems," "a show about the ephemeral nature of black childhood joy when you're forced to grow up in stressful circumstances," a show about "escaping your negative circumstances and embracing who you are in order to make something of yourself," and a "cop show" solving Coogie's murder.[67] Criticisms like this reveal how Black art about the streets is often interpreted through the lens of non-Black forms. This criticism tries to locate *The Chi* in relation to shows like *The Wire*. However, *The Chi* is hard to place precisely because it avoids pigeonholing the streets in the way other shows have done.

I argue that *The Wire* is proof that while White America might accept that the criminals they imagine in the city are in fact human, or that certain individuals living in the streets are doing their best to overcome the odds, it is much more reticent to believe that the streets themselves have been mischaracterized. In contrast, *The Chi* attempts to contest the derogatory view of the streets by constructing an image of the streets as a mosaic of people and communities. The show does not try to explain how the brother of a drug dealer can be a carefree Black boy or why an aspiring chef might contemplate murder because these complexities rarely demand explanation when they are not tied to Blackness. Instead, it offers these characters up as a reflection of reality. Moreover, while *The Chi* acknowledges that the streets do indeed pose certain threats to Black life, it also points out how the streets foster community. Much like the character Coogie, the streets can be the source of both tragedy and joy. By weaving together a tapestry of the streets replete with complex characters who both fit and transcend stereotypical perceptions of urban Blackness, *The Chi* projects one of the most holistic views of the streets seen on television.

New Ways of Visualizing the Streets

Despite the fact that de jure urban segregation ended more than fifty years ago, the realities of how urban space has been racialized and delineated from White, middle-class suburbia are reflected in the films and television shows produced within the last thirty years. While the hood genre films of the 1990s opened the door for Black urban representation and provided a humanizing look at Black urban male youth, these movies also often reinforced cultural perceptions of otherness and spatial belonging among White Americans. Furthermore, as critics such as Jaqueline Jenkins and S. Craig Watkins have argued, these films worked to commodify Black urban life for White viewers.

Still, it would be unjust to cast these films as wholly unproductive. *Boyz n the Hood* not only challenged conceptions of Black male youth as superpredators but also paved the way for future depictions of Black masculinity that truly diverge from dominant ideologies and expectations. Although it took twenty-five years, *Moonlight* continued the hood genre's work by presenting viewers with a complex view of Black urban life as more than its socioeconomic conditions. Likewise, Lena Waithe's *The Chi* takes on the gritty, urban realist television genre and turns it into something *The Wire* could never be. Waithe's show captures the nuanced reality of Black urban life in all its joys and sorrows. What these television shows and films reveal is that, despite the proliferation of stereotypical urban representation, the people who grew up in these spaces are beginning to challenge conventions by telling their own stories. These writers and artists are unafraid of engaging both the troubling and the liberating aspects of the hood genre. Their embrace of complexity is a hopeful sign that we might one day see the streets, and the people who live there, for what they are.

Conclusion

As I am writing this, people across the world are protesting police violence in response to the murder of George Floyd on May 25, 2020. What started as a local uprising in Minneapolis has become a global struggle. From the moment the Third Precinct Police Station was set on fire, an event that was live streamed across news outlets and social media platforms, the movement against White supremacy, systemic racism, and anti-Blackness has only grown. Countless videos of police violence are circulating online and various people, from hacktivists like Anonymous to Korean Pop fans, have joined Black activists in mobilizing online and in the streets. Our current moment encompasses much of my argument about the streets in terms of how they shape Black life and that they remain a contested territory. As protestors take over these spaces, chanting "Whose streets? Our streets!" this reality becomes even clearer.

Beyond the obvious connection of being a Black person, this uprising is personal to me for several reasons. In the middle of this book project, I moved back to the Twin Cities after being away for most of my adult life. I remember talking to my mother about whether I would move to Minneapolis or Saint Paul and her telling me that, for now, she could not bring herself to live in Minneapolis because it holds too many painful memories. Her comments made me think about the role of geographic memory in how and where we feel free. I feel similarly about the Twin Cities in general. After years of living abroad and on the West Coast, the thought of moving back felt repressive. It was not that the West Coast was any less racist, but that the geography of Twin Cities is tied to my first experiences of racism and anti-Blackness. It does not help that the Minneapolis–Saint Paul metro area is consistently ranked one of the top five worst cities for Black Americans.[1]

The basis of this ranking is largely due to the gross geographic segregation and economic disparities that continue to characterize the Twin Cities today. According to the most recent census data, Black households in the Twin Cities earn 44 percent of what White households earn. This is the second greatest income disparity in any metro area in the nation. Similarly, only 1 in 4 Black households own their home. In contrast, at 76 percent, White homeownership rates in the Twin Cities are among the highest in the country.[2] The irony that such racial disparities exist while Minneapolis and Saint Paul continue to be labeled the most livable cities in America is not lost on me.[3] In fact, these rankings highlight the contrasting realities of White and Black space, even within the same geographic area. They also beg the question, livable for whom?

As I join with others in protesting George Floyd's murder and police violence, I cannot help but think that we are not only protesting the nature of his death, but also the conditions of his life, the conditions of the streets. As I discussed in chapter 1, the racialized economic disparities in the Twin Cities are merely one piece of a national problem. As I look back at some of the more recent writing, music, and film examined in this book, it seems like a distinct shift has taken place culturally and politically over the past four years. In many ways, the Obama era, despite its tendency to supplant the realities of White supremacy with positive narratives of postracism, carved out the kind of discursive space George Lipsitz describes in *How Racism Takes Place*.[4] Films and television shows such as *Moonlight* and *The Chi* are examples of the cultural production that seized upon America's post-Obama moment to tell new, complex, and countercultural narratives about the streets. While these Black artists depicted the streets in countercultural ways to the broader American imaginary in one way, the election of Donald Trump did so in another. The White supremacist push to "make America great again" represents a return to the overtly negative narratives of the streets that thrived under Reaganism. The murders of George Floyd, Breonna Taylor, Ahmaud Arbery, and Tony McDade are emblematic of the relative freedom White supremacy has under these narratives to police and extinguish Black life today. It is not that Black lives were less threatened when Obama was president, but that they were not as openly preyed upon.

Trump's version of Reaganism reveals that, contrary to how the Obama era was perceived, we have not moved that far from historically derogatory understandings of the streets. The streets are still framed as a problem to be solved, this time through explicit national calls for anti-Black violence. When the president uses terms like "thugs" to describe Black people, makes statements like, "when the looting starts, the shooting starts" and other similar calls for violence against Black people, the delineation between the streets, where Blackness resides, and the rest of America is clear.[5] In the sections that follow, I look at possibilities for redress and a future where the streets no longer signify the limitation of Black life.

Redess and Reparations

Recently, I was teaching on the subject of U.S. housing policy and the racial wealth gap. I often try to pique my students' interest in the topic by framing this history as equally impactful on Black Americans as that of slavery and mass incarceration. After I had made my case by discussing how housing and geographic segregation have affected everything from education to public perceptions of Blackness, one of my students asked, "How do we even begin to undo something so overwhelming?" I myself have often felt overwhelmed by the great extent to which geographic segregation continues to impact Black life. I want, however, to resist the temptation to throw up my hands and simply say, "Well, that's a travesty." Instead, I would like to walk through the ways in which scholars, politicians, and activists have thought about redress and reparations, before offering my own suggestions.

Much of the conversation on reparations has revolved around the issue of slavery. In 1973, Boris Bittker, a legal professor at Yale University, put a rough price on reparations for slavery. Bittker claimed that reparations should focus on closing the racial wealth gap. As such, if one multiplied the average difference in per capita income between White and Black Americans (he used income, rather than wealth, in his calculation), one would arrive at the figure of $34 billion.[6] While Bittker's method leaves something to be desired, it is commendable that he was willing and able to take the first step of discussing reparations in concrete terms. More recently, another legal scholar, Charles Ogletree, has argued for a more holistic understanding of reparations. Instead of economic reparations, Ogletree suggests we pursue a "program of job training and public works that takes racial justice as its mission but includes the poor of all races."[7]

The pursuit of reparations is not limited to the work of legal scholars. Congressman John Conyers Jr. (D-MI) spent much of his career trying to get the federal government to engage in the topic of reparations by introducing bill H.R. 40. Given the struggle Conyers had getting the bill on the floor, one would assume it proposed some extreme measure of reparations. In reality, H.R. 40 simply proposes to establish a "Commission to Study and Develop Reparation Proposals for African-Americans" that would examine the government's role in institutionalizing slavery, as well as the history of discrimination against Black people in the colonies and the United States from 1619 to the present. Eventually, the commission would recommend "appropriate remedies" to Congress.[8] Despite the modest nature of this request, H.R. 40

was not introduced to Congress until 2017, well over a quarter century after Conyers first attempted to introduce the bill.

Ta-Nehisi Coates argues that the fact that "HR 40 has never—under either Democrats or Republicans—made it to the House floor suggests our concerns are rooted not in the impracticality of reparations but in something more existential. If we conclude that the conditions in North Lawndale and black America are not inexplicable but are instead precisely what you'd expect of a community that for centuries has lived in America's crosshairs, then what are we to make of the world's oldest democracy?"[9] What Coates, Conyers, and others reveal is that discussions of reparations are about far more than economic practicality. Rather, they are about reconciling the narrative of American democracy and equality with the reality of Black life. Moreover, these examples largely revolve around reparations for slavery (Coates extends his analysis to housing segregation as well). As such, the controversy and pushback that surround these discussions illustrate the difficulty America has in facing the history of White supremacy, even in its most egregious form.

The difficulty of discussing redress and reparations only increases when we turn to an issue such as housing and geographic segregation. In the 1960s and 1970s, there were some efforts to rectify the issue. One of the largest efforts came in the form of a report written by the National Advisory Committee on Civil Disorders, better known as the Kerner Commission, which I return to later. Other, more local efforts included city planning. For instance, in Chicago there was a proposal to build scatter-site public housing, which would be integrated with predominantly White middle-class neighborhoods. The Department of Housing and Urban Development (HUD), however, did not support these efforts. In most White neighborhoods, the building of new housing projects was still subject to the alderman's approval. Of the requests made to build this housing and integrate White neighborhoods in Chicago, more than 99 percent were vetoed by local aldermen. When this issue was brought to Chicago mayor Richard Daley, he refused to support integration efforts. Instead, he argued, public housing should only be built where it is deemed acceptable.

In 1976, the issue of geographic integration in Chicago eventually made its way to the U.S. Supreme Court, where Robert Bork, the solicitor general under President Gerald Ford, argued that HUD's practices were justified. Bork claimed that efforts to redress geographic segregation would have "an enormous practical impact on innocent communities who have to bear the burden of the housing, who will have to house a plaintiff class from Chicago, which they wronged in no way."[10] His argument is revealing in a number of ways. For one, Bork frames the issue of dealing with geographic segregation entirely from the perspective of White suburban America. He does so by depicting White suburbanites as hardworking victims of efforts to take advantage of their well-earned spatial possession. Second, Bork uses the language of social conservatism to further delineate the Black urban "plaintiff class" and the "innocent communities" of White suburbia. In doing so, he frames the federal government as equally culpable for forcing integration through "big government" policy.

What is, of course, ironic about Bork's statement is that he makes no complaint about the decades-long "big government" policies that made the creation of "innocent [White] communities" possible. What is most revealing about the 1976 Supreme Court case, and Robert Bork's defense of geographic segregation, is that it illustrates a historical trend in America. Less than ten years before this case, President Lyndon B. Johnson signed the Fair Housing Act. As a nation, we are comfortable formally recognizing Black civil rights and acknowledging that decades of practicing housing segregation were a mistake. Bork demonstrates, though, that we are far less comfortable with any efforts to redress these realities. Although the Supreme Court ordered HUD to construct its proposed housing projects in predominantly White neighborhoods, HUD found a way around this by not constructing the housing at all.

The same year as the Chicago HUD case, the Contract Buyers League (CBL) of Chicago received a verdict on its lawsuit against predatory lenders. For anyone who has read Coates's essay "The Case for Reparations," the story of the CBL is a familiar one. The league was made up of the 85 percent of Black Chicago residents who were targeted by predatory lenders. These lenders would purchase homes in Black neighborhoods and sell them under contract terms that all but guaranteed default. In 1968, the CBL sued contract sellers and demanded restitution for the money spent on these predatory contracts, as well as money spent maintaining properties that were never really theirs. In a true pursuit of equitable restitution, the CBL asked for 6 percent interest on this money, minus the cost of a reasonable rental rate for the units during the time they were occupied by the plaintiffs. What is interesting about the league's demands is that in addition to economic reparations, the CBL asked the court to pronounce that the contract sellers had "acted willfully and maliciously and that malice is the gist of this action."[11] Unsurprisingly, the CBL lost its case. As Coates observes, the ruling against the CBL illustrates the seeming impossibility of securing reparations.[12] Still, the ten years or so that the CBL spent in pursuit of reparations demonstrate that conversations about concrete forms of redress are not new, nor are they hard to trace back to concrete examples of racial injustice.

In contrast to both Coates and the CBL, Richard Rothstein proposes another lens through which to consider reparations for the history of U.S. housing discrimination and geographic segregation. In *The Color of Law*, Rothstein suggests that this is really an issue about constitutional actions because, while the government policies and laws enforcing geographic segregation were not always illegal, they were most certainly unconstitutional. Rothstein suggests that "by failing to recognize that we now live with the severe, enduring effects of *de jure* segregation, we avoid confronting our constitutional obligation to reverse it. . . . . 'Let bygones be bygones' is not a legitimate approach if we wish to call ourselves a constitutional democracy."[13]

While Rothstein offers a new point of entrance into conversations about reparations and redress, some aspects of his argument are troubling. For one, Rothstein takes up a narrative of collective responsibility and duty to ourselves that fails to acknowledge the power dynamics involved in these histories. He suggests that "few of us may be the direct descendants of those who perpetuated a segregated system or those who were its most exploited victims." As such, he concludes that "African Americans cannot await rectification of past wrongs as a gift, and white Americans collectively do not owe it to African Americans to rectify them."[14] Rothstein fails to understand housing segregation as more than a set of discriminatory policies. As such, his analysis of its multigenerational impact is limited.

Yet, as I have argued throughout this book, the streets are much more than the physical neighborhoods created through U.S. housing policy. Their impact on Black Americans has only grown since the policies responsible for creating them were first instituted. The racial wealth gap, derogatory perceptions of urban Blackness, educational inequality, social isolation, and a host of other by-products of geographic segregation reach far beyond "a few direct descendants." Similarly, the argument that only those who enforced such policies are responsible for them is fallacious, at best. After having the social, cultural, and economic scales systematically weighed in favor of White America, it is unjust to claim that the beneficiaries of these actions bear no responsibility in redressing them. Moreover, to do so is not a gift but a debt.

Although I do not fully agree with Rothstein's logic, I do agree that practices of geographic segregation were indeed unconstitutional; more important, I agree with Rothstein's explanation as to why this is significant.

Rothstein argues that "although most African Americans have suffered under this *de jure* system, they cannot identify, with the specificity a court case requires, the particular point at which they were victimized."[15] He goes on to cite an example of African American veterans who never even applied for federally insured mortgages because they were aware that their applications would be denied due to their race. As a result, they never accumulated the capital represented by homeownership and all the benefits that go along with it. Because these veterans never even filled out an application, their descendants have no legal proof of discrimination. Yet anyone who closely examines the practices and cultural ethos of the time will logically conclude that they were, in fact, systematically excluded from these privileges. Rothstein's point, and one with which I agree, is that although African Americans today may not be able to make a legal case to rectify these past injustices, they can advocate for their redress on the basis of unconstitutionality. Whichever framework one takes up, the point is that redress is both necessary and possible.

The Kerner Commission

One of the most comprehensive efforts to strategize redress for geographic segregation came in the form of a study conducted by the National Advisory Committee on Civil Disorders, typically referred to as the Kerner Commission. Rather than working through the possibility of reparations and redress, the commission, which was chaired by Otto Kerner, assumed America's ability to do so and focused instead on the question of what this should look like. Published in 1968, just a month before Martin Luther King Jr.'s assassination and the signing of the Fair Housing Act, the commission's report was part of President Johnson's effort to better understand the causes behind riots such as the one that took place in Detroit in 1967. Although the commission, which was described as both bipartisan and nonpartisan, set out to investigate the causes and nature of race riots in the United States, its report ended up being a systematic examination of the causes of and potential solutions to urban poverty.

In addition to the ways in which the Kerner Commission's words ring true today, the report is evidence that the notion of systemic redress for geographic segregation did not appear out of thin air. Rather, in the wake of decades of government policies and practices that created and reinforced geographic segregation, leaders within the U.S. government, business sectors, and nonprofits managed to acknowledge the need to tackle this issue through social, cultural, and economic means. To be clear, the Kerner Commission was primarily concerned with reform. Still, the types of redress outlined in the report signal the larger need for radical action.

Much of the Kerner Commission's report discusses the city as "the focus of racial disorder." While the report argues that the immediate responsibility for peace and order in the city lies with community leaders, it also recognizes that events of social unrest are "not simply a problem of the racial ghetto or the city . . . they are symptoms of social ills that have become endemic in our society and now affect every American."[16] Because these riots are symptoms of a larger social problem, the process of addressing them is not about "rewarding the rioters," but rather understanding America's responsibility for social unrest in Black space.[17] Thus, the commission framed the issue of redress as an American problem, rather than a Black one. Similarly, despite the fact that the report uses the language of civil disorder, which echoes certain ideologies about policing Blackness, one of the most surprising and impressive aspects is the way it identifies the social, cultural, and economic origins of protest riots rather than simply attributing them to faulty racial character.

Seemingly aware of the pushback it would receive, the Kerner Commission addressed the potential critiques of its recommended action plan. The first issue the commission tackled was how to pay for these programs. Because this question continues to be central to most rejections of proposals for reparations, the commission's answer is worth noting. The commission claimed that "the Nation has substantial financial resources . . . enough to make an important start on reducing our critical 'social deficit,' in spite of a war and in spite of current budget requirements."[18] I find this last part of the commission's claim, that we can afford redress "in spite of a war," to be the most revealing. The condition of the United States being engaged in an expensive war, or other military efforts, is not an exceptional occurrence. In fact, it has been a regular part of our history since the Kerner Commission report was written. As such, it should not be used as an excuse to push away efforts to apply federal funds toward restitution for geographic segregation. If the government can justify military spending under the logic of protecting American democracy, why can it not use that same logic to rectify the ways in which that promise was gutted historically for Black Americans?

Rather than leave the question of redress in vague terms, the final section of the Kerner Commission's report offers a series of recommendations for national action that focus primarily on employment, welfare, education, and housing programs. Before providing detailed policy recommendations, however, the commission framed its proposal within a greater need for social and ideological change. As stated in the report, "The need is not so much for the Government to design new programs as it is for the Nation to generate new will."[19] Part of this involves addressing how geographic segregation creates social conditions that are internalized by those living in urban Black spaces. Recognizing this, one of the commission's three key objectives was "removing the frustration of powerlessness among the disadvantage by providing the means to deal with the problems that affect their own lives and by increasing the capacity of our public and private institutions to respond to those problems."[20] The report also argues for communication and educational efforts that would "destroy stereotypes, halt polarization, end distrust and hostility, and create common ground for efforts toward common goals of public order and social justice."[21] In essence, the Kerner Commission understood redress as something that must function not only on a programmatic level but also on a cultural and ideological one. This approach works to simultaneously promote institutional change and deconstruct racial myths about urban Blackness.

In terms of its more programmatic recommendations, the Kerner Commission report outlines practical steps toward addressing the vast unemployment and underemployment resulting from geographic segregation and divestment from Black neighborhoods. To rectify this, the report suggests the creation of new job training programs, the recruitment of Black employees, and greater dissemination of knowledge about job and career paths. The goal of such programs would be to provide greater social mobility in both the private and public sectors. The report does more than just suggest job training and counseling programs, however. It calls for the creation of 2 million new jobs—1 million in the public sector and 1 million in the private sector—over the three years that followed the report's publication. These jobs would be designed specifically for meeting the needs of underemployed and unemployed Black urban inhabitants. The report also suggests a stimulation of investment in Black urban spaces through tax credits and greater support for Black business ownership.[22]

Similar to the commission's recommendations for employment, its report offers a detailed action plan for addressing racialized educational disparities. After providing a detailed analysis of how these disparities were continuing to grow and isolate Black urban children in 1968, despite the ruling of *Brown v. Board of Education* (1954), the Kerner Commission's report makes several pragmatic recommendations. For one, it outlines a need for programs that foster trust and understanding between community members and school administrators, such as hiring community liaisons, teaching aides, and tutors. This suggestion seems to recognize the need for an educational approach that does not further reinforce racialized power disparities.

In addition to programs that place community members in schools, the report argues for systemic programs that facilitate greater access to higher education and vocational training. It also calls for increased budgets, higher-quality teacher training (so that those who work in inner-city schools are of the same quality as those working in the suburbs), year-round educational programs, and greater attention to pedagogical approaches.[23] What is most notable about the Kerner Commission's approach to educational inequality is that it goes beyond the sole suggestion of integration. In fact, the commission recognized that "no matter how great the effort toward desegregation, many children of the ghetto will not, within their school careers, attend integrated schools."[24] The fact that, more than fifty years later, the public school system in America continues to be highly segregated makes the commission's words truer today than they were in 1968.

The Kerner Commission's discussion of the welfare system is significant because, in addition to providing practical recommendations, the commission also addressed policies that reinforce racist stereotypes. Among other recommendations, the commission's report calls for greater welfare provisions, at least enough to bring Black Americans to the threshold of the poverty line. What is particularly interesting, though, is the call to remove the so-called man-in-the-house rule, which refers to a policy that limits welfare access to women and children who do not have a male head of household. More important, this policy is one of the ways that racial stereotypes such as the welfare queen are systematically reinforced. The Kerner Commission seemed to be aware of this. Overall, it argued for programs that support Black families as they attempt to work, build lives, and move out of poverty.[25]

The final issue addressed in the Kerner Commission report is housing. Rather than make blanket suggestions, the report begins by reviewing the history of the FHA and how its programs barred Black people from homeownership and access to decent housing. In response, the report proposes the construction of better-quality public housing. This suggestion is not meant to reinforce Black use of public housing, but rather to replace existing subpar housing. The report is practical in its recognition of the fact that until the racial wealth gap is closed, quality public housing is a necessity.

In an effort to redress the FHA's discriminatory practices, the commission argued for "an expanded and modified below-market interest rate program," as well as incentives for new home construction. Both of these measures were meant to increase Black homeownership. The commission also suggested a federal write-down of interest rates on loans to private builders to make private loans more readily available for would-be Black homeowners. With all of these efforts, the commission was suggesting a proactive focus on geographic integration.[26]

I find the final line of the Kerner Commission's report to be particularly poignant today: "It is time now to end the destruction and the violence, not only in the streets of the ghetto but in the lives of the people."[27] While the report may have been referring to the destruction and violence of race riots, in this book I have tried to frame these as a response to the systemic destruction of and violence against Black people that stems from the creation of the streets. The overlapping recommendations of the Kerner Commission, the product of a bipartisan attempt at reform, and Black revolutionary groups such as The Black Panther Party, make it abundantly clear that redress must begin by meeting the radical demand for "land, bread, housing, education, clothing, justice and peace."[28]

Where Do We Go from Here?

Just over fifty years ago, Martin Luther King Jr. asked, "Why is equality so assiduously avoided?" When King posed this question, he already knew the answer. Having gotten much of liberal White America on board with desegregation and the granting of certain legal rights to Black Americans, King now turned to America's greatest stumbling block: economic equality. As King explained then, and as is true today, "The absence of brutality and unregenerated evil is not the presence of justice . . . the discount education given the Negroes will in the future have to be purchased at full price . . . jobs are harder and costlier to create than voting rolls."[29] What King points out, and what I wish to reiterate, is that the history of anti-Black racism in America is a deeply economic one. We cannot claim racial equality without facing the necessity for economic reparations.

To be clear, there are concrete strategies that can at least begin the process of redress. I agree with urban historian N. D. B. Connolly's argument that "we need a new blueprint, at a policy and political level, that reverse engineers the state-sponsored taking of black people's futures, one that halts social processes that have made it in every group's interests not to be black, look black, talk black, learn black, or live black."[30] While Connolly's focus is slightly different than mine, I agree that any attempt at redress must consider the economic, social, and cultural ways in which geographic segregation has impacted Black life.

Educational disparities between Black and White Americans could be one starting point for redress. A number of scholars have demonstrated the impact of geographic segregation on educational opportunity.[31] While some have suggested that busing inner-city kids to the suburbs is the solution, I would argue that this ultimately reinforces social isolation and public perceptions of urban Blackness. As someone who has personal experience with such programs, I can confirm that they often demand greater emotional and cultural labor from students of color while also creating a sense of distance and dislocation from one's home community. Beyond this, such programs do little to actually build long-lasting systemic change. Instead, urban schools (as well as other predominantly Black schools—gentrification has shifted the location of Black space, but the experiences and meanings associated with it remain) need increased funding. Just like the government-subsidized home loans that later developed into increased property values and wealth for White school districts, the government should subsidize the educational costs necessary for equitable education. This means greater social and economic investment in education as a public good and a commitment to equitable access. We must go beyond salary incentives and diversity hires to bring about radical change. We must also change the narratives within education itself. Many of the ideologies around urban Blackness that I have explored are still perpetuated through public education today.

Broad economic redress also means public investment in Black homeownership as a means to economic self-determination as well as ownership of Black space. This might take the form of subsidized loans or lower property taxes since, as George Lipsitz has demonstrated, property tax rules are just one of the many examples where White homeownership has driven legal policy.[32] However, economic redress could take more radical forms that truly rectify the way Black people were divested of homeownership through redlining and other racist practices. The point is that redress is not about the unfair redistribution of wealth from "hardworking White Americans" to "urban criminals and welfare queens." It is about correcting a stark historical injustice with quantifiable outcomes.

While much of the conversation on redress and reparations focuses on the federal government, and for good reason, this is not the sole avenue for change. As I discussed in chapter 1, local governments and communities often enforced geographic segregation through city planning and covenants. These same powers can be used today to work toward racial equity. What would it look like for states and cities to invest in racially integrated neighborhoods where Black people are homeowners? What would it look like for homeowners' associations to write clauses that promote social, cultural, and economic equity? These are the kinds of questions that will get us started on the path to full redress.

The way foreword is uncertain because those in power have not yet dared to imagine what freedom from these inequities might look like. Despite the many efforts to build a movement around redress and reparations, many continue to put off this conversation and claim that the cost is too high. I would argue that the cost of *not* doing anything is much higher. The realities of anti-Black racism are conspicuous parts of news and social media trends. From the criminality of holding a barbeque in a park, or selling water without a permit, to the numerous deaths of Black people at the hands of police and the overwhelmingly disproportionate number of Black people living as legal slaves of the state in prisons, the impact of American anti-Black racism has only grown since the civil rights era. Who knows, if we had taken the advice of Boris Bittker in the 1970s, perhaps we would have stemmed the exponential growth in the racial wealth gap since then. Instead, the cost of reparations today is even higher, and the longer we continue to argue that we are not responsible for past generations' actions, the greater, in fact, that responsibility will become.

Another form of resistance to redress and reparations comes from those who feel that this is no longer the responsibility of ordinary Americans. I find it baffling, however, that one could bemoan the expense of reparations for Americans without any recognition of the enormous national profit generated by centuries of free labor provided by enslaved Black people, or the subsidized wages of Black labor that continue to exist today. For anyone who exclaims, "My family immigrated later" or "We never owned slaves, why should I have to pay for others' sins?," I pose three questions. First, do you not continue to benefit from the structural, cultural, and social benefits of Whiteness created by these historical practices? Second, will you not at least ask yourself why it is so difficult for you to acknowledge these continued inequalities, and why have you had such a visceral reaction against the notion of racial equity? Third, even if you claim neither benefit nor responsibility, is it not your duty as a moral human being to pursue equity and redress for those who have been dispossessed and disenfranchised?

I pose these questions to highlight the fact that, arguably, it is not that the cost of reparations is too high for Americans economically, but rather that it is too high ideologically. As Coates puts it, "The idea of reparations is frightening not simply because we might lack the ability to pay. The idea of reparations threatens something much deeper—America's heritage, history, and standing in the world. . . . The popular mocking of reparations as a harebrained scheme authored by wild-eyed lefties and intellectually unserious black nationalists is fear masquerading as laughter."[33] It seems that America—White America in particular—is unwilling to pay the price of reckoning with the concrete origins and contemporary impact of the streets on Black life, especially when this reckoning involves economic change.

I am not the first person to make this claim. As a legal scholar, Kimberlé Crenshaw examines the ways in which racial ideologies are instituted and systematized. Yet, in addition to systemic change, she argues that "to bring a fundamental challenge to the way things are, whites would have to question not just their own subordinate status, but also both the economic and the racial myths that justify the status quo. . . . A challenge to the legitimacy of continued racial inequality would force whites to confront myths about equality of opportunity that justify for them whatever measure of economic success they may have attained."[34] Like Coates, Crenshaw understands that full redress will require institutional, cultural, and ideological change. An equitable response to the creation of the streets requires that, in addition to rectifying the economic and social disparities produced, Americans understand how the streets continue to shape perceptions of U.S. Blackness in everything from consumer habits to moral character. This begins with the kind of reckoning described by Coates, something I hope *How the Streets Were Made* helps facilitate.

Notes

Introduction

1. Evans, Twitter post.
2. Coates, *We Were Eight Years in Power*, 153.
3. Coates, 153.
4. Coates, *The Beautiful Struggle*, 115.
5. Coates, *We Were Eight Years in Power*, 153.
6. Coates, *The Beautiful Struggle*, 68.
7. Massey and Denton, *American Apartheid*, 18.
8. Myrdal, *An American Dilemma*, 618.
9. Clark, *Dark Ghetto*, 11.
10. Anderson, *Code of the Street*, 10.
11. Massey and Denton, *American Apartheid*, 19. It is worth noting that Massey and Denton are not discounting the reality of reservations or other racially segregated neighborhoods. Rather, they posit that the combination of racial, social, and economic isolation without any sense of sovereignty or ownership is a unique set of circumstances that applies primarily to Black Americans.
12. Conley, *Being Black, Living in the Red*; Massey and Denton, *American Apartheid*; Powell, Kearney, and Kay, *In Pursuit of a Dream Deferred*; Rothstein, *The Color of Law*; Shapiro, *The Hidden Cost*.
13. Lipsitz, *How Racism Takes Place*, 5.
14. Lipsitz, 6.
15. Kraus, Rucker, and Richeson, "Americans Misperceive Racial Economic Equality."
16. Lipsitz, *How Racism Takes Place*, 13.
17. Hegel, *The Philosophy of History*, 92.
18. Hegel, 91.
19. Hegel, 93.
20. Senghor, *The Foundations of "Africanité."* Even in his challenge to Hegel, Senghor assumes an African essentialism. Still, he uses this to argue against the inferiority assumed by Hegel. See also Camara, "The Falsity of Hegel's Theses on Africa" for a succinct analysis of how Negritude refutes Hegel's claims.
21. See Kirby, *Indifferent Boundaries*; Gilmore, "Fatal Couplings of Power and Difference"; McKittrick, *Demonic Grounds*.
22. McKittrick, *Demonic Grounds*, x.
23. Coates, *Between the World and Me*, 110–111.
24. Frazier, *The Negro Family in the United States*.
25. Moynihan, *The Negro Family*, 5.
26. Moynihan, of course, does not use this term, nor does he fully recognize how this systemic process worked. See Patterson, *Slavery and Social Death*.

27. Moynihan, *The Negro Family*, 16.
28. Moynihan, 17.
29. Moynihan, 19.
30. See Rainwater and Yancey, *The Moynihan Report and the Politics of Controversy*.
31. Coates, *We Were Eight Years in Power*, 227–230.
32. Jefferson, *Notes on the State of Virginia*, 153.
33. Lewis, *La Vida*; Lewis, "The Culture of Poverty."
34. Lewis, "The Culture of Poverty," 19.
35. Murray, *Losing Ground*; Mead, *Beyond Entitlement*.
36. Watkins, *Representing*, 17.
37. Watkins, 29–30.
38. Dallek, *Ronald Reagan*, xxiii–xxiv.
39. Davis, "Race and Criminalization."
40. Watkins, *Representing*, 36.
41. Collins, *Black Feminist Thought*, 88.
42. Dilulio, "The Coming of the Super-predators."
43. Watkins, *Representing*, 37.
44. Smith, "Ethnic Images."
45. Eggers and Massey, "The Structural Determinants of Urban Poverty"; Wilson, *The Truly Disadvantaged*; Watkins, *Representing*.
46. Massey and Denton, *American Apartheid*, 8.
47. Massey and Denton, 2.
48. See Hall, "Race, Culture, and Communications"; Hall, *Representation*; Williams, *Marxism and Literature*.
49. Coates, "The Case for Reparations."

Chapter One

1. Coates, "The Case for Reparations."
2. Cedric Robinson's theory of racial capitalism argues that racism has been an essential part of capitalism's development. Coates's argument situates geographic segregation as a specific component of this.
3. See, for example, Jackson, *Crabgrass Frontier*; Massey and Denton, *American Apartheid*; Rothstein, *The Color of Law*; Shapiro, *The Hidden Cost*.
4. Smith, "Ethnic Images."
5. Massey and Denton, *American Apartheid*, 18.
6. Massey and Denton, 20.
7. Massey and Denton, 24–25; Demerath and Gilmore, "The Ecology of Southern Cities."
8. For example, texts such as Frederick Douglass's *Narrative* and Harriet Jacobs's *Incidents in the Life of a Slave Girl* detail northern racism before 1900. Likewise, Thomas Sugrue's *Sweet Land of Liberty* details the history of northern anti-Blackness.
9. Katzman, *Before the Ghetto*, 81–103; Kusmer, *A Ghetto Takes Shape*, 35–52.
10. Massey and Denton, *American Apartheid*, 30–31.

11. Lieberson, *A Piece of the Pie*, 266; Massey and Denton, *American Apartheid*, 33.
12. Drake and Cayton, *Black Metropolis*, 176–178.
13. Massey and Denton, *American Apartheid*, 35; Rothstein, *The Color of Law*, 139–151.
14. Rothstein, *The Color of Law*, viii.
15. Rothstein, 18.
16. Fishel, "The Negro in the New Deal Era."
17. Quoted in Chappell, *A Stone of Hope*, 10.
18. Rothstein, *The Color of Law*, 20.
19. Hirsch, "Choosing Segregation"; Hirsch, "The Last and Most Difficult Barrier."
20. Rothstein, *The Color of Law*, 18.
21. Rothstein, 21.
22. U.S. Housing Administration, *Manual on Policy and Procedures, 1937*, 7–8.
23. Rothstein, *The Color of Law*, 31; Hirsch, "Searching for a 'Sound Negro Policy'"; Julian and Daniel, "Separate and Unequal"; von Hoffman, "A Study in Contradictions," 309.
24. Truman, "Statement by the President upon Signing the Housing Act of 1949."
25. Rothstein, *The Color of Law*, 32; Hirsch, "Searching for a 'Sound Negro Policy,'" 401–406, 417–418.
26. U.S. Commission on Civil Rights, *Housing*, 109–116.
27. Rothstein, *The Color of Law*, 32–33.
28. Hirsch, "Choosing Segregation," 218.
29. Abrams, "The New 'Gresham's Law of Neighborhoods,'" 327; Hirsch, "The Last and Most Difficult Barrier," 59–60.
30. Rothstein, *The Color of Law*, 44.
31. Rothstein, 46; Rice, "Residential Segregation by Law"; Thornbrough, "Segregation in Indiana," 598–599.
32. Kushner, *Apartheid in America*, 562–566; McGovney, "Racial Residential Segregation by State Court Enforcement," 6–11; *Corrigan v. Buckley*; Philpott, *The Slum and the Ghetto*, 189–193.
33. *Shelley v. Kraemer*.
34. Whitten, *The Atlanta Zone*, 10.
35. Rothstein, *The Color of Law*, 46.
36. Freund, *Colored Property*, 76–78.
37. Freund, 73–74; Hancock, "The New Deal and American Planning," 200–201; Rothstein, *The Color of Law*, 51.
38. Rothstein, *The Color of Law*, 48.
39. Flint, *Zoning and Residential Segregation*, 50, 103–119, 207, 322, 345–347, 394; Gordon, *Mapping Decline*, 122–128; Rothstein, *The Color of Law*, 50.
40. Drake and Cayton, *Black Metropolis*, 210–211.
41. See Loewen, *Sundown Towns*.
42. Finney, *Black Faces, White Spaces*, 60–61.
43. Collin and Collin, "Urban Environmentalism and Race," 227–230; Rothstein, *The Color of Law*, 56–58. Also see President Clinton's Executive Order 12898.

44. Quoted in Rothstein, *The Color of Law*, 127.

45. Massey and Denton, *American Apartheid*, 44–56; Mohl, "Planned Destruction," 226–245; Rothstein, *The Color of Law*, 126–131.

46. Massey and Denton, *American Apartheid*, 55–56.

47. Hirsch, *Making the Second Ghetto*, 252–254.

48. Massey and Denton, *American Apartheid*, 57.

49. Better Homes in America, "Announcing the Inauguration," 17.

50. Gries and U.S. Department of Agriculture, *How to Own Your Home*; Hutchinson, "Building for Babbitt," 194.

51. Jackson, *Crabgrass Frontier*, 196–197.

52. Hoover, "Address to the White House Conference," 572.

53. Hoover, 572.

54. Hoover, 572.

55. Freund, *Colored Property*, 115.

56. McEntire, *Residence and Race*, 245.

57. Rothstein, *The Color of Law*, 64.

58. Jackson, *Crabgrass Frontier*, 196–203.

59. Jackson, 196–203.

60. Both Katznelson and Frydl have written works that outline the way Black veterans were systematically denied these benefits. See Katznelson, *When Affirmative Action Was White*; Frydl, *The G.I. Bill*.

61. Hays, *The Federal Government and Urban Housing*; Jackson, *Crabgrass Frontier*, 203–208.

62. Quoted in Jackson, *Crabgrass Frontier*, 208.

63. *Race: The Power of an Illusion*; Rothstein, *The Color of Law*, 64.

64. Coates, "The Case for Reparations."

65. Jackson, *Crabgrass Frontier*, 208.

66. Federal Housing Association, *Underwriting Manual*, 1–2.

67. Massey and Denton, *American Apartheid*, 45.

68. Massey and Denton, 44.

69. *Race: The Power of an Illusion*.

70. Jackson, *Crabgrass Frontier*, 208–209, 238; *Levitt v. Division against Discrimination*.

71. *Levitt v. Division against Discrimination*.

72. Quoted in Rothstein, *The Color of Law*, 69.

73. Rothstein, *The Color of Law*, 69, 141; Goodwin, *No Ordinary Time*, 329–330; *Race: The Power of an Illusion*.

74. Rothstein, *The Color of Law*, 97–98.

75. Helper, *Racial Policies and Practices*, 172–182; Hirsch, *Making the Second Ghetto*, 31–33; Massey and Denton, *American Apartheid*, 38–39.

76. Blockbusting involved profiting off Black people's desire to escape ghettoization and White people's fear of integration. For excellent discussions of the history of blockbusting, see Philpott, *The Slum and the Ghetto*, 149–153, 163–164; Hirsch, *Making the Second Ghetto*, 34–35.

77. Drake and Cayton, *Black Metropolis*, 576–577; Massey and Denton, *American Apartheid*, 39.

78. Helper, *Racial Policies and Practices*, 321–337; Massey and Denton, *American Apartheid*, 50.

79. U.S. Bureau of the Census, *Statistical Abstract of the United States, 1956*; U.S. Bureau of the Census, *Statistical Abstract of the United States, 1966*; U.S. Bureau of the Census, *Statistical Abstract of the United States, 1976*.

80. Hirsch, "Choosing Segregation," 211–214.

81. Allport, *The Nature of Prejudice*, 74.

82. Schuman, Steeh, and Bobo, *Racial Attitudes in America*, 74–75.

83. Schuman, Steeh, and Bobo, 74–75.

84. U.S. Commission on Civil Rights, *Housing*, 36–37, 42, 49–51, 45.

85. U.S. National Advisory Commission on Civil Disorders, *Report of the National Advisory Commission on Civil Disorders*, 2.

86. U.S. National Advisory Commission on Civil Disorders, 22.

87. Farley, *Blacks and Whites*, 130–171; Massey and Denton, *American Apartheid*, 60–61.

88. Farley, *Blacks and Whites*, 56–81; Farley and Allen, *The Color Line*, 283–358; Massey and Denton, *American Apartheid*, 61.

89. Massey and Denton, *American Apartheid*, 62–67.

90. Massey and Denton, 62–67.

91. Clay, "The Process of Black Suburbanization"; Farley, "The Changing Distribution of Negroes"; Lake, *The New Suburbanites*.

92. Massey and Denton, "Hypersegregation in U.S. Metropolitan Areas," 373. For a discussion of the empirical methods used to measure hypersegregation, see Massey and Denton, "The Dimensions of Residential Segregation"; White, "The Measurement of Spatial Segregation."

93. Massey and Denton, *American Apartheid*, 77.

94. Quoted in Massey and Denton, 94.

95. Massey, *Categorically Unequal*, 73–74.

96. Massey and Denton, *American Apartheid*, 100–105; Wienk et al., *Measuring Racial Discrimination in American Housing Markets*; Yinger and U.S. Department of Housing and Urban Development, *Housing Discrimination Study*, 23–43.

97. U.S. Department of Housing and Urban Development, "Housing Discrimination against Racial and Ethnic Minorities 2012," 68.

98. U.S. Department of Housing and Urban Development, 68.

99. U.S. Bureau of the Census, "Quarterly Residential Vacancies and Homeownership"; Flippen, "Unequal Returns to Housing Investments?"

100. Lipsitz, *How Racism Takes Place*, 106–109; Rothstein, *The Color of Law*, 113.

101. Rothstein, *The Color of Law*, 109–111.

102. Countrywide, a subsidiary of Bank of America, was one of the primary lending companies responsible for such loans during the first decade of the 2000s. See U.S. Department of Housing and Urban Development, "Prepared Remarks."

103. *Race: The Power of an Illusion*.

104. Jones, "The Racial Wealth Gap."

105. *Race: The Power of an Illusion*.

106. Lipsitz, *How Racism Takes Place*, 4; Shapiro, Meschede, and Sullivan, "The Racial Wealth Gap Increases Fourfold."

107. Quoted in Shapiro, *The Hidden Cost*, 5.
108. Lipsitz, *How Racism Takes Place*, 4–5.
109. Kraus, Rucker, and Richeson, "Americans Misperceive Racial Economic Equality."
110. Jones, "The Racial Wealth Gap."
111. Addo, Houle, and Simon, "Young, Black, and (Still) in the Red."
112. Kraus, Rucker, and Richeson, "Americans Misperceive Racial Economic Equality," 10329.
113. *Race: The Power of an Illusion*.
114. Lipsitz, *How Racism Takes Place*, 5; Rothstein, "How the U.S. Tax Code Worsens the Education Gap"; Shapiro, Meschede, and Sullivan, "The Racial Wealth Gap Increases Fourfold."
115. Massey et al., "The Puzzle of Minority Underachievement."
116. Quoted in Acevedo-Garcia and Osypuk, "Impacts of Housing and Neighborhoods on Health," 197.
117. Bor et al., "Police Killings and Their Spillover"; Smith, "Facing the Dragon."
118. Sharkey, *Stuck in Place*, 39.

Chapter Two

1. Dingle, *Black Enterprise Titans of the B.E. 100s*, 15.
2. Johnson and Bennett, *Succeeding against the Odds*, 180–181.
3. Weems, *Desegregating the Dollar*, 75.
4. D'Rozario and Williams, "Retail Redlining."
5. Hayward, *How Americans Make Race*, 120–122.
6. General Records of the Own Your Own Home Campaign, U.S. Housing Corporation, 1917–1952.
7. Luken and Vaughan, ". . . Be a Genuine Homemaker *in Your Own Home*," 1611.
8. General Records of the Own Your Own Home Campaign, U.S. Housing Corporation, 1917–1952.
9. Luken and Vaughan, ". . . Be a Genuine Homemaker *in Your Own Home*," 1611.
10. Central Intelligence Agency, *The Kitchen Debate*, 1–4.
11. Central Intelligence Agency, 1.
12. Central Intelligence Agency, 1.
13. Sivulka, *Soap, Sex, and Cigarettes*, 204.
14. DuBois, *The Philadelphia Negro*, 121.
15. Stuart, *An Economic Detour*, xxiii.
16. Drake and Cayton, *Black Metropolis*, 443–445.
17. Marchand, *Advertising the American Dream*, 64.
18. Weems, *Desegregating the Dollar*, 1.
19. Kassarjian, "The Negro and American Advertising," 29–39.
20. Sullivan, "Don't Do This—If You Want to Sell Your Products to Negros!," 46–47.
21. "National Negro Market," 34.
22. "Food, Clothing Get Most of Negroes' $10 Billion," 50.
23. Quoted in Weems, *Desegregating the Dollar*, 42.

24. *The Secret of Selling the Negro.*
25. *The Secret of Selling the Negro.*
26. *The Secret of Selling the Negro.*
27. *The Secret of Selling the Negro.*
28. Weems, *Desegregating the Dollar*, 70.
29. Johnson and Bennett, *Succeeding against the Odds*, 277–280.
30. *The Secret of Selling the Negro.*
31. Johnson, "Why Negroes Buy Cadillacs," 34.
32. Wilkerson, *The Warmth of Other Suns*, 299–301.
33. Haring, "Selling to Harlem," 17–18.
34. Batten, Barton, Durstine & Osborn, Inc., *Proposed Operational Plan*, 1.
35. Batten, Barton, Durstine & Osborn, Inc., 1.
36. Archer, "How to Sell Today's Negro Woman," 49.
37. Hughes, "*Ebony*'s Nativity," 42.
38. *Ebony* advertisement, *Advertising Age*, 7.
39. Johnson, "Editorial Concept," 161.
40. Johnson and Bennett, *Succeeding against the Odds*, 152–153.
41. Johnson and Bennett, 159.
42. Walker, *Style and Status*, 16.
43. Walker, 13.
44. "Six Ways," 128.
45. "Six Ways," 128.
46. "Michigan's Ghetto Buster," 55.
47. "Michigan's Ghetto Buster," 55.
48. "I Sold a House to a Negro," 92.
49. "I Sold a House to a Negro," 92.
50. "I Sold a House to a Negro," 92.
51. "I Sold a House to a Negro," 93–93.
52. "I Sold a House to a Negro," 94.
53. "I Sold a House to a Negro," 99.
54. "I Sold a House to a Negro," 99–100.
55. "I Sold a House to a Negro," 94.
56. "I Sold a House to a Negro," 94.
57. Bennett, "The White Problem," 29.
58. Bims, "Housing—The Hottest Issue in the North," 93.
59. Bennett, "The White Problem," 30.
60. Young, "The High Cost of Discrimination," 51.
61. Bennett, "The White Problem," 30.
62. Bennett, 29.
63. Bennett, 32.
64. Bennett, 32.
65. Bennett, 36.
66. Johnson, "A Statement from the Publisher," 19.
67. "Message from Truman," 21.

68. "Message from Hoover," 21.
69. Johnson, "A Statement from the Publisher," 19.
70. Johnson, "*Ebony*'s Fifteenth Birthday," 159.
71. Johnson, 159.
72. Johnson's Wax advertisement, *Ebony*, 103.
73. Nadinola advertisement, *Ebony*, 10.
74. Bennett, "The Negro Woman," 94.
75. Kwate, "Retail Messages in the Ghetto Belt," 48.

Chapter Three

1. Coates, *Between the World and Me*, 110–111.
2. Although I do not analyze it in this chapter, perhaps the most obvious example of Black authors doing this kind of work is Gwendolyn Brooks's poetry collection *A Street in Bronzeville*.
3. Lipsitz, *How Racism Takes Place*, 61.
4. Drake and Cayton, *Black Metropolis*, 385.
5. Drake and Cayton, 379–397.
6. DuBois, *The Philadelphia Negro*, 5.
7. See, for example, Hopkins, *Contending Forces*; Chesnutt, "The Wife of His Youth"; Chesnutt, "A Matter of Principle"; Johnson, *Black Manhattan*.
8. Locke, "Enter the New Negro," 5.
9. Scruggs, *Sweet Home*.
10. Scruggs, 4–5.
11. Holladay, *Ann Petry*, 9–10.
12. Holladay, 10.
13. Shockley, "Buried Alive," 441.
14. Petry, *The Street*, 1–2.
15. Petry, 2.
16. Petry, 2.
17. Petry, 2.
18. Petry, 2.
19. Petry, 436.
20. Petry, 250.
21. Petry, 251–252.
22. Petry, 57.
23. Petry, 60.
24. Petry, 67.
25. Petry, 32.
26. Petry, 37–38.
27. Petry, 43.
28. Petry, 28.
29. Petry, 28.
30. Petry, 78.
31. Petry, 426.

32. Petry, 388.
33. Petry, 389.
34. See Patterson, *Slavery and Social Death*.
35. Petry, *The Street*, 327.
36. Petry, 328.
37. Petry, 329.
38. Petry, 331.
39. Petry, 57.
40. Baldwin, *The Fire Next Time*, 6.
41. Baldwin, 7.
42. Baldwin, 7.
43. Field, *James Baldwin*, 2–3.
44. Field, 72–73.
45. Baldwin, *The Fire Next Time*, 16.
46. Baldwin, 20.
47. Baldwin, 24.
48. Baldwin, 28.
49. Baldwin, 30–31.
50. Baldwin, 30–31.
51. Baldwin, 39.
52. Baldwin, 76.
53. Baldwin, 20.
54. Baldwin, 23.
55. Baldwin, 24.
56. Baldwin, 50.
57. Baldwin, 78–79.
58. Shakur, *Assata*, 153.
59. Coates, *Between the World and Me*, 15–16.
60. Baldwin, *The Fire Next Time*, 26–27.
61. Coates, *Between the World and Me*, 82.
62. Coates, 82.
63. Shapiro, *The Political Sublime*, 65.
64. Coates, *Between the World and Me*, 82.
65. Coates, 14.
66. Coates, 14.
67. The performance of power as part of the culture of the streets is something Elijah Anderson explores in *Code of the Streets*.
68. See Alvarez, *The Power of the Zoot*.
69. Coates, *We Were Eight Years in Power*, 155.
70. Coates, *Between the World and Me*, 22.
71. Coates, 23.
72. Coates, 14–15.
73. Singh, *Black Is a Country*, 203.
74. Coates, *Between the World and Me*, 30.
75. Coates, 25.

76. Coates, 33.

77. For an in-depth discussion of civil and social death, as well as incarceration as neoslavery, see Alexander, *The New Jim Crow*; Childs, *Slaves of the State*; Davis, *Are Prisons Obsolete?*; James, *The New Abolitionists*; and Patterson, *Slavery and Social Death*.

78. Malcolm X, "The Ballot or the Bullet."

79. Shakur, *Assata*, 60.

80. Shakur, 90.

81. Jordan Davis, a seventeen-year-old high school student, was shot and murdered at a gas station in Jacksonville, Florida, in 2012. His murderer, Michael David Dunn, opened fire on Davis and his friends while they were sitting in their car because they would not agree to turn down their music, which Dunn described as "rap crap" or "thug music." Jordan's mother, Lucy McBath, was recently elected to Congress after running on a gun reform platform.

Chapter Four

1. Coates, *The Beautiful Struggle*, 101.
2. Forman, *The 'Hood Comes First*, 3.
3. Forman, xvii.
4. Forman, xvi.
5. Forman, 35–42.
6. Hip-hop is typically defined by its four main components: break dancing, disc jockeying, graffiti, and rap. However, as many have argued, a number of other elements such as dress and politics may be considered fundamental to the genre. This expanded understanding of hip-hop makes sense given the subgenres that have emerged around themes such as social consciousness, materialism, gangs, and regional identity. In this chapter, I extend the traditional understanding of hip-hop by demonstrating the streets' centrality to the genre.
7. Forman, *The 'Hood Comes First*, 42.
8. Keyes, *Rap Music and Street Consciousness*, 122.
9. Plunz, *A History of Housing in New York City*, 257, 267–273.
10. Chang, *Can't Stop, Won't Stop*, 13–15.
11. Chang, 13.
12. Many of these gangs first emerged in response to violence perpetrated by White groups that did not want people of color moving into formerly White ethnic neighborhoods. However, these gangs evolved and began engaging in other activities, including petty theft and in some cases drug distribution. A host of factors influenced the development of these gangs, including the flooding of Black and Brown communities with drugs by outside sources.
13. Quoted in Wallace and Wallace, *A Plague on Your Houses*, 22.
14. Moynihan, "Memorandum."
15. Kotlowski, *Nixon's Civil Rights*, 173.
16. Chang, *Can't Stop, Won't Stop*, 67–87; Neal, "Postindustrial Soul"; Nelson, *Hip Hop America*.
17. Chang, *Can't Stop, Won't Stop*, 67–87.

18. Chang, 67.
19. Chang, 77–78.
20. Quoted in Chang, 78. What is notable about this origin story is that hip-hop is tied to the streets, but it is not exclusively African American. Both Herc and La Rock are Jamaican. Another hip-hop pioneer, Grandmaster Flash (Joseph Saddler), is from Barbados. Beyond these Caribbean connections, hip-hop's origins can also be traced to Latinx music.
21. Gosa, "The Fifth Element," 58.
22. Grandmaster Flash emerged on the hip-hop scene around 1977. He was also known for public shows, experimental use of electric percussion, beatboxing, and scratching.
23. Chang, *Can't Stop, Won't Stop*, 89–108.
24. Hager, "Afrika Bambaataa's Hip-Hop," 14.
25. Hager, 15.
26. Quoted in Hager, 17.
27. Hager, 18.
28. Hager, 15.
29. Gosa, "The Fifth Element," 60.
30. Quoted in Hager, "Afrika Bambaataa's Hip-Hop," 20.
31. Rose, "Hip Hop on Trial."
32. Perry, *Prophets of the Hood*, 41.
33. Perry, 42.
34. Dyson, *Know What I Mean?*, xxi.
35. Dyson, 6.
36. Coleman, *Check the Technique*, 211.
37. Furman and Furman, *Heart of Soul*, 86.
38. The Fugees, "Red Intro," *The Score*.
39. Coleman, *Check the Technique*, 215.
40. Coleman, 215.
41. Coleman, 218.
42. The Fugees, "Ready or Not," *The Score*.
43. The Fugees.
44. Coleman, *Check the Technique*, 217.
45. The Fugees, "The Beast," *The Score*; The Fugees, "Fu-Gee-La," *The Score*.
46. The Fugees, "No Woman No Cry," *The Score*.
47. Fiasco, "Words I Never Said," *Lasers*.
48. Riley, "Lupe Fiasco Calls Obama a 'Terrorist.'"
49. Fiasco, "Interview."
50. "Lupe Fiasco: Rapping Outside the Box."
51. "Lupe Fiasco: Rapping Outside the Box," 152.
52. "Lupe Fiasco: Rapping Outside the Box."
53. Sawjani, "Lupe Fiasco."
54. Crosley, "The Unclassifiable Lupe Fiasco."
55. Crosley.
56. Fiasco, "The Cool," *Lupe Fiasco's Food & Liquor*.

57. Solarsk, "Lupe Fiasco Talks The Cool, Cheeseburgers, Retirement."
58. Fiasco, "The Coolest," *Lupe Fiasco's The Cool*.
59. Fiasco.
60. Fiasco.
61. Fiasco, "Streets on Fire," *Lupe Fiasco's The Cool*.
62. Fiasco.
63. Fiasco.
64. Quoted in Gosa, "The Fifth Element," 122–123.
65. Fiasco, "Put You on Game," *Lupe Fiasco's The Cool*.
66. Fiasco.
67. Fiasco.
68. Fiasco.
69. Wilson, Usinger, and Lucas, "All You Need to Know"; Haithcoat, "Born and Raised in Compton."
70. Lamar, "XXX," *DAMN*.
71. Lamar.
72. Ahmed, "When Kendrick Lamar Delivered a Classic."
73. Dyson, *Know What I Mean?*, xvii.
74. Love, "Good Kids, Mad Cities," 320.
75. Lamar, "Good Kid," *Good Kid, M.A.A.D. City*.
76. Lamar.
77. Lamar, "m.A.A.d. City," *Good Kid, M.A.A.D. City*.
78. Lamar.
79. Lamar, "Backseat Freestyle Annotations."
80. Lamar, "Swimming Pools (Drank)," *Good Kid, M.A.A.D. City*.

Chapter Five

1. McCarthy et al., "Race, Suburban Resentment, and the Representation of the Inner City," 163.
2. Silk and Silk, *Racism and Anti-racism in American Popular Culture*, 174–175.
3. Newton, "He Won't Bleed Me," B.
4. Massood, *Black City Cinema*, 117.
5. For more on blaxploitation films, see Martinez, Martinez, and Chavez, *What It Is, What It Was!*; Koven, *Blaxploitation Films*; Howard, *Blaxploitation Cinema*.
6. *BadAsssss Cinema*.
7. Edwards, "Realer Than Reel," 1.
8. Watkins, *Representing*, 171.
9. Diawara, *Black American Cinema*, 230.
10. Watkins, *Representing*, 176.
11. Diawara, "Noir by Noirs."
12. Massood, *Black City Cinema*, 146.
13. Gillespie, *Film Blackness*, 7.
14. Fisher, "'America's Worst Nightmare,'" 229.
15. Jones, *The Dispossessed*, 270.

16. Watkins, *Representing*, 175.
17. Bulman, "Teachers in the 'Hood."
18. Massood, "Street Girls with No Future?," 242.
19. hooks, *Black Looks*, 120.
20. Moynihan, *The Negro Family*.
21. Dilulio, "The Coming of the Super-predators."
22. Singleton, "The Fire This Time," 74–75.
23. Watkins, *Representing*, 189.
24. Antonio, *Contemporary African American Cinema*, 40.
25. *Boyz n the Hood*.
26. Massood, *Black City Cinema*, 162.
27. Bradshaw, "A Visually Ravishing Portrait of Masculinity"; Lee, "It's Impossible to Be Vulnerable"; Orr, "It's Painful Watching the Male Crisis Onscreen."
28. Gillespie, *Film Blackness*, 121.
29. Cooper, "Hear How 'Moonlight' Got Its Sound."
30. Scott, "'Moonlight.'"
31. Aguirre, "*Moonlight*'s Cinematographer on Filming the Most Exquisite Movie of the Year."
32. Buckley, "Naomie Harris Explains How 'Moonlight' Avoided Crack-Addict Stereotypes."
33. *Moonlight*.
34. Quoted in Massood, "Street Girls with No Future?," 234.
35. Massood.
36. *Just Another Girl on the I. R. T.*
37. *Just Another Girl on the I. R. T.*
38. *Just Another Girl on the I. R. T.*
39. *Just Another Girl on the I. R. T.*
40. Antonio, *Contemporary African American Cinema*, 72.
41. Rafferty, "Tunnel Vision."
42. Taubin, "Girl N the Hood," 17.
43. Quoted in Phillips, "Growing Up Black and Female," 87.
44. Healy, "Fly Girls on Film," 24.
45. See, for example, García, "Baltimore in *The Wire*"; Lipsitz, *How Racism Takes Place*; Williams, "The Lost Boys of Baltimore."
46. Gates, "Must Buppiehood Cost Homeboy His Soul?," 11.
47. Williams, "The Lost Boys of Baltimore," 58.
48. France, "Idris Elba 'Too Street' to Play James Bond."
49. France.
50. In "Home Rooms" from season four, Omar worries that the collapse of the Barksdale organization, his previous opposition, has made him soft.
51. Williams, "The Lost Boys of Baltimore," 59.
52. Williams, 59.
53. Levine, *Forms*, 132.
54. Levine, 132–133. Levine also addresses the networks and hierarchies depicted in the show.

55. Levine, 135.
56. Levine, 136.
57. Williams, *On the Wire*, 31.
58. Kia Corthron cowrote an episode of *The Wire*.
59. Obama has stated that he is a "huge fan" of *The Wire*.
60. Lipsitz, *How Racism Takes Place*, 115–116.
61. Williams, *On the Wire*, 177–183.
62. Gross, "'The Chi' Creator Lena Waithe."
63. Hyman, "With 'The Chi,' Lena Waithe Heads Home."
64. Hyman.
65. William Lee and Nina Metz provide weekly recaps and criticism for the *Chicago Tribune*.
66. "Today Was a Good Day."
67. Ray-Harris, "*The Chi* Finds a Compelling Story."

Conclusion

1. Comen, "For Black Americans Moving to a New City."
2. U.S. Bureau of the Census, "American Community Survey."
3. "125 Best Places to Live in the U.S."
4. Lipsitz, *How Racism Takes Place*, 61.
5. Trump, Twitter post.
6. Bittker, *The Case for Black Reparations*.
7. Quoted in Coates, "The Case for Reparations."
8. Commission to Study and Develop Reparation Proposals for African-Americans Act, H.R. 40, 2–5.
9. Coates, "The Case for Reparations."
10. Quoted in Rothstein, *The Color of Law*, 35.
11. Coates, "The Case for Reparations."
12. Coates.
13. Rothstein, *The Color of Law*, xi.
14. Rothstein, xv–xvi.
15. Rothstein, xi.
16. U.S. National Advisory Commission on Civil Disorders, *Report of the National Advisory Commission on Civil Disorders*, 229.
17. U.S. National Advisory Commission on Civil Disorders, 231.
18. U.S. National Advisory Commission on Civil Disorders, 229.
19. U.S. National Advisory Commission on Civil Disorders, 230.
20. U.S. National Advisory Commission on Civil Disorders, 230.
21. U.S. National Advisory Commission on Civil Disorders, 230.
22. U.S. National Advisory Commission on Civil Disorders, 232–236.
23. U.S. National Advisory Commission on Civil Disorders, 244–251.
24. U.S. National Advisory Commission on Civil Disorders, 243.
25. U.S. National Advisory Commission on Civil Disorders, 252–257.
26. U.S. National Advisory Commission on Civil Disorders, 257–263.

27. U.S. National Advisory Commission on Civil Disorders, 265.
28. Dr. Huey P. Newton Foundation, "The Black Panther Party's Ten-Point Program."
29. King, *Where Do We Go from Here?*, 4–6.
30. Connolly, "The Case for Repair, Part 2."
31. See Kozol, *Savage Inequalities*; Sharkey, *Stuck in Place*; Shapiro, *The Hidden Cost*; Powell, Kearney, and Kay, *In Pursuit of a Dream Deferred*. Nikole Hannah Jones has also written a number of good essays on this topic. See, for example, "The Resegregation of Jefferson County" or "Choosing a School for My Daughter."
32. Lipsitz, *How Racism Takes Place*, 3.
33. Coates, "The Case for Reparations."
34. Crenshaw, "Race, Reform, and Retrenchment," 1380–1381.

Bibliography

Abrams, Charles. "The New 'Gresham's Law of Neighborhoods'—Fact or Fiction." *Appraisal Journal* 10 (July 1950): 324–328.

Acevedo-Garcia, Dolores, and Theresa L. Osypuk. "Impacts of Housing and Neighborhoods on Health: Pathways, Racial/Ethnic Disparities, and Policy Directions." In *Segregation: The Rising Cots for America*, edited by James Carr and Nandinee Kutty, 197–236. New York: Routledge, 2008.

Addo, Fenaba R., Jason N. Houle, and Daniel Simon. "Young, Black, and (Still) in the Red." *Race and Social Problems* 8 (March 2016): 64–76.

Aguirre, Abby. "*Moonlight*'s Cinematographer on Filming the Most Exquisite Movie of the Year." *Vogue*, December 20, 2016. https://www.vogue.com/projects/13514953/moonlight-cinematographer-james-laxton/.

Ahmed, Insanul. "When Kendrick Lamar Delivered a Classic with *Good Kid, M.A.A.D. City*, Nobody Saw it Coming. Now That the Whole World Is Watching, Can He Outdo Himself?" *Complex*, August/September 2014. http://www.complex.com/covers/kendrick-lamar-interview-turn-the-page-2014-cover-story/.

Alexander, Michelle. *The New Jim Crow: Mass Incarceration in the Age of Colorblindness*. New York: New Press, 2012.

Allport, Gordon. *The Nature of Prejudice*. Boston: Addison-Wesley, 1954.

Alvarez, Luis. *The Power of the Zoot: Youth Culture and Resistance during World War II*. Berkeley: University of California Press, 2008.

Anderson, Elijah. *Code of the Street: Decency, Violence, and the Moral Life of the Inner City*. New York: W. W. Norton, 1999.

Antonio, Sheril D. *Contemporary African American Cinema*. New York: Peter Lang, 2002.

Archer, Elsie. "How to Sell Today's Negro Woman." *Sponsor* 20 (July 25, 1966): 49.

BadAsssss Cinema: A Bold Look at 70's Blaxploitation Films. Directed by Isaac Julien. New York: Docurama, 2002. DVD.

Baldwin, James *The Fire Next Time*. London: Vintage, 1992.

Balshaw, Maria. *Looking for Harlem: Urban Aesthetics in African-American Literature*. New York: Pluto Press, 2001.

Batten, Barton, Durstine & Osborn, Inc. *Proposed Operational Plan for the B. F. Goodrich Tire Co. in the Negro Market*. New York: Batten, Barton, Durstine & Osborn, 1960.

Bennett, Lerone, Jr. "The Negro Woman." *Ebony*, September 1963, 86–94.

———. "The White Problem." *Ebony*, August 1965, 29–36.

Better Homes in America. "Announcing the Inauguration." *Delineator*, October 1922, 16–17.

Bims, Hamilton J. "Housing—The Hottest Issue in the North." *Ebony*, August 1965, 93–100.

Bittker, Boris. *The Case for Black Reparations*. Boston: Beacon Press, 2003.
Bor, Jacob, Atheendar S. Venkataramani, David R. Williams, and Alexander C. Tsai. "Police Killings and Their Spillover Effects on the Mental Health of Black Americans: A Population-Based, Quasi-experimental Study." *Lancet* 392 (July 2018): 302–310. https://doi.org/10.1016/S0140-6736(18)31130-9.
Boyz n the Hood. Directed by John Singleton. Los Angeles: Columbia Pictures, 1991. DVD.
Bradshaw, Peter. "A Visually Ravishing Portrait of Masculinity." *Guardian*, February 16, 2017. https://www.theguardian.com/film/2017/feb/16/moonlight-review-masculinity-naomie-harris.
Buckley, Cara. "Naomie Harris Explains How 'Moonlight' Avoided Crack-Addict Stereotypes." *New York Times*, December 16, 2016. https://www.nytimes.com/2016/12/16/movies/naomie-harris-moonlight-avoided-addict-stereotypes.html.
Bulman, Robert C. "Teachers in the 'Hood: Hollywood's Middle-Class Fantasy." *Urban Review* 34 (September 2002): 251–276.
Camara, Babacar. "The Falsity of Hegel's Theses on Africa." *Journal of Black Studies* 36 (September 2005): 82–96.
Central Intelligence Agency. *The Kitchen Debate*. U.S. Embassy, Moscow, Soviet Union. July 24, 1959. https://www.cia.gov/library/readingroom/docs/1959-07-24.pdf.
Chang, Jeff. *Can't Stop, Won't Stop: A History of the Hip-Hop Generation*. London: Picador, 2005.
Chappell, David L. *A Stone of Hope: Prophetic Religion and the Death of Jim Crow*. Chapel Hill: University of North Carolina Press, 2005.
Chesnutt, Charles. "A Matter of Principle." In *Charles W. Chesnutt: Stories, Novels, and Essays*, 149–168. New York: Library of America, 2002.
———. "The Wife of His Youth." In *Charles W. Chesnutt: Stories, Novels, and Essays*, 101–112. New York: Library of America, 2002.
Childs, Dennis. *Slaves of the State: Black Incarceration from the Chain Gang to the Penitentiary*. Minneapolis: University of Minnesota Press, 2015.
Chin, Elizabeth. *Purchasing Power: Black Kids and American Consumer Culture*. Minneapolis: University of Minnesota Press, 2001.
Clark, Kenneth B. *Dark Ghetto: Dilemmas of Social Power*. New York: Harper and Row, 1965.
Clay, Phillip L. "The Process of Black Suburbanization." *Urban Affairs Quarterly* 14 (February 1979): 405–424.
Coates, Ta-Nehisi. *The Beautiful Struggle: A Memoir*. New York: Spiegel and Grau, 2008.
———. *Between the World and Me*. New York: Spiegel and Grau, 2015.
———. "The Case for Reparations." *The Atlantic*, June 2014. https://www.theatlantic.com/magazine/archive/2014/06/the-case-for-reparations/361631/.
———. *We Were Eight Years in Power: An American Tragedy*. New York: One World, 2017.
Coleman, Brian. *Check the Technique: Liner Notes for Hip-Hop Junkies*. New York: Villard, 2007.

Collin, Robert W., and Robin Morris Collin. "Urban Environmentalism and Race." In *Urban Planning and the African American Community: In the Shadows*, edited by Marsha Ritzdorf and June Manning Thomas, 220–237. Thousand Oaks, CA: Sage, 1997.

Collins, Patricia Hill. *Black Feminist Thought: Knowledge, Consciousness, and the Politics of Empowerment*. New York: Routledge, 2008.

Comen, Evan. "For Black Americans Moving to a New City, These are Some of the Worst Places to Settle." *Wall 24/7*, November 8, 2019. https://www.usatoday.com/story/money/2019/11/08/moving-the-worst-us-cities-for-black-americans/40553101/.

Commission to Study and Develop Reparation Proposals for African-Americans Act. H.R. 40. 115th Cong., 2017.

Conley, Dalton. *Being Black, Living in the Red: Race, Wealth, and Social Policy in America*. Berkeley: University of California Press, 1999.

Connolly, "The Case for Repair, Part 2." *Urban History Association Blog*, May 24, 2014. https://urbanhistorians.wordpress.com/2014/05/24/the-case-for-repair-part-2/.

Cooper, Michael. "Hear How 'Moonlight' Got Its Sound." *New York Times*, February 21, 2017. https://www.nytimes.com/2017/02/21/arts/music/moonlight-movie-score-music-oscars.html.

Corrigan v. Buckley, 271 U.S. 323 (1926).

Crenshaw, Kimberlé. "Race, Reform, and Retrenchment: Transformation and Legitimation in Antidiscrimination Law." *Harvard Law Review* 101 (May 1988): 1331–1387.

Crosley, Hillary. "The Unclassifiable Lupe Fiasco." *Billboard*, November 27, 2007. https://www.billboard.com/articles/news/1047214/the-unclassifiable-lupe-fiasco.

Dallek, Robert. *Ronald Reagan: The Politics of Symbolism*. Cambridge, MA: Harvard University Press, 1984.

Davis, Angela. *Are Prisons Obsolete?* New York: Seven Stories Press, 2003.

———. "Race and Criminalization: Black Americans and the Punishment Industry." In *The House That Race Built*, edited by Wahneema Lubiano, 264–279. New York: Vintage, 1997.

Demerath, Nicholas, and Harlan W. Gilmore. "The Ecology of Southern Cities." In *The Urban South*, edited by Rupert B. Vance, 135–164. Chapel Hill: University of North Carolina Press, 1954.

Diawara, Manthia. *Black American Cinema*. New York: Routledge, 1993.

———. "Noir by Noirs: Towards a New Realism in Black Cinema." *African American Review* 27 (Winter 1993): 525–537.

Dilulio, John, Jr. "The Coming of the Super-predators." *Weekly Standard*, November 27, 1995. https://www.weeklystandard.com/john-j-dilulio-jr/the-coming-of-the-super-predators.

Dingle, Derek. *Black Enterprise Titans of the B.E. 100s: Black CEOs Who Redefined and Conquered American Business*. New York: Wiley, 1999.

Douglass, Frederick. *Narrative of the Life of Frederick Douglass, An American Slave, Written by Himself*. New York: W. W. Norton, 2007.

Drake, St. Clair, and Horace R. Cayton. *Black Metropolis: A Study of Negro Life in a Northern City*. Chicago: University of Chicago Press, 1993.

Dr. Huey P. Newton Foundation. "The Black Panther Party's Ten-Point Program: March 29, 1972." In *Black Panther Party: Service to the People Programs*, edited by David Hilliard, 74–77. Albuquerque: University of New Mexico Press, 2016.

D'Rozario, Denver, and Jerome D. Williams. "Retail Redlining: Definitions, Theory, Typology, and Measurement." *Journal of Macromarketing* 25 (2005): 175–186.

DuBois, W. E. B. *The Philadelphia Negro: A Social Study*. Philadelphia: University of Pennsylvania Press, 1996.

Dyson, Michael Eric. *Know What I Mean? Reflections on Hip-Hop*. New York: Basic Civitas Books, 2007.

Ebony advertisement. *Advertising Age* 23 (October 1950): 7.

Edwards, Timothy J. "Realer Than Reel: *Menace II Society* and the 1990s Hood Film Cycle." *Kino: The Western Undergraduate Journal of Film Studies* 2 (2011): 1–5.

Eggers, Mitchell L., and Douglas S. Massey. "The Structural Determinants of Urban Poverty: A Comparison of Whites, Blacks, and Hispanics." *Social Science Research* 20 (September 1991): 217–255.

Evans, Duanecia. Twitter post. March 31, 2019, 7:34 P.M. https://twitter.com/Duanecia/status/1112513511555506176.

Farley, Reynolds. *Blacks and Whites: Narrowing the Gap?* Cambridge, MA: Harvard University Press, 1984.

———. "The Changing Distribution of Negroes: The Emergence of Black Suburbs." *American Journal of Sociology* 75 (January 1970): 512–529.

Farley, Reynolds, and Walter R. Allen. *The Color Line and the Quality of Life in America*. New York: Russell Sage Foundation, 1987.

Federal Housing Association. *Underwriting Manual*. Washington, DC: Government Printing Office, 1955.

Fiasco, Lupe. "About." *Lupe Fiasco*. http://lupefiasco.com/#about. Accessed February 25, 2018.

———. "Interview." *The Colbert Report*, May 9, 2011. http://www.cc.com/video-clips/d8bi6b/the-colbert-report-lupe-fiasco.

———. *Lasers*. 1st & 15th; Atlantic, 2011. CD.

———. *Lupe Fiasco's Food & Liquor*. 1st & 15th; Atlantic, 2006. CD.

———. *Lupe Fiasco's The Cool*. 1st & 15th; Atlantic, 2007. CD.

Field, Douglas. *James Baldwin*. Tavistock, UK: Northcote House, 2011.

Finney, Carolyn. *Black Faces, White Spaces: Reimagining the Relationship of African Americans to the Great Outdoors*. Chapel Hill: University of North Carolina Press, 2014.

Fishel, Leslie H., Jr. "The Negro in the New Deal Era." *Wisconsin Magazine of History* 48 (Winter 1964–1965): 111–126.

Fisher, Celeste A. "'America's Worst Nightmare': Reading the Ghetto in a Culturally Diverse Context." In *Say It Loud! African-American Audiences, Media, and Identity*, edited by Robin R. Means Coleman, 229–248. New York: Routledge, 2002.

Flint, Barbara Jane. *Zoning and Residential Segregation: A Social and Physical History, 1910–40*. Chicago: University of Chicago Press, 1977.

Flippen, Chenoa. "Unequal Returns to Housing Investments? A Study of Real Housing Appreciation among Black, White, and Hispanic Households." *Social Forces* 82 (June 2004): 1523–1551.

"Food, Clothing Get Most of Negroes' $10 Billion." *Advertising Age* 18 (March 24, 1947): 50.

Forman, Murray. *The 'Hood Comes First: Race, Space, and Place in Rap and Hip-Hop*. Middletown, CT: Wesleyan University Press, 2002.

France, Lisa Respers. "Idris Elba 'Too Street' to Play James Bond." CNN, September 1, 2015. https://www.cnn.com/2015/09/01/entertainment/idris-elba-bond-anthony-horowitz-feat/index.html.

Frazier, E. Franklin. *The Negro Family in the United States*. New York: Citadel Press, 1948.

Freund, David. *Colored Property: State Policy and White Racial Politics in Suburban America*. Chicago: University of Chicago Press, 2007.

Frydl, Kathleen. *The G.I. Bill*. New York: Cambridge University Press, 2009.

The Fugees. *The Score*. Ruffhouse; Columbia Records, 1996. CD.

Furman, Leah, and Elina Furman. *Heart of Soul: The Lauryn Hill Story*. New York: Ballantine Books, 1999.

García, Alberto N. "Baltimore in *The Wire* and Los Angeles in *The Shield*: Urban Landscapes in American Drama Series." *International Journal of TV Serial Narratives* 3 (2017): 51–60.

Gates, Henry Louis, Jr. "Must Buppiehood Cost Homeboy His Soul?" *New York Times*, March 1, 1992.

General Records of the Own Your Own Home Campaign, U.S. Housing Corporation, 1917–1952. Record Group 3, box 5. U.S. National Archives and Records Administration, College Park, MD.

Gillespie, Michael Boyce. *Film Blackness: American Cinema and the Idea of Black Film*. Durham, NC: Duke University Press, 2016.

Gilmore, Ruth Wilson. "Fatal Couplings of Power and Difference: Notes on Racism and Geography." *Professional Geographer* 54 (February 2002): 15–24.

Goodwin, Doris Kearns. *No Ordinary Time: Franklin and Eleanor Roosevelt: The Home Front in World War II*. New York: Simon and Schuster, 1995.

Gordon, Colin. *Mapping Decline: St. Louis and the Fate of the American City*. Philadelphia: University of Pennsylvania Press, 2008.

Gosa, Travis L. "The Fifth Element: Knowledge." In *The Cambridge Companion to Hip Hop*, edited by Justin A. Williams, 56–70. Cambridge: Cambridge University Press, 2015.

Gries, John, and U.S. Department of Agriculture. *How to Own Your Home*. Washington, DC: Better Homes in America, 1929.

Gross, Terry. "'The Chi' Creator Lena Waithe Says Television 'Taught Me How to Dream.'" *National Public Radio*, January 11, 2018. https://www.npr.org/2018/01/11/577311653/the-chi-creator-lena-waithe-says-television-taught-me-how-to-dream.

Hager, Steven. "Afrika Bambaataa's Hip-Hop." In *And It Don't Stop: The Best American Hip-Hop Journalism of the Last 25 Years*, edited by Raquel Cepeda, 10–26. New York: Faber and Faber, 2004.

Haithcoat, Rebecca. "Born and Raised in Compton." *LA Weekly*, January 20, 2011. http://www.laweekly.com/music/born-and-raised-in-compton-kendrick-lamar-hides-a-poets-soul-behind-pussy-and-patron-2168759.

Hall, Stuart. "Race, Culture, and Communications: Looking Backward and Forward at Cultural Studies." *Rethinking Marxism* 5 (1992): 10-18.

———. *Representation: Cultural Representations and Signifying Practices*. London; Thousand Oaks, CA: Sage in Association with the Open University, 1997.

Hancock, John. "The New Deal and American Planning: The 1930s." In *Two Centuries of American Planning*, edited by Daniel Schaffer, 197-230. London: Mansell, 1988.

Haring, H. A. "Selling to Harlem," *Advertising and Selling*, October 1928, 17-18.

Hays, R. Allen. *The Federal Government and Urban Housing*. Albany: State University of New York Press, 2012.

Hayward, Clarissa Rile. *How Americans Make Race: Stories, Institutions, Spaces*. New York: Cambridge University Press, 2013.

Healy, Mark. "Fly Girls on Film." *New York Magazine*, January 25, 1993, 24.

Hegel, G. W. F. *The Philosophy of History*. Buffalo, NY: Prometheus, 1991.

Helper, Rose. *Racial Policies and Practices of Real Estate Brokers*. Minneapolis: University of Minnesota Press, 1969.

Hirsch, Arnold R. "Choosing Segregation: Federal Housing Policy between *Shelley* and *Brown*." In *From Tenements to the Taylor Homes: In Search of an Urban Housing Policy in Twentieth-Century America*, edited by John F. Bauman, Roger Biles, and Kristin M. Szylvian, 206-225. University Park: Pennsylvania State University Press, 2000.

———. "'The Last and Most Difficult Barrier': Segregation and Federal Housing Policy in the Eisenhower Administration, 1953-1960." *Poverty and Race Research Action Council*, March 2005, 1-74.

———. *Making the Second Ghetto: Race and Housing in Chicago, 1940-1960*. Chicago: University of Chicago Press, 1998.

———. "Searching for a 'Sound Negro Policy': A Racial Agenda for the Housing Acts of 1949 and 1954." *Housing Policy Debate* 11 (January 2000): 393-441.

Holladay, Hilary. *Ann Petry*. New York: Twayne, 1996.

hooks, bell. *Black Looks: Race and Representation*. New York: Routledge, 2015.

Hoover, Herbert. "Address to the White House Conference on Home Building and Home Ownership, 1931." In *Public Papers of the Presidents of the United States: Herbert Hoover: Containing the Public Messages, Speeches, and Statements of the President*, 572-574. Washington, DC: United States Printing Office, 1976.

Hopkins, Pauline. *Contending Forces: A Romance Illustrative of Negro Life North and South*. Carbondale: Southern Illinois University Press, 1978.

Howard, Josiah. *Blaxploitation Cinema: The Essential Reference Guide*. Surrey: FAB Press, 2008.

Hughes, Langston. "*Ebony*'s Nativity." *Ebony*, November 1965, 40-48.

Hutchinson, Janet. "Building for Babbitt: The State and the Suburban Home Ideal." *Journal of Policy History* 9 (April 1997): 184-210.

Hyman, Dan. "With 'The Chi,' Lena Waithe Heads Home in Search of the Real Chicago." *New York Times*, January 2, 2018. https://www.nytimes.com/2018/01/02/arts/television/lena-waithe-the-chi.html.

"I Sold a House to a Negro: Florida Real Estate Broker Loses Her License in Brave Fight for Residential Desegregation." *Ebony*, October 1963, 92-100.

Jackson, Kenneth T. *Crabgrass Frontier: The Suburbanization of the United States*. New York: Oxford University Press, 1985.
Jacobs, Harriet. *Incidents in the Life of a Slave Girl*. New York: Open Road, 2016.
James, Joy. *The New Abolitionists: (Neo) Slave Narratives and Contemporary Prison Writings*. Albany: State University of New York Press, 2005.
Jefferson, Thomas. *Notes on the State of Virginia, 1743-1826*. Chapel Hill: University of North Carolina Press, 2006.
Johnson, James Weldon. *Black Manhattan*. New York: Alfred A. Knopf, 1930.
Johnson, John H. "*Ebony*'s Fifteenth Birthday." *Ebony*, November 1960, 159.
———. "Editorial Concept of *Ebony* Has Been Deepened, Enriched." *Ebony*, November 1960, 161.
———. "A Statement from the Publisher." *Ebony*, September 1963, 19.
———. "Why Negroes Buy Cadillacs." *Ebony*, September 1949, 34.
Johnson, John H., and Lerone Bennett Jr. *Succeeding against the Odds*. New York: Warner Books, 1989.
Johnson's Wax advertisement. *Ebony*, September 1963, 103.
Jones, Jacqueline. *The Dispossessed: America's Underclasses from the Civil War to the Present*. New York: Basic Books, 1992.
Jones, Janelle. "The Racial Wealth Gap: How African-Americans Have Been Shortchanged Out of the Materials to Build Wealth." *Economic Policy Institute*, February 13, 2017. https://www.epi.org/blog/the-racial-wealth-gap-how-african-americans-have-been-shortchanged-out-of-the-materials-to-build-wealth/.
Jones, Nikole Hannah. "Choosing a School for My Daughter." *New York Times*, June 11, 2016. https://www.nytimes.com/2016/06/12/magazine/choosing-a-school-for-my-daughter-in-a-segregated-city.html.
———. "The Resegregation of Jefferson County." *New York Times*, September 6, 2017. https://www.nytimes.com/2017/09/06/magazine/the-resegregation-of-jefferson-county.html.
Julian, Elizabeth K., and Michael M. Daniel. "Separate and Unequal: The Root and Branch of Public Housing Segregation." *Clearinghouse Review* 23 (1989): 666–668.
Just Another Girl on the I. R. T. Directed by Leslie Harris. 1993. New York: Miramax Films, 1993.
Kassarjian, Harold H. "The Negro and American Advertising, 1946-1965." *Journal of Marketing Research* 6 (February 1969): 29-39.
Katzman, David M. *Before the Ghetto: Black Detroit in the Nineteenth Century*. Urbana: University of Illinois Press, 1973.
Katznelson, Ira. *When Affirmative Action Was White: An Untold History of Racial Inequality in Twentieth-Century America*. New York: W. W. Norton, 2005.
Keyes, Cheryl Lynette. *Rap Music and Street Consciousness*. Urbana: University of Illinois Press, 2002.
King, Martin Luther, Jr. *Where Do We Go from Here: Chaos or Community?* Boston: Beacon Press, 1968.
Kirby, Kathleen. *Indifferent Boundaries: Spatial Concept of Human Subjectivity*. New York: Guilford Press, 1996.

Kotlowski, Dean J. *Nixon's Civil Rights: Politics, Principle, and Policy*. Cambridge, MA: Harvard University Press, 2001.

Koven, Mikel J. *Blaxploitation Films*. Harpenden, UK: Kamera, 2010.

Kozol, Jonathan. *Savage Inequalities: Children in America's Schools*. New York: Broadway Paperbacks, 2012.

Kraus, Michael W., Julian M. Rucker, and Jennifer A. Richeson, "Americans Misperceive Racial Economic Equality." *Proceedings of the National Academy of Sciences of the United States of America* 114 (September 2017): 10324–10331. https://doi.org/10.1073/pnas.1707719114.

Kushner, James A. *Apartheid in America: An Historical and Legal Analysis of Contemporary Racial Segregation in the United States*. Greene County, IL: Carrollton Press, 1980.

Kusmer, Kenneth L. *A Ghetto Takes Shape: Black Cleveland, 1870–1930*. Urbana: University of Illinois Press, 1976.

Kwate, Naa Oyo A. "Retail Messages in the Ghetto Belt." In *Race and Retail: Consumption across the Color Line*, edited by Mia Bay and Ann Fabian, 44–66. New Brunswick, NJ: Rutgers University Press, 2015.

Lake, Robert. *The New Suburbanites: Race and Housing in the Suburbs*. New Brunswick, NJ: Transaction Publishers, 2012.

Lamar, Kendrick. "Backseat Freestyle Annotations." *Genius*, 2013. https://genius.com/2339578.

———. *DAMN*. Top Dawg, 2017. CD.

———. *Good Kid, M.A.A.D. City*. Aftermath, 2012. CD.

Lee, Benjamin. "It's Impossible to Be Vulnerable." *Guardian*, September 15, 2016. https://www.theguardian.com/film/2016/sep/15/its-impossible-to-be-vulnerable-how-moonlight-reflects-being-a-black-gay-man-in-the-us.

Levine, Caroline. *Forms: Whole, Rhythm, Hierarchy, Network*. Princeton, NJ: Princeton University Press, 2015.

Levitt & Sons Inc. v. Division against Discrimination, 363 U.S. 418 (1960).

Lewis, Oscar. "The Culture of Poverty." *American* 215 (October 1966): 19–25.

———. *La Vida: A Puerto Rican Family in the Culture of Poverty—San Juan and New York*. New York: Random House, 1966.

Lieberson, Stanley. *A Piece of the Pie: Black and White Immigrants since 1880*. Berkeley: University of California Press, 1980.

Lipsitz, George. *How Racism Takes Place*. Philadelphia: Temple University Press, 2011.

Locke, Alain. "Enter the New Negro." *Survey Graphic*, March 1925, 1–6.

Loewen, James W. *Sundown Towns: A Hidden Dimension of American Racism*. New York: Touchstone, 2006.

Love, Bettina. "Good Kids, Mad Cities: Kendrick Lamar and Finding Inner Resistance in Response to Ferguson USA." *Cultural Studies, Critical Methodologies* 16 (March 2016): 320–323.

Luken, Paul C., and Suzanne Vaughan. ". . . Be a Genuine Homemaker *in Your Own Home*: Gender and Familial Relations in State Housing Practices, 1917–1922." *Social Forces* 83, no. 4 (June 2005): 1603–1625.

"Lupe Fiasco: Rapping Outside the Box." *Ebony*, December 2006, 152.

Malcolm X. "The Ballot or the Bullet." Speech, Detroit, Michigan, April 12, 1964. https://archive.org/details/EducationRadioMalcolmXstheBallotOrTheBullet.

Marchand, Roland. *Advertising the American Dream: Making Way for Modernity, 1920-1940*. Berkeley: University of California Press, 1985.

Martinez, Gerald, Diana Martinez, and Andres Chavez. *What It Is, What It Was! The Black Film Explosion of the '70s in Words and Pictures*. New York: Hyperion, 1998.

Massey, Douglas S. *Categorically Unequal: The American Stratification System*. New York: Russell Sage Foundation, 2007.

Massey, Douglas S., Camille Z. Charles, Garvey Lundy, and Mary J. Fischer. "The Puzzle of Minority Underachievement." In *The Source of the River: The Social Origins of Freshmen at America's Selective Colleges and Universities*, edited by Douglas Massey, 1-19. Princeton, NJ: Princeton University Press, 2011.

Massey Douglas S., and Nancy Denton. *American Apartheid: Segregation and the Making of the Underclass*. Cambridge, MA: Harvard University Press, 1993.

———. "The Dimensions of Residential Segregation." *Social Forces* 67 (December 1988): 281-315.

———. "Hypersegregation in U.S. Metropolitan Areas: Black and Hispanic Segregation along Five Dimensions." *Demography* 26 (August 1989): 373-393.

Massood, Paula J. *Black City Cinema: African American Urban Experiences in Film*. Philadelphia: Temple University Press, 2003.

———. "Street Girls with No Future? Black Women Coming of Age in the City." In *Contemporary Black American Cinema: Race, Gender and Sexuality at the Movies*, 232-250. New York: Routledge, 2012.

McCarthy, Cameron, Alida Rodriquez, Shuaib Meecham, Stephen David, Carrie Wilson-Brown, Heriberto Godina, K. E. Supryia, and Ed Buendia. "Race, Suburban Resentment, and the Representation of the Inner City in Contemporary Film and Television." In *Beyond Silence Voices: Class, Race, and Gender in United States Schools*, edited by Lois Weis and Michelle Fine, 163-174. Albany: State University of New York Press, 2005.

McEntire, Davis. *Residence and Race: Final and Comprehensive Report to the Commission on Race and Housing*. Berkeley: University of California Press, 1960.

McGovney, Dudley O. "Racial Residential Segregation by State Court Enforcement of Restrictive Agreements, Covenants or Conditions in Deeds Is Unconstitutional." *California Law Review* 33 (March 1945): 5-39.

McKittrick, Katherine. *Demonic Grounds: Black Women and the Cartographies of Struggle*. Minneapolis: University of Minnesota Press, 2006.

Mead, Lawrence. *Beyond Entitlement: The Social Obligation of Citizenship*. New York: Free Press, 1986.

"Message from Hoover." *Ebony*, September 1963, 21.

"Message from Truman." *Ebony*, September 1963, 21.

"Michigan's Ghetto Buster." *Ebony*, February 1963, 55-60.

Mohl, Raymond A. "Planned Destruction: The Interstates and Central City Housing." In *From Tenements to the Taylor Homes: In Search of an Urban Housing Policy in Twentieth-Century America*, edited by John F. Bauman, Roger Biles, and

Kristin M. Szylvian, 226–245. University Park: Pennsylvania State University Press, 2000.

Moonlight. Directed by Barry Jenkins. Miami: A24 and Plan N Entertainment, 2016.

Moynihan, Daniel P. "Memorandum." National Archives and the Nixon Foundation. https://www.nixonlibrary.gov/virtuallibrary/releases/jul10/53.pdf. Accessed April 4, 2018.

———. *The Negro Family: The Case for National Action*. Westport, CT: Greenwood Press, 1981.

Murray, Charles A. *Losing Ground: An American Social Policy, 1950–1980*. New York: Basic Books, 1984.

Myrdal, Gunnar Rose. *An American Dilemma*. New York: McGraw-Hill, 1964.

Nadinola advertisement. *Ebony*, September 1963, 10.

"National Negro Market Study Shows $12,000,000,000 Expenditures." *Publishers Weekly* 152 (July 1947): 34–35.

Neal, Mark Anthony. "Postindustrial Soul: Black Popular Music at the Crossroads." In *What the Music Said: Black Popular Music and Black Public Culture*, 125–159. New York: Routledge, 1999.

Nelson, George. *Hip Hop America*. New York: Penguin Books, 1999.

Newton, Huey P. "He Won't Bleed Me: A Revolutionary Analysis of 'Sweet Sweetback's Baadasssss Song.'" *Black Panther* 6 (June 1971): A–L.

Obama, Barack. "President Obama Interviews the Creator of 'The Wire' David Simon." *Medium*, March 27, 2015. https://medium.com/@ObamaWhiteHouse/president-obama-interviews-the-creator-of-the-wire-david-simon-40fb7bd29b18.

"158 Negro Newspapers Study Racial Market." *Printer's Ink* 216 (August 23, 1946): 98.

"125 Best Places to Live in the U.S." *U.S. News*, April 6, 2019. https://realestate.usnews.com/places/rankings/best-places-to-live?src=usn_pr.

Orr, Deborah. "It's Painful Watching the Male Crisis Onscreen." *Guardian*, February 18, 2017. https://www.theguardian.com/commentisfree/2017/feb/18/film-therapy-masculinity-manchester-by-the-sea-moonlight.

Patterson, Orlando. *Slavery and Social Death: A Comparative Study*. Cambridge, MA: Harvard University Press, 1982.

Perry, Imani. *Prophets of the Hood: Politics and Poetics in Hip Hop*. Durham, NC: Duke University Press, 2004.

Petry, Ann. *The Street: A Novel*. Boston: Mariner Books, 1998.

Phillips, Julie. "Growing Up Black and Female: Leslie Harris's *Just Another Girl on the IRT*." *Cineaste* 19 (March 1993): 86–87.

Philpott, Thomas Lee. *The Slum and the Ghetto: Neighborhood Deterioration and Middle-Class Reform, 1880–1930*. New York: Oxford University Press, 1978.

Plunz, Richard. *A History of Housing in New York City*. New York: Columbia University Press, 2016.

Powell, John A, Gavin Kearney, and Vina Kay. *In Pursuit of a Dream Deferred: Linking Housing and Education Policy*. New York: Peter Lang, 2001.

Race: The Power of an Illusion. Produced by Larry Adelman, Christine Herbes-Sommers, Tracy Heather Strain, Llewellyn M. Smith, Jean Cheng, and Natatcha Estébanez. San Francisco: California Newsreel, 2003. DVD.

Rafferty, Terrence. "Tunnel Vision." *New Yorker*, March 22, 1993. http://archives.newyorker.com/?i=1993-03-22#folio=CV1.

Rainwater, Lee, and William L. Yancey. *The Moynihan Report and the Politics of Controversy: A Trans-action Social Science and Public Policy Report*. Cambridge, MA: MIT Press, 1967.

Ray-Harris, Ashley. "*The Chi* Finds a Compelling Story." *AV Club*, March 4, 2018. https://www.avclub.com/the-chi-finds-a-compelling-story-in-one-of-its-quietest-1823507930.

Rice, Roger L. "Residential Segregation by Law, 1910–1917." *Journal of Southern History* 34 (May 1968): 179–199.

Riley, Marcus. "Lupe Fiasco Calls Obama a 'Terrorist.'" NBC Chicago, June 8, 2011. https://www.nbcchicago.com/news/politics/123467904.html.

Robinson, Cedric J. *Black Marxism: The Making of the Black Radical Tradition*. Chapel Hill: University of North Carolina Press, 2000.

Rose, Tricia. "Hip Hop on Trial." *Versus Debates*, June 27, 2012. https://www.youtube.com/watch?v=r3-7YoxG89Q.

Rothstein, Richard. *The Color of Law: A Forgotten History of How Our Government Segregated America*. New York: Liveright Publishing, 2017.

———. "How the U.S. Tax Code Worsens the Education Gap." *New York Times*, April 25, 2001, A17.

Sawjani, Archna. "Lupe Fiasco: Thought Process." *XXL*, December 17, 2007. http://www.xxlmag.com/news/2007/12/lupe-fiasco-thought-process/.

Schuman, Howard, Charlotte Steeh, and Lawrence Bobo. *Racial Attitudes in America: Trends and Interpretations*. Cambridge, MA: Harvard University Press, 1985.

Scott, A. O. "'Moonlight': Is This the Year's Best Movie?" *New York Times*, October 20, 2016. https://www.nytimes.com/2016/10/21/movies/moonlight-review.html.

Scruggs, Charles. *Sweet Home: Invisible Cities in the Afro-American Novel*. Baltimore: Johns Hopkins University Press, 1993.

The Secret of Selling the Negro. Directed by Wayne A. Langston. 1954. SARRA Production. https://www.youtube.com/watch?v=E8PBrhFN35c.

Senghor, Léopold. *The Foundations of "Africanité" or "Négritude" and "Arabité."* Paris: Présence Africaine, 1971.

Shakur, Assata. *Assata: An Autobiography*. Chicago: Zed Books, 1987.

Shapiro, Michael J. *The Political Sublime*. Durham, NC: Duke University Press, 2018.

Shapiro, Thomas M. *The Hidden Cost of Being African American: How Wealth Perpetuates Inequality*. New York: Oxford University Press, 2005.

Shapiro, Thomas M., Tatjana Meschede, and Laura Sullivan. "The Racial Wealth Gap Increases Fourfold." *Institute on Assets and Social Policy*, May 2010, 1–4.

Sharkey, Patrick. *Stuck in Place: Urban Neighborhoods and the End of Progress toward Racial Equality*. Chicago: University of Chicago Press, 2013.

Shelley v. Kraemer, 334 U.S. 1 (1948).

Shockley, Evie. "Buried Alive: Gothic Homelessness, Black Women's Sexuality, and (Living) Death in Ann Petry's 'The Street.'" *African American Review* 40 (Fall 2006): 439–460.

Silk, Catherine, and John Silk. *Racism and Anti-racism in American Popular Culture: Portrayals of African-Americans in Fiction and Film*. Manchester: Manchester University Press, 1990.

Singh, Nikhil Pal. *Black Is a Country: Race and the Unfinished Struggle for Democracy*. Cambridge, MA: Harvard University Press, 2004.

Singleton, John. "The Fire This Time." *Premier*, July 1992, 74–75.

Sivulka, Juliann. *Soap, Sex, and Cigarettes: A Cultural History of American Advertising*. Belmont, CA: Wadsworth, 1998.

"Six Ways to Stop Negro Crime." *Ebony*, November 1959, 128–129.

Smith, Christen A. "Facing the Dragon: Black Mothering, Sequelae, and Gendered Necropolitics in the Americas." *Transforming Anthropology* 24 (April 2016): 31–48.

Smith, Tom. "Ethnic Images." *GSS Technical Report* 19 (December 1990): 1–18. https://www.researchgate.net/publication/237471758_Ethnic_Images.

Solarsk, Matthew. "Lupe Fiasco Talks The Cool, Cheeseburgers, Retirement." *Pitchfork*, December 13, 2007. https://lupethefiasco.blogspot.com/2007/11/.

Stuart, M. S. *An Economic Detour: A History of Insurance in the Lives of American Negroes*. College Park, MD: McGrath, 1940.

Sugrue, Thomas. *Sweet Land of Liberty: The Forgotten Struggle for Civil Rights in the North*. New York: Random House, 2008.

Sullivan, David J. "Don't Do This—If You Want to Sell Your Products to Negros!" *Sales Management* 52 (March 1943): 46–47.

Taubin, Amy. "Girl N the Hood." *Sight and Sound* 3 (August 1993): 16–17.

Thornbrough, Emma Lou. "Segregation in Indiana during the Klan Era of the 1920s." *Journal of American History* 47 (March 1961): 594–618.

"Today Was a Good Day." *The Chi*. Directed by Darren Grant. Chicago: Showtime Network, 2018.

Truman, Harry S. "Statement by the President Upon Signing the Housing Act of 1949." *Public Papers of the Presidents of the United States*. Washington, DC: Government Printing Office, 1949.

Trump, Donald J. Twitter post. May 28, 2020, 11:53 P.M. https://twitter.com/byjoelanderson/status/1052684215119015937.

U.S. Bureau of the Census. "American Community Survey: Data Profiles, 2018." https://www.census.gov/acs/www/data/data-tables-and-tools/data-profiles/. Accessed June 8, 2020.

———. "Quarterly Residential Vacancies and Homeownership." July 26, 2018. https://www.census.gov/housing/hvs/files/currenthvspress.pdf.

———. *Statistical Abstract of the United States, 1956*. Washington, DC: Government Printing Office, 1956.

———. *Statistical Abstract of the United States, 1966*. Washington, DC: Government Printing Office, 1966.

———. *Statistical Abstract of the United States, 1976*. Washington, DC: Government Printing Office, 1976.

U.S. Commission on Civil Rights. *Housing: 1961 United States Commission on Civil Rights Report*. Washington, DC: Government Printing Office, 1961.

U.S. Department of Housing and Urban Development. "Housing Discrimination against Racial and Ethnic Minorities 2012." *Urban Institute*, June 2013, 1–190.

———. "Prepared Remarks of Secretary Shaun Donovan during the Countrywide Settlement Press Conference." December 21, 2011. https://archives.hud.gov/remarks/donovan/speeches/2011-12-21.cfm.

U.S. Housing Administration. *Manual on Policy and Procedures*. Washington, DC: Government Printing Office, 1937.

U.S. National Advisory Commission on Civil Disorders. *Report of the National Advisory Commission on Civil Disorders*. Washington, DC: Government Printing Office, 1968.

von Hoffman, Alexander. "A Study in Contradictions: The Origins and Legacy of the Housing Act of 1949." *Housing Policy Debate* 11 (2000): 299–326.

Walker, Susannah. *Style and Status: Selling Beauty to African American Woman, 1920–1975*. Lexington: University Press of Kentucky, 2007.

Wallace, Deborah, and Rodrick Wallace. *A Plague on Your Houses: How New York Was Burned Down and Public Health Crumbled*. New York: Verso, 1998.

Watkins, S. Craig. *Representing: Hip Hop Culture and the Production of Black Cinema*. Chicago: University of Chicago Press, 1998.

Weems, Robert E., Jr. *Desegregating the Dollar: African American Consumerism in the Twentieth Century*. New York: New York University Press, 1998.

White, Michael J. "The Measurement of Spatial Segregation." *American Journal of Sociology* 88 (March 1983): 1008–1018.

Whitten, Robert Harvey, and Atlanta City Planning Commission. *The Atlanta Zone: Report Outlining a Tentative Zone Plan for Atlanta*. Atlanta: City Planning Commission, 1992.

Wienk, Ronald E., Clifford E. Reid, John C. Simonson, and Frederick J. Eggers. *Measuring Racial Discrimination in American Housing Markets*. Washington, DC: U.S. Department of Housing and Urban Development, 1979.

Wilkerson, Isabel. *The Warmth of Other Suns: The Epic Story of America's Great Migration*. New York: Vintage, 2010.

Williams, James S. "The Lost Boys of Baltimore: Beauty and Desire in the Hood." *Film Quarterly* 62 (Winter 2008): 58–63.

Williams, Linda. *On the Wire*. Durham, NC: Duke University Press, 2014.

Williams, Raymond. *Marxism and Literature*. Oxford: Oxford University Press, 1977.

Wilson, Kate, Mike Usinger, and John Lucas. "All You Need to Know." *Straight*, August 1, 2017. https://www.straight.com/music/943516/all-you-need-know-about-kendrick-lamar-vancouver.

Wilson, William J. *The Truly Disadvantaged: The Inner City, the Underclass, and Public Policy*. Chicago: University of Chicago Press, 1987.

Yinger, John, and U.S. Department of Housing and Urban Development. *Housing Discrimination Study: Incidence of Discrimination and Variation in Discriminatory Behavior*. Washington, DC: U.S. Department of Housing and Urban Development, Office of Policy Development and Research, 1991.

Young, Whitney, Jr. "The High Cost of Discrimination." *Ebony*, August 1965, 51–54.

Index

Page numbers in italic refer to figures.

Academy Awards, 129, 135
advertising. *See* marketing
Advertising the American Dream (Marchand), 51
Afrika Bambaataa, 102–105
American Dream: in Coates, 92, 97; family and, 79; homeownership and, 45–46, 48; in literature, 78–79, 81, 83–85, 92, 97; in Lupe Fiasco, 116; Manifest Destiny and, 30; marketing and, 62, 72; in music, 116; Nixon and, 50
Amos 'n Andy Show, The (television program), 128
Anderson, Elijah, 5, 179n67
appraisals, home, 31–32
Arbery, Ahmaud, 157
Archer, Elsie, 60
art: Black spatial experience in, 99; as expression of humanity, 129; ghettoization of, 100; hip-hop as, 105–106, 123; non-Black forms in interpretation of Black, 153
"Art of Peer Pressure, The" (Lamar), 120
Asghedom, Ermias Joseph. *See* Hussle, Nipsey
assimilation, 59, 63, 69, 96
Atlanta, 26, 52
authenticity, 126–127, 136, 145

"Backseat Freestyle" (Lamar), 120–121
Baldwin, James, 77–78, 87–92, 98
"Beast, The" (Fugees), 110
Beautiful Struggle, The (Coates), 3, 99–100
beauty products, 52, 63, 73, 74
Beloved (Morrison), 77

Bennett, Lerone, Jr., 68–69, 73
Berger, Fred, 135
Better Homes in America (BHA), 29–30
Bettman, Alfred, 26
Between the World and Me (Coates), 2, 7–8, 78, 92–97, 106, 110
BHA. *See* Better Homes in America (BHA)
Birth of a Nation, The (film), 86
"Bitch Don't Kill My Vibe" (Lamar), 118
Bittker, Boris, 158, 168
Black Arts Movement, 17
Black consumerism, 51, 54–55, 58–61, 75
Black Faces, White Spaces (Finney), 27
Black imaginary, 97–98
Black Looks (hooks), 128
Black Metropolis (Drake and Cayton), 17, 76
Black nationalism, 17, 119, 125, 131, 133, 140, 169
Blackness: in Coates, 97–98; as contagion, 86; criminalization of, 11–12; economic risk and, 36; in film, 127; Fugees and, 107; Harlem and, 77; in Lamar, 118; in Lupe Fiasco, 114; in Petry, 86; street as connected to, 38–39; in *The Wire*, 150
"black-on-black crime," 76
Black Panther Party, 102, 112
Black radicalism, 111–112, 125
blaxploitation films, 125
blockbusting, 34, 65, 174n76
Book of Eli, The (film), 135
Bork, Robert, 159–160
Boyz n the Hood (film), 124, 128–135

brand consciousness, 58–60
Britell, Nicholas, 136
Bronx River Project, 103–104
Brooks, Gwendolyn, 178n2
Brown v. Board of Education, 164–165
Bulman, Robert C., 127
busing, 167

Cabrera, Nathan, 113
Campbell, Clive. *See* DJ Kool Herc
Can't Stop, Won't Stop (Chang), 101–102
capitalism: in hip-hop, 115; homeownership and, 45–46; marketing and, 57; predatory, 105; racial, 172n2; racialized, 116; sexism in, 50
"Case for Reparations, The" (Coates), 15
Cayton, Horace R., 17, 51, 76
CBL. *See* Contract Buyers League (CBL)
Challenge to Liberty, The (Hoover), 71
Chang, Jeff, 101–102
Charles, Camille Z., 42
Chenault, John, 66–68
Chesnutt, Charles, 16, 77
Chi, The (television program), 124, 145, 150–155, 157
Christianity, 88–91, 110, 116
civil rights consumerism, 69–73, 70
civil rights movement, 35–43
Clark, Kenneth B., 4
class solidarity, 46
Coates, Ta-Nehisi, 2–3, 7–8, 15, 32, 78, 92–100, 106, 110, 146, 159–160, 168–169
Cocke, Erle, 36
Code of the Street (Anderson), 5, 179n67
Coke La Rock, 103
Collins, Patricia Hill, 11
Color of Law, The (Rothstein), 19–20, 161
Common (hip-hop artist), 150–51
communism, 45–46
Connolly, N. D. B., 166–67
conservativism, 10–11, 24, 57, 160
constitutionality, 19–20
construct, sociocultural: streets as, 1–2

consumerism. *See* Black consumerism; civil rights consumerism; marketing
Contract Buyers League (CBL), 160–161
Conyers, John, Jr., 158
"Coolest, The" (Fiasco), 114
Coolidge, Calvin, 29
Countrywide, 40, 175n102
covenants, housing, 25–26
Crenshaw, Kimberlé, 169
Cross Bronx Expressway, 28, 101–102

Daley, Richard, 159
DAMN (Lamar), 117
Dangerous Minds (film), 127
Davis, Jordan, 180n81
Dead Presidents (film), 135
Del Rio, James, 65
Democratic Party, 23, 38, 112, 159
Denton, Nancy, 4–5, 12–13, 17–18, 32–33, 37, 171n11
Desegregating the Dollar (Weems), 57
DiIulio, John J., Jr., 11–12, 129
Division of Slum Clearance, 24
DJ Kool Herc, 102–103
DJ Red Alert, 107
Donovan, Kevin. *See* Afrika Bambaataa
Donovan, Shaun, 40
Do the Right Thing (film), 125–126
Drake, St. Clair, 17, 51, 76
D'Rozario, Denver, 45
drugs. *See* War on Drugs
DuBois, W. E. B., 16, 51, 77
Dunn, Michael David, 180n81
Dyson, Michael Eric, 106, 118, 123

Ebony (magazine), 44, 54, 61–69, 64, 69–71, 70, 71–72, 74
economic illiteracy, 44–45
economic zoning, 26
education, 96, 127–128, 167
Edwards, Timothy, 125–126
Eisenhower, Dwight, 24, 71
Elba, Idris, 146
Ellison, Ralph, 77
employment competition, 17–18

equity, home, 31, 39–40
Espionage Act, 45
ethnic enclaves, 18
Evans, Duanecia, 1

Fair Housing Act of 1968, 13, 19, 35–37, 160, 162, 165–66
family, 8, 46–50, 47, 49; American Dream and, 79; in film, 133; homeownership and, 30; marketing and, 55–56, 72–73; slavery and, 9, 86; violence and, 93
FDIC. *See* Federal Deposit Insurance Corporation (FDIC)
Federal Deposit Insurance Corporation (FDIC), 36
Federal Housing Act of 1934, 5
Federal Housing Administration (FHA), 31–32
FHA. *See* Federal Housing Administration (FHA)
Fiasco, Lupe, 100–101, 111–116
films: blaxploitation, 125; hood genre, 124–140; masculinity in, 129–140; urban high school, 127–128; women in, 128–129; youth culture and, 126–127
Finney, Carolyn, 27
Fire Next Time, The (Baldwin), 78, 87–92
Fischer, Mary J., 42
Floyd, George, 156–157
Ford, Gerald, 159
Forman, Murray, 99–100
Foster, Joseph Pershing, 59
Foxy Brown (film), 125
Frazier, E. Franklin, 8
"Fu-Gee-La" (Fugees), 108, 109
Fugees, 100–101
furniture, 63–65, 64
Fusco, Joy, 149

gangs, 102, 180n12
gangster rap, 105. *See also* hip-hop
Gates, Henry Louis, Jr., 145
gaze, White, 124, 127, 150

gender roles, 46–48, 47
gentrification, 42, 131–132, 167
geographies, racialized, 4–8, 23, 125
ghetto. *See* streets
ghettoization: of Black art, 100; as Black issue, 5; blockbusting and, 174n76; segregation and, 100
"ghetto loans," 39–40
G.I. Bill, 31
Gillespie, Michael Boyce, 126–127
Gilmore, Ruth Wilson, 7
Good Kid, M.A.A.D. City (Lamar), 100–101, 117–123
Go Tell It on the Mountain (Baldwin), 77
Grandmaster Flash, 181n20, 181n22
Great Migration, 16–18
Griffin, Junius, 125

Hager, Steven, 103–104
Hall, Stuart, 13
Harder They Come, The (film), 108
Haring, H. A., 59
Harlem, 68, 77–87
Harlem Renaissance, 17, 56
Hegel, Georg Wilhelm Friedrich, 6–7, 171n20
Helper, Rose, 34
"He Say/She Say" (Fiasco), 113
Hill, Lauryn, 107
hip-hop: Black spatial experience and, 99; in Coates, 99–100; commercialization of, 105; components of, 180n6; criticism of, 106; Cross Bronx Expressway and, 101–102; cultural nationalist, 105; history of, 101–106; violence and, 105–106; women in, 102–103. *See also* music
HOLC. *See* Home Owners' Loan Corporation (HOLC)
Holladay, Hilary, 79
home appraisals, 31–32
homeownership, 5–6, 28–35, 38–39, 51, 72, 167
Home Owners' Loan Corporation (HOLC), 30–31

Index 203

Homestead Act of 1862, 5
Homicide: Life on the Street (television program), 149
homosexuality, 98, 136–137, 139–140, 146–147
hood. *See* streets
hooks, bell, 128
Hoover, Herbert, 29–30, 71
Hopkins, Pauline, 77
Horowitz, Jordan, 135, 146
housing: covenants, 25–26; equity, 31, 39–40; Great Migration and, 17–18; public, 20–25, 33, 65–66, 103–104; subsidization, 23, 28–35, 40
Housing Act of 1949, 23–24
How Racism Takes Place (Lipsitz), 5, 157
Hughes, Albert, 134–135
Hughes, Allen, 134–135
Hughes, Langston, 61
Hussle, Nipsey, 1

Ickes, Harold, 21–22
illiteracy, economic, 44–45
Illmatic (Nas), 100
imaginary: American, 97; Black, 97–98; geographic, 25; racial, 4; spatial, 5–6, 149; White, 76, 86–87, 128
immigrant enclaves, 18
Immigration Act of 1918, 45
individualism, 11, 80, 128
industrial zones, 27
In Moonlight Black Boys Look Blue (McCraney), 135
Invisible Man (Ellison), 77
isolation: community and, tension between, 77–78; education and, 167; in Petry, 80; spatial, 42

Jay-Z, 1, 111
J. Brother, 105
Jean, Wyclef, 107, 110
Jefferson, Thomas, 9
Jenkins, Barry, 135–137
Jim Crow, 8, 17. *See also* segregation
Johnson, James Weldon, 77

Johnson, John, 44, 54, 58, 61–62, 71
Johnson, Lyndon B., 9, 13, 19, 35, 160, 162
Juice (film), 126, 128
Just Another Girl on the I. R. T. (film), 124, 141–144

Kennedy, John F., 71
Kerner, Otto, 36
Kerner Commission, 36–37, 159, 162–166
Keyes, Cheryl L., 101
Khrushchev, Nikita, 48, 50
King, Martin Luther, Jr., 166
Kirby, Kathleen, 7
Kitchen Debate, 50
KRS-One, 115

La La Land (film), 135–136
Lamar, Kendrick, 99–101, 117–123
Lasers (Fiasco), 111
law and order, 11
Lean on Me (film), 127
Lee, Spike, 125–126
Lee, William, 184n65
lending, predatory, 34, 160
Levine, Caroline, 148
Levitt, William, 33
Levittown, New York, 33
Lewis, Oscar, 9
Lipsitz, George, 5–6, 40–41, 76, 157, 167
Locke, Alain, 77
Long Island, 33
Los Angeles Police Department, 1
Love, Monie, 102
Luken, Paul C., 48
Lundy, Garvey, 42
Lupe Fiasco's Food & Liquor (Fiasco), 113
Lupe Fiasco's The Cool (Fiasco), 100–101, 111–116

"m.A.A.d. City" (Lamar), 99, 119–120
Malcolm X, 96
Manifest Destiny, 30
Marchand, Roland, 51

marketing: of beauty products, 63; in *Ebony*, 44, 62–63; of furniture, 63–65, 64; and homeownership, 45–50, 47, 49, 72; and Negro market, 50–61; racialized divergence in, 44–45; racist imagery in, 51–52, 58; research, 52–53; segregation and, 54; surveys, 52–53; women and, 60
masculinity, 46–48, 47, 129–140, 147–148
Massey, Douglas, 4–5, 12–13, 17–18, 32–33, 37, 42, 171n11
Massood, Paula, 128
McBath, Lucy, 180n81
McCraney, Tarell Alvin, 135
McDade, Tony, 157
McKittrick, Katherine, 7
MC Lyte, 102
McQuillar, Tayannah Lee, 105
Mead, Lawrence, 10
Menace II Society (film), 128, 135
Mereday, Robert, 33–34
Metz, Nina, 184n65
Michel, Samuel Prakazrel, 107
Minneapolis, 1–2, 156–157
Moonlight (film), 124, 127, 135–140, 157
Moore, Elizabeth, 66–68
Morrison, Toni, 77
mortgages, 30–31, 39–40, 165–166, 175n102
Moses, Robert, 101
Moynihan, Daniel Patrick, 8–10, 36, 102, 128–129, 171n26
Murray, Charles, 10
music, 95; ads for musical instruments, 52; in Coates, 95, 99–100; racialized space and, 6. *See also* hip-hop
Myrdal, Gunnar, 4–5

NAREB. *See* National Association of Real Estate Boards (NAREB)
Nas (hip-hop artist), 100
National Advisory Commission on Civil Disorders, 36–37, 159

National Association for the Advancement of Colored People (NAACP), 21, 25
National Association of Real Estate Boards (NAREB), 46, 66
National Housing Act of 1934, 31
nationalism, Black, 17, 119, 125, 131, 133, 140, 169
Native Son (Wright), 77
Negro market, 50–61
New Deal, 15, 21, 28, 31
New Jack City (film), 128
"New Negro," 56, 58, 77
Newton, Huey, 125
Nixon, Richard, 9, 48, 50, 102
"No Woman, No Cry" (Fugees), 110–111
N.W.A., 100

Obama, Barack, 2, 111, 157
Olmsted, Frederick Law, Jr., 26
ownership. *See* homeownership
Own Your Own Home campaign, 46–48

patriotism, 11, 20, 29–30, 35, 46, 84
Perry, Imani, 105–106
personification, 79, 81, 112, 116, 138
Petry, Ann, 78–87, 97–98
Philadelphia Negro, The (DuBois), 51, 77
Poetic Justice (film), 124, 126
police violence, 92–93, 110, 119, 126, 156–157
Political Sublime, The (Shapiro), 93
poverty: Blackness and, 69; compounding of, 43; consumerism and, 75; Cross Bronx Expressway and, 28; in "culture of poverty" thesis, 9; cycle of, 10; in film, 125, 128, 140; in hip-hop, 100, 110, 122; Kerner Commission and, 162, 165; low point in, 37; public housing and, 20, 71; racialization of, 22–23, 88; segregation and, 15–16; spatial isolation and, 43. *See also* wealth
Powell, John A., 42
Pras (hip-hop artist), 107

Index   205

predatory lending, 34, 160
property value, 31, 38–39, 67, 167
public housing, 20–25, 33, 65–66, 103–104
Public Works Administration (PWA), 21–23
Puerto Ricans, 9
"Put You On Game" (Fiasco), 115–116
PWA. *See* Public Works Administration (PWA)

Queen Latifah, 102
queerness, 98, 136–137, 139–140, 146–147
Quinn, Eithne, 105

racial capitalism, 172n2
"racial equity formula," 24, 71
racialized geographies, 4–8, 22, 125
racialized space, 5–7
racial zoning, 25–27, 32, 34, 71. *See also* redlining
radicalism, Black, 111–112, 125
Rafferty, Terrence, 143
Rap Music and Street Consciousness (Keyes), 101
RCA. *See* Research Company of America (RCA)
"Ready or Not" (Fugees), 108–109
Reaganism, 10–11, 157
redlining, 6, 31–32, 39–40, 45, 67, 150, 167
redress, 158–162, 167
religion, 88–91, 110, 116
reparations, 158–162, 168–169
Republican Party, 11, 23–24, 112, 159
Research Company of America (RCA), 52–53
respectability, 56, 62–63, 97, 105, 121, 142–143, 153
"retail redlining," 45
"reverse redlining," 39–40
Richards, Franklin, 35
Robinson, Cedric, 172n2
Roc Nation, 1

Roosevelt, Franklin D., 13, 21, 29–31. *See also* New Deal
Rose, Tricia, 105–106
Rothstein, Richard, 19–21, 161–162
Russian Revolution of 1917, 45

sapphire stereotype, 128–29
Score, The (Fugees), 100–101, 106–111, 109
Scott, A. I., 136
Scruggs, Charles, 77
Secret of Selling the Negro, The (film), 54–57
Sedition Act, 45
segregation, 164–165; after civil rights movement, 35–43; in Coates, 2–3; constitutionality of, 19–20; covenants in, 25–26; in "culture of segregation" theory, 12–13; ethnic enclaves vs., 18; in Kerner Commission, 36–37; local housing, 25–28; marketing and, 54; in Moynihan Report, 8; perseverance of, 37–38; poverty and, 15–16; in public housing, 22; public opinion on, 35; slavery vs., 17; uniqueness of Black, 13; violence and, 18, 32
Senghor, Leopold, 6, 171n20
Servicemen's Readjustment Act of 1944, 31
sexism, 50
Shaft (film), 125
Shakur, Assata, 96
Shanté, Roxanne, 102
Shapiro, Michael J., 93
Shelley v. Kramer, 34–35
She's Gotta Have It (film), 125–126
Shockley, Evie, 79
Simon, David, 145, 148–149
Singleton, John, 124, 129
Sivulka, Juliann, 51
skin lightening creams, 73, 74
slavery: Black geographies and, 6; in Coates, 96; family and, 9, 86; Great Migration and, 17; Moynihan Report and, 8; reparations for, 158–163;

segregation *vs.*, 17; White supremacy and, 7; women and, 73
slum clearance, 24, 27–28. *See also* urban renewal
Smith, Tom, 12
Snoop Dogg, 105
Soap, Sex, and Cigarettes (Sivulka), 51
social mobility, 10, 17, 25, 34, 41–43, 59, 61, 72–73, 82–84, 96–97, 110, 130, 142, 164
solidarity, 22, 46, 110
Soviet Union, 50
space(s): coding of, in policy, 22–24; delineation of Black and White, 6; economic zoning and, 26; racialized, 5–7
spatial experience, 99
spatial imaginary, 5–6, 149
spatial isolation, 42–43
Stevens, Sapphire, 128
Straight Out of Brooklyn (film), 128
Straight Outta Compton (N.W.A.), 100
Street, The (Petry), 78–87, 97–98
"Street Girls with No Future?" (Massood), 128
Street in Bronzeville, A (Brooks), 178n2
streets: of the *vs.* from the, 3; in Anderson, 5; in Baldwin, 87–92; in Black imaginary, 97–98; Blackness and, 38–39; in blaxploitation films, 125; in *Boyz n the Hood*, 129–135; in *The Chi*, 145, 150–154; in Clark, 4–5; in Coates, 2–3, 7–8, 92–97; consumer of, 73–75; in DuBois, 77; in *Ebony*, 65–69; in Fugees *The Score*, 106–111, *109*; grime of, 80; in hood genre films, 124–140; in *Just Another Girl on the I.R.T.*, 141–144; in Kerner Commission, 162–166; in Lamar, 117–123; liminality of, 4; in Lupe Fiasco, 111–116; in *Moonlight*, 135–136; in Myrdal, 4–5; in Petry, 78–87; public discourse on, 8–13; racialized geographies of, 4–8; as sociocultural construct, 1–2; as transnational, 106–111, *109*; in *The Wire*, 145–50
"Streets on Fire" (Fiasco), 114–115
Stuart, M. S., 51
Style and Status (Walker), 63
subprime mortgages, 39–40, 175n102
subsidization, housing, 23, 28–35, 40
suburbia, 28–35, 60, 80, 84, 101, 125, 127–128, 160
Sullivan, David, 52
sundown towns, 27
superpredator thesis, 11–12, 129, 154
Sweet Sweetback's Baadasssss Song (film), 125
"Swimming Pools (Drank)" (Lamar), 121–123
syphilis, 27

Taubin, Amy, 143
tax policy, 11, 40–41, 164, 167
Taylor, Breonna, 157
television, 125, 144–154
Trout, Robert, 55–56
Truman, Harry, 23–24, 71
Trump, Donald, 157

urban renewal, 23, 27–28, 101, 150
U.S. Housing Authority (USHA), 23

value, property, 31, 38–39, 67, 167
Vaughan, Suzanne, 48
Veterans Administration (VA), 31
violence, 3–4, 93–95, 105–106; Black space and, 27; in Coates, 93–95; family and, 93; in film, 127–135, 140, 142, 144; gang, 180n12; in hip-hop, 100–101, 104–111, 116–119, 122–123; in Petry, 79, 82, 85–86; police, 92–93, 110, 119, 126, 156–157; racism and, 12; segregation and, 18, 32; in television, 145, 147, 151–153; youth and, 11

Waithe, Lena, 150–151
Walker, Susannah, 63

Wallace, Henry, 28
Warmth of Other Suns, The (Wilkerson), 59
War on Drugs, 11, 145
Watkins, S. Craig, 10, 126–127
wealth: American Dream and, 78; consumerism and, 45; gap, 4, 6, 41–43, 158, 161, 165, 168; homeownership and, 31, 40; housing equity in, 40; policies impacting, 40–41; redistribution of, 167; subsidies and, 6, 40, 42, 167. *See also* poverty
Weeks, Sinclair, 57
Weems, Robert, Jr., 57
welfare queen, 11, 126, 165, 167
welfare state, 10
We Were Eight Years in Power (Coates), 2
White gaze, 124, 127, 150
Whiteness: in Baldwin, 90; betterment and, 73; in hip-hop, 110; in literature, 83–84; marketing and, 60, 73; in Petry, 83–84; Public Works Administration and, 22; reparations and, 168; subsidization and, 5; suburbia and, 25, 80
Whites: homeownership marketed to, 46; in public housing, 20–21; in suburbia, 28–35, 60
White supremacy, 159; in Baldwin, 89–90; blaxploitation films and, 125; Christianity and, 90; in Coates, 2; concept of streets as rooted in, 3–4; Harlem and, 87; hip-hop and, 105; Obama and, 157; racialized space and, 6–7

Whitten, Robert, 26
Wilkerson, Isabel, 59
Williams, Jerome D., 45
Williams, Linda, 149–150
Williams, Pharrell, 119
Williams, Raymond, 13
Wire, The (television program), 124, 144–150
women: in blaxploitation films, 125; brand consciousness and, 60; in film, 125, 128–129, 133, 142; in hip-hop, 102–103; homeownership and, 48; Kerner Commission and, 165; Kitchen Debate and, 50; marketing to, 60, 73; Moynihan Report and, 8; in Petry, 85; poverty and, 165; respectability politics and, 143; welfare queen and, 11, 126, 165, 167; welfare queen stereotype and, 11, 165, 167
World War I, 18, 20
World War II, 14, 15, 23–24, 33, 89
Wright, Richard, 77

"XXX" (Lamar), 117–118

Young, Whitney, 68
Young Lords Party, 102
youth culture, 95–96, 126–127. *See also* hip-hop

zoning, racial, 25–27, 32, 34, 71. *See also* redlining
Zulu (film), 103

www.ingramcontent.com/pod-product-compliance
Lightning Source LLC
Chambersburg PA
CBHW030735250426
43671CB00035B/406